End-of-Life Ethics:
A Case Study Approach

**Edited by Kenneth J. Doka, Amy S. Tucci,
Charles A. Corr, & Bruce Jennings**

*Foreword by Richard B. Fife,
The Foundation for End of Life Care*

**HOSPICE FOUNDATION
OF AMERICA**

This book is part of Hospice Foundation of America's *Living with Grief®* series.

Special thanks to the Foundation for End of Life Care for its support of the
2012 *End-of-Life Ethics* Program

This book is part of HFA's *Living with Grief*® series.

Ordering information:

Call Hospice Foundation of America: 800-854-3402

Or write:
Hospice Foundation of America
1710 Rhode Island Avenue, NW #400
Washington, DC 20036

Or visit HFA's Web site:
www.hospicefoundation.org

Managing Editor: Lisa McGahey Veglahn
Layout and Design: The YGS Group

Publisher's Cataloging-in-Publication
(Provided by Quality Books, Inc.)

End-of-life ethics: a case study approach /
   edited by Kenneth J. Doka ... [et al.]; foreword by Richard B. Fife.
   p. cm. -- (Living with grief series)
   Includes bibliographical references and index.
   LCCN 2011942172
   ISBN 978-1-893349-14-8

   1. Terminal care--Moral and ethical aspects.
   I. Doka, Kenneth J. II. Hospice Foundation of America.
   III. Series: Living with grief.

R726.E53 2012   179.7
                                 QBI12-600013

Dedication

To everyone who has had to make difficult decisions about end-of-life care
For themselves or those they love

To our colleagues in hospice and palliative care
In mindful appreciation of their caring and deep ethical sensitivity

And

To William Lamers, MD
Hospice pioneer and longtime Medical Consultant to HFA
For his unfailing dedication and substantial contribution to the development
of hospice

Contents

Acknowledgments

As always, we begin by thanking the small but immensely productive workforce of the Hospice Foundation of America, as well as HFA's supportive Board of Directors. Special recognition goes to our managing editor Lisa McGahey Veglahn, who kept us on deadline and carefully reviewed all aspects of editing and production.

Rather than each of the four editors offering their individual comments, we wish together to acknowledge one another for a collegial process. Four hands in a brew can result in bitter arguments. Instead, we were fortunate to find this process savory. We need to thank all the authors who responded to tight deadlines. Each editor also would like to thank their families and friends for their patience as we worked to publish a complex book in such a short time. You know who you are!

The development of the book was itself an interesting and fascinating dialogue. With four editors, a managing editor, and near two dozen prominent authors, we had intense discussions amongst ourselves of the underlying ethical issues in each chapter. Such is the nature of ethics—if we all agreed, all the time, there would be no ethical dilemmas and no reason for an HFA *Living with Grief®* program or book.

As always, we wish to recognize the continuing legacy of the late Jack Gordon, founder and former chair of The Hospice Foundation of America and David Abrams—former president, current board member, and always friend.

— Kenneth J. Doka, Amy S. Tucci, Charles A. Corr, and Bruce Jennings

Foreword

Richard B. Fife

On April 15, 1975, I was working on a doctorate degree at Drew University in Madison, New Jersey. The university is located just a few miles from the Newton Memorial Hospital, where on that day a bright and energetic 21-year-old woman named Karen Ann Quinlan would be rushed to the emergency room. At the time she was already in a deep coma and in what would later be called a persistent vegetative state. It would be weeks before those of us on the campus would hear anything about this remarkable young woman. It would be months before her name would become a household word and the events surrounding her would begin to change the course of health care around the country and even around the world.

Thirty-five years later, on April 15, 2010, Dr. Kenneth Doka, one of this book's editors, and I were giving ethics presentations to a New Jersey state gathering of palliative care nurses at the invitation of Rutgers University. My presentation was focused on case studies of three Catholic women—Karen Ann Quinlan, Nancy Cruzan, and Terri Schiavo. As I began my presentation on Karen Ann Quinlan, I noticed that her mother was sitting near the front of the audience. Julia Duane Quinlan speaks at conferences across the country on ethics, end-of-life care, hospice, and the importance of her daughter's landmark case. Following the presentation Ms. Quinlan invited Ken and me to join her for dinner. I asked her what she thought was the most important part of the legal fight surrounding her daughter. She answered that question by talking about how the case had become so closely identified with the "right to die." In spite of this, she said that this was not what they were trying to accomplish in their legal battle. Instead, they were fighting for the right to remove an artificial life-support system that seemed to offer no hope of success. In her book she states, "we felt to choose not to prolong life artificially was the ultimate respect for human life. Death was not desired, only accepted" (Quinlan, 2005, p. 75). Indeed, after the respirator was finally removed, Karen Ann would live almost a decade in her suspended state. Ms. Quinlan said that they were talking about respect for life, not the "right to die." She acknowledged that prior to her daughter's case there was very little discussion on the particular issue of the right to die.

In an earlier Hospice Foundation of America publication on ethics and end-of-life care, Bruce Jennings and Alan Meisel strongly acknowledge the importance of the landmark case of Karen Ann Quinlan. They point out that there had been important legal rulings on a patient's right to give or withhold consent to medical treatment in the decades prior to 1975; but they go on to say that "the law of end-of-life care began in the mid-1970s with the case of Karen Ann Quinlan in New Jersey" (Jennings and Meisel, 2005, p. 64). In the legal case *In re Quinlan*, 1976, the legal basis for the ruling would be focused on the issue of privacy, but, as Jennings and Meisel point out, it "was taken to mean that competent individuals had a right to control their own medical decisions" (Jennings and Meisel, 2005, p. 64). In this case, this was true even if the patient was in a permanent persistent vegetative state. The patient did not forfeit the rights; they just had to be exercised by a surrogate. In the Quinlan case, the surrogate would be Karen Ann's father. What made this such a landmark case was that it was "the first time that an individual's right to refuse life-sustaining medical treatment was affirmed by an American appellate-level court" (Jennings and Meisel, 2005, p. 65).

As someone who has developed and trained hospice ethics committees since 1991, I stress that ethics committees should use a principle-based approach. That is, they should look at the situation in the light of well-established ethical principles. These principles are generally recognized as beneficence, nonmaleficence, autonomy, justice, and fidelity. The principles of beneficence and nonmaleficence are not the same, but they do share much common ground. Beneficence speaks to what is of most benefit to the patient while nonmaleficence usually means "do no harm."

However, the Quinlan case would help establish autonomy as the dominant ethical principle over the next several decades. Prior to that case, what was "best for the patient" was generally decided by the physician or the institution. That importance would be highlighted in the tragic case of Nancy Cruzan in Missouri in the mid-1980s. Nancy Cruzan was a 23-year-old woman who was involved in a single car accident. She was left in a persistent vegetative state. After her parents accepted that she would never regain consciousness, they asked the court to allow the removal of life-support equipment, including artificial nutrition and hydration. However, as Nancy had never completed an advance directive, both the hospital and the court were reluctant to allow a discontinuation of life support. It was a reluctance that would keep Nancy in a suspended state of consciousness for years. Hers would be the first patient rights and right-to-die case that would make it all the way to the Supreme Court. The only question that was put before the Supreme Court was: "Can the state of Missouri require clear and convincing evidence of Nancy's own wishes in deciding whether to grant permission to Nancy's parents" (Clarke, 1994, p. 96). In 1990, the Supreme Court ruled in favor of Nancy's parents; from that landmark case would emerge the federal Patient Self-Determination Act, which became effective on December 1, 1991. This act would go a long way to somewhat ensure *informed* consent and the dominance of autonomy as guiding principles.

As autonomy was often viewed as the prime ethical principle in medical ethics, it would point the way for those who would advocate physician-assisted suicide. For many, the right to die is seen as the extrapolation of the principle of autonomy—one should be able to choose the moment and means of one's death. In 1997 there were two cases before the Supreme Court in relation to the right to die and assisted suicide. One was *Washington v. Glucksberg* and the other was *Vacco v. Quill*. In both cases the Supreme Court ruled that there is not a constitutional right to aid in dying. However, they allowed that states may (or may not) "choose to criminalize physician involvement in a patient's willful hastening of his/her own death (commonly termed Physician Assisted Suicide—PAS)" (NHPCO, 2005, p. 1). Indeed, one state, Oregon, had already passed a law in 1994 that legalized physician-assisted suicide; that law would go into effect in 1997. In 2008 voters in Washington would pass a PAS initiative commonly referred to as the Death with Dignity Act. In 2009 the Supreme Court of Montana would hand down a decision that would permit PAS, although this measure did not have the safeguards or guidelines of the bills in Oregon and Washington. PAS measures were defeated very narrowly in Maine (51% to 49%) and California (54% to 46%); and PAS was defeated by a large margin in Michigan (71% to 29%). By 2011, only three states in North America would have laws allowing physician-assisted suicide under certain established guidelines.

Yet medical ethics are never static, but continue to evolve. Each new case— Quinlan, Cruzan, Schiavo—has stretched our understanding of end-of-life ethics, created new challenges and controversies, and changed or clarified laws. This book, published by the Hospice Foundation of America, looks at end-of-life ethics in innovative ways. First, by primarily taking a case study approach, the book reinforces the reality that it is cases—real-life cases that occur in hospices and other institutions offering palliative and end-of-life care—that cause us to apply, review, and sometimes, reconsider, our ethics. Second, the book acknowledges that ethics continue to evolve, suggesting perhaps that a more communal ethos—what will this decision mean to others surviving the death?—may challenge the primacy of autonomy even as it remains a key ethical principle. Finally, the book affirms that because of the strong moral and spiritual traditions of hospice; because of the compassion of hospice and respect for life; and because hospice has always been seen as not just for the dying but for the living, end-of-life ethics will always be a concern. For from the very beginning of modern hospice, its founder, Dame Cicely Saunders, taught that dying is a natural process that is neither to be hastened nor delayed. Yet, dying should never be devoid of hope. If not hope for a cure, hospice can offer hope for something else—hope for the suffering to be controlled; hope for emotional support; hope for resolving some family relations; hope for relieving feelings of guilt; hope for the quality of life to be improved and measured.

Richard B. Fife, PhD, MDiv, is a United Methodist minister, president of the Foundation for End of Life Care, and a founding and sustaining member of the Duke Institute for Care at the End of Life. An activist minister, he has written about his encounters with racism in the 1960s, his participation in civil rights marches with Dr. King and other civil rights leaders as a student, and five years of participating with William Sloane Coffin and the Riverside Disarmament program in the 1980s. He served several United Methodist churches in Florida before becoming vice-president of Bioethics and Pastoral Care for 15 years with VITAS Healthcare, establishing the first corporate ethics committee in a national hospice and developing and training ethics committees in over 40 hospices. He participated on the panel for the Hospice Foundation of America's (HFA) 2005 Living With Grief® program on Ethics. Among his writings are chapters on ethics, ethical dilemmas, diversity, and spirituality that he has written for previous HFA Living with Grief® books.

REFERENCES

Clarke, D. B. (1994). The Patient Self-Determination Act. In J. Monagle & D. Thomasma (Eds.), *Health Care Ethics: Critical Issues for the 21St Century.* Gaithersburg, MD: Aspen Publishers.

Jennings, B., & Meisel, A. (2005). Ethics, End-of-Life Care, and the Law: Overview. In K. J. Doka, B. Jennings, & C. A. Corr (Eds.), *Living with Grief: Ethical Dilemmas at the End of Life.* Washington, DC: The Hospice Foundation of America.

NHPCO (National Hospice and Palliative Care Organization). (2005). Commentary and Resolution on Physician Assisted Suicide. Arlington, VA: NHPCO. http://www.nhpco.org/files/public/PAS_Resolution_Commentary.pdf

Quinlan, J. D. (2005). *Karen Ann's Mother Remembers: My Joy, My Sorrow.* Cincinnati, OH: St. Anthony Messenger Press.

Principles of Bioethics

We often think of ethics as the unchanging principles that guide our personal and professional lives. In reality, ethics are always evolving. This evolution may result from technological advances that present new possibilities and pose new ethical dilemmas. Changes in ethical stances may also arise from broad social changes and emerging sensitivities that challenge prior consensus. In addition, our ethics can be influenced by generational shifts in the values of different generational cohorts. For example, the current emphasis on autonomy as a prime ethical value, and some of its manifestations such as the advocacy of physician-assisted suicide, reflect the strong emphasis on individuality valued by aging Baby Boomers.

This is certainly true in end-of-life ethics. Here tremendous advances in medical technology have shattered a prior consensus on when life begins and ends. All the major cases in end-of-life ethics—Quinlan, Cruzan, Schiavo— hinged on that question. In addition, generational differences, changing social trends, and cultural factors have all created new prisms to review end-of-life ethics.

Bruce Jennings's chapter opens this section. Jennings begins by acknowledging the ways that technological, generational, social, and cultural changes have challenged the dominant ethical paradigm in end-of-life ethics. He notes that the end-of-life reform movement has changed the nature of end-of-life care. To Jennings, two key strategies of this movement have been to create alternative systems of care such as hospice and palliative care, and to empower patients to make their own choices for end-of-life care. The movement toward better end-of-life care also altered our ethical calculus, replacing the value of beneficence with that of autonomy. In other words, a system once built around physician paternalism has given way to a more consumer-driven, individualistic approach. Jennings sees in hospice the roots of a more holistic, ecological model that places ethical decision making in a more familial and communal ethos.

Nancy Berlinger too emphasizes the communal aspect of ethics. To Berlinger *solidarity* is a key ethical principle—a principle that emphasizes "we are all in this together." But such an ethos goes hand-in-hand with an emphasis on *justice*. As her case example indicates, it is difficult to be "in this together" when there is differential access to care and treatment options.

Berlinger's chapter is the first chapter to utilize a case study approach—a major emphasis in this book. In using cases, the editors wish to emphasize that ethics evolve as we deal with the myriad of real-life situations that daily confront end-of-life care.

CHAPTER 1

From Rights to Relationships: The Ecological Turn in Ethics Near the End of Life

Bruce Jennings

Perhaps no single area of medical care has received more ethical and legal attention in recent years than the care of the dying or "end-of-life care." I use this term broadly to include hospice and palliative care, but also the use of all manner of life-saving and life-sustaining medical treatment for persons who are in an advanced stage of chronic, progressive, incurable disease. Such conditions (chronic heart, vascular, and pulmonary disease; cancer; dementia; and frailty) characterize the dying of the vast majority of Americans today at increasing old age (Lynn, 2004). Current forms of intensive, high-technology modes of medical and surgical management rescue many from premature death from acute life-threatening illness, such as trauma or infection. Such treatments also allow many patients to survive acute emergencies that punctuate the early and middle stages of many chronic illnesses. But this same form of medical management becomes increasingly problematic when employed in the context of end-of-life care (Teno et al., 2004).

Taking these two focal points of end-of-life care—technological medical management to prolong life and palliative care to support quality of life—as my orientation in this chapter, I provide a brief analysis of the ethical goals and strategies underlying efforts to improve end-of-life care during the past three decades. Emerging from the recognition of some of the shortcomings of prior approaches, there is today a new orientation taking shape in end-of-life care that reflects what might be called a "relational" perspective on the situation, needs, and agency of the person at the end of life (Mackenzie and Stoljar, 2000). This I refer to as the ecological turn in ethics near the end of life. It offers a revised understanding of the goals of end-of-life care and of the ethical standards and communication requirements of end-of-life treatment planning and decision making. In biology and environmental science, ecology is the study of the systemic interaction and interdependency of various organisms among themselves and with their inorganic environment. Social ecology applies this same systems viewpoint to the complex nexus of social and cultural relations among human beings, with their extraordinarily diverse and powerful cognitive, affective, and communicative capacities (Code, 2006).

My thesis is that the principal task of the next few years in the end-of-life care domain will be to shift toward this ecological perspective and away from the now prevailing individualistic perspective (Jennings, 2008). This shift will allow us to refine the decision-making processes and tools that are already in place and to devise new and more culturally sensitive, family systems-oriented strategies of communication and care planning. In certain respects, this kind of perspectival shift has already begun (Browning and Solomon, 2006; Dubler and Liebman, 1994; Meier, Isaacs, and Hughes, 2010; Morrissey, 2011; Morrissey and Jennings, 2006; Sabatino, 1999, 2010; Schneider, 1998). But ethical and conceptual clarity will be needed to guide this shift if it is to realize its full potential, and also to protect against the undue erosion of important patient-centered rights and values. Patient's rights should be reconstrued, but they should not be rejected. It is important to insist on this distinction, for it is not a mere semantic quibble at a time of concerted, often less than careful or discerning, financial cost-containment policy measures targeted at end-of-life care.

THE EVOLUTION OF END-OF-LIFE CARE

At the time of the Karen Ann Quinlan case in 1975, the law and ethics of forgoing life-sustaining treatment were *terra incognita*. Thirty-five years later (not that long as ethics and the law go) court rulings and statutes at the federal level and in all 50 states had created a widely accepted framework for decision making near the end of life.

How did we get to where we are today? Beginning in the 1960s, new technologies were coming on line to prolong life-functions in critically and terminally ill patients—mechanical ventilators, intensive care units, kidney dialysis, and the like. These were, for the most part, "half-way" technologies (in Lewis Thomas's phrase) because they could stave off death and prolong biological functions of life, but could not necessarily restore the patient to a meaningful mode of being alive (Thomas, 1974).

In the wake of this technological transformation of end-of-life treatment, two realizations occurred. First, it became evident that, for perhaps the majority of patients at the end of life, the exact timing and circumstances of one's death was no longer beyond anyone's control but had become in fact the result of specific decisions and choices made by those caring for (health care professionals) and speaking for (usually family) the patient. Second, thoughtful leaders in medicine, and many family members who had observed the new end-of-life care firsthand, gradually became aware that the experience of dying (for the individual, for the family, and also at times for health care providers) was often a horror. Too many Americans were dying unnecessarily bad deaths—deaths with inadequate palliative support, inadequate compassion, and inadequate human presence and witness; deaths preceded by a dying marked by fear, anxiety, loneliness, and isolation; and deaths that effaced dignity and denied individual self-control and choice.

Not surprisingly, a movement for reform took shape aiming to improve end-of-life care. This movement was based on the belief that bad dying was avoidable because it does not reside in dying or death per se, but in a poorly managed dying. Our powerful new technology was not being used wisely and judiciously but had succumbed to a kind of technological imperative. Aggressive interventions were not being adequately informed or guided by the patient's own wishes and values. Reductionistic medical perspectives, which were the flip side of the new technology and the medical training that went along with it, were displacing more holistic perspectives; this made it more difficult to see "the patient as person," as one leading bioethicist aptly put it (Ramsey, 1970). Palliative care was not a priority of mainstream medicine, and the hospice model was only beginning to develop for a limited number of people, such as cancer patients who had "failed" chemotherapy.

Over time the end-of-life care reform movement devised two major strategies for change. The first of these can be called the *patient empowerment strategy*. Working mainly through the medium of the law, but also through ethical persuasion and education within medicine, new norms and decision-making standards were put in place to empower and enable individuals to set the terms of their own medical care at the end of life (Meisel, 1993; National Center for State Courts, 1993). The law and ethics embraced the right of an individual to consent to or forgo all forms of medical care, and they embraced the use of advance directives to keep the wishes of the individual at the center of the decision-making process if and when the patient lost the capacity to make medical decisions.

The second approach was the *alternative care system strategy*. Working mainly through the medium of health care policy and medical/nursing education, the task of improving care for the dying was approached by building a different type of institutional system and model for the delivery of end-of-life care. This system of hospice and palliative care is based on the principles of quality of life, dignity, and the relief of suffering (Field and Cassel, 1997; Cassel and Foley, 1999). The goal of the system strategy is to orient end-of-life care toward dignity, comfort, symptom management, and meaningful life closure rather than technological intervention to prolong the duration of life.

Looking back today, however, one would have to concede that this reform movement has had mixed success. Many expectations and hopes have not been realized, and unexpected obstacles have arisen that make improving end-of-life care more difficult than we thought.

But progress has been real, nonetheless. Today people have much more control of their medical care at the end of life, the technological imperative has been bridled to some extent, and palliative care is taken more seriously in the medical mainstream. Well over one million people who die each year receive hospice services for some period of time (often too short) before death. Deaths in hospitals and nursing homes are preceded by more deliberate decision-making processes in which advance directives, medical orders done in consultation with the patient or authorized family surrogates, and constructive advice given by an ethics consultation service and/or a palliative care consultation service all play a more regular and reliable role. Many people are fortunate enough to die with pain kept to a minimum, surrounded by the people they love, in a setting attentive to their spiritual, emotional, and physical needs. That is progress.

By achieving individual empowerment and a more holistic quality of living-while-dying system of end-of-life care, reformers working over several decades have believed that ordinary people and their families would embrace both enhanced patient autonomy and hospice with open arms. However, the public and cultural response has not been what the end-of-life care reform movement had expected. The allure of life-extending medical technology has remained very strong as it has improved and even as it has gotten much more expensive (Callahan, 2000). Cultural, ethnic, and religious diversity has called some of the reform movement's assumptions about autonomy and empowerment into question (Koenig and Gates-Williams, 1995). Persons with long-term disabilities have also challenged assumptions about what constitutes quality of life (Asch, 2001). Racial and class disparities in access and quality of end-of-life care remain a shameful reality in the American health care system.

As recently as 2004, the Schiavo case in Florida demonstrated the political volatility that decisions to forgo life-sustaining technology (in that case artificial nutrition and hydration) still have (Eisenberg, 2005). And in 2009 something as seemingly noncontroversial as encouraging physicians to have conversations with their patients about advance directives and end-of-life care wishes was stigmatized as a proposal to create government-mandated "death panels." The fact that such statements are thought to be (and are) politically effective attests to the reality that after more than three decades of widespread publicity and social discussion, there still remains widespread ignorance among the general public concerning the process of end-of-life care. Those who have been empowered apparently haven't gotten the news.

TOWARD A RELATIONAL, ECOLOGICAL PARADIGM

I believe that a crucial shortcoming of end-of-life care reform is that the patient empowerment strategy and the alternative system strategy have failed to converge successfully. The two strategies have more or less run parallel to one another from the 1970s on without sufficient interactive learning and self-correction. That is beginning to change—indeed, that convergence is what the ecological turn is all about—but the earlier inability to converge was not simply fortuitous. It was caused by deep-seated factors in American culture and in the health care system, factors that remain strong today.

It is striking that in the United States these two strategies were virtually contemporaneous in their origins. Both were not only expert-driven, top-down reform strategies, but also bottom-up social movements—the hospice movement and the so-called "right to die" movement—that arose out of widespread grassroots dissatisfaction with mainstream medicine. The system approach began in 1973 with the importation of the hospice concept into the United States by Florence Wald at Yale University, who had worked and studied with Cicely Saunders at St. Christopher's Hospice in London. Mainstream oncology was manifestly failing to provide adequate support and continuity of care to cancer patients in the terminal phase of their illness. Hospice was designed to remedy that systemic defect; it was created to provide symptom control, palliative relief from suffering, and meaningful presence and human refuge to dying patients and their families (Corless and Foster, 1999). At virtually the same time, in 1975, the family of Karen Ann Quinlan in New Jersey turned to the courts in search of a solution to what they considered a denial of dignity for their daughter by the power of a new life-sustaining technology, mechanical ventilation. The New Jersey Supreme Court ruled that

Karen, who was permanently unconscious after sustaining catastrophic anoxic brain injury, had a right to refuse life-sustaining medical treatment under the circumstances (*In re Quinlan*, 1976).

The hospice movement developed an alternative model of cancer care to better meet the needs of patients and families who were being abandoned by mainstream treatment systems, and created community-based, non-profit agencies to deliver this care. Hospice was supported by out-of-pocket patient and family payment and by charitable funding until the creation of the Medicare Hospice Benefit (MHB) in 1982 and the concomitant development of private insurance coverage (Hoyer, 1998). Over time, enrollment has grown and hospice has undergone increasing professionalization and quality improvement. It has assumed a business orientation as larger for-profit organizations have entered the hospice marketplace. In the 1990s a parallel palliative care initiative, not specifically funded but also not constrained by Medicare eligibility requirements, arose and has been growing significantly, especially in hospital settings (Morrison and Meier, 2011).

Hospice and palliative care today offers a well-proven, effective therapeutic model that prevents and manages suffering, maintains quality of life, and reduces illness burden in populations with serious or life-threatening illnesses. This care takes a multidimensional, multidisciplinary approach and is grounded in a holistic bio-psycho-social-spiritual conception of care. In principle, hospice and palliative care is beneficial to anyone living with virtually any form of chronic, progressive, life-limiting illness (not only cancer) and is relevant throughout the entire course of the disease (not just in the final six months of life). Both the individual patient and the family are considered the unit of care. This model aims to promote ongoing communication to support shared decision making and advance care planning that is sensitive to culture, religion, and other value concerns. It provides comfort and relief from suffering through expert symptom control and management of psychosocial and spiritual needs. It provides practical help in the home and expert management of active dying and its aftermath. It also offers support for family while they are engaged in caregiving and experiencing grief and bereavement. Access to this therapeutic model has grown substantially in the past decade but is still limited by policy rules and economic and cultural factors (Jennings, Ryndes, D'Onofrio, and Baily, 2003).

The right-to-die movement was not focused so much on a new therapeutic model (although it shared with hospice and palliative care many of the same aims), but rather on legal empowerment to protect individual patients from both the Scylla of overly aggressive treatment due to the technological imperative and medical paternalism and the Charybdis of inadequate treatment due to discrimination, disrespect, and neglect (Webb, 1997). This movement has been remarkably successful in altering the legal and clinical landscape of the United States through judicial action and legislative reform strategies. The constitutional right to refuse life-sustaining medical treatment has been clearly and repeatedly affirmed by courts at the highest levels. Laws authorizing advance medical directives and surrogate decision making for incapacitated patients have been enacted in every state. Ethics committees to oversee decision making in accordance with patients' rights have been established in virtually every sizable hospital, and rights protections are required by health care accreditation standards nationwide (Meisel and Cerminara, 2004).

For patients rejected by the mainstream medical system, hospice provided a refuge where an interdisciplinary model of palliative care could provide relief and dignity. The right-to-die movement established the principle of the individual's right to refuse medical treatment in the service of his or her dignity and autonomy as a person. In effect, it provided freedom from a mainstream medical system that would not let the patient go and offered a legal power to place the patient (or those acting on behalf of her wishes) effectively in charge of her own medical treatment.

Until recently, most of the action in the end-of-life care arena has come from the individualistic, empowerment orientation of the right-to-die movement. Yet, I would argue that it is the systems and holistic perspective of hospice that actually contains the seeds of the new ecological orientation now taking shape. The ecological turn in end-of-life care has taken a long time to emerge because hospice has not influenced mainstream end-of-life care very much.

There are several reasons for this. As a counter-cultural movement and as an alternative care system largely composed of small, community-based agencies offering primarily home-based services, hospice had little direct contact or influence with larger medical centers and physicians in specialized practice. In 1982 the creation of the Medicare Hospice Benefit (MHB) created a large source of new funding for hospice programs and expanded access to these services. But this expansion did not bring about a broader application of the hospice model of care because the hospice philosophy became equated— mistakenly in my view—with the conditions of the MHB. Hospice came to be regarded not as a model for end-of-life care generally, but rather as a kind of last resort alternative, after life-extending medical treatments had become futile or unduly burdensome and after a decision had been made to forgo them (Jennings et al., 2003). And this was assumed to be appropriate only during the last six months of life, even though at roughly the same time many courts were ruling that such a short duration of life expectancy was not a precondition for the legal and ethical right to refuse life-sustaining treatment. This hiving off of a more relational and holistic approach to end-of-life care until after the rest of medical care had run its course, as it were, was a key factor in making the individualistic, empowerment orientation the sole focus for end-of-life care ethics in mainstream medical settings.

One important facet of the current emergence of an ecological paradigm is the breakdown of this artificial separation, thanks to the development in many hospitals of specialized palliative care consultation services. These programs promote an ecological approach in ways that can fit into the cultural ethos and institutional patterns of hospital–based medical practice. In this way a more holistic, hospice-like, model can become a part of the decision-making process in end-of-life care when life-prolonging measures are still under consideration by patients and families. Hospice programs treating patients funded by Medicare will remain cut off from other portions of the end-of-life care system until Medicare policy is changed, but their philosophical, therapeutic orientation is spreading through palliative care programs into the length and breadth of end-of-life care.

However, if hospice as an embodiment of a new kind of end-of-life care system contains the seeds of an ecological orientation, and if palliative care programs are helping to reorient end-of-life care beyond the present scope of hospice narrowly defined, an even more important factor is bringing about change in end-of-life care today. Change is being brought about by the practical failure of many of the basic tenets of the individualistic empowerment paradigm itself.

This paradigm is based on the principle that the dying person is, ironic as this may seem, an independent and unencumbered self, unmoored from a context of relational meaning. Our legal structures for end-of-life decision making are grounded in the principle that the dying individual should choose, and all others—physicians, families, and judges—should defer to (facilitate, support, carry out) those choices. This core conception is coming to be recognized as a profound oversimplification (Schneider, 1998). It overlooks, or is indifferent to altogether, the fact that individuals die, as they live, in a web of vital and complex relationships. What happened in life, and what happens in dying, is shaped by and shapes those relationships. An individualistic framing in terms of privacy, rights, and autonomy makes it difficult to appreciate both how bedside decision making takes place in a number of different social contexts (the family, the hospital or clinical ethos, the surrounding community) and why it is important to focus on choices among various systems of care rather than on microchoices about the uses of medical technology one at a time and crisis by crisis. In order to improve end-of-life care, liberation of the patient from heavy-handed medical paternalism is a necessary but far from sufficient accomplishment.

Thus to frame end-of-life care as first and foremost an issue of individual rights and empowerment is to misconstrue the cultural meaning of care and to slice thin the moral responsibilities of family members as caretakers for the dying. The end of life is not the best time to micromanage one's own medical care and to wage battles on behalf of independent selfhood. Caring, family solidarity, mutual respect, love, and attentiveness to the dying person are the qualities most needed at that time. The empowerment paradigm has been rather suspicious of families and embraces the legal fiction that they are and should be empty conduits of the patient's wishes (Nelson, 1992; Nelson and Nelson, 1995). Mothers and fathers, brothers and sisters, and companions all lose their deep, long-lived ties with the dying person and become "surrogates" or "proxies"—cold, artificial terms to denote an impersonal role.

PRINCIPLES THAT FACILITATE HUMAN FLOURISHING

Still, there is no gainsaying the importance of having a paradigm for end-of-life care, some legal regime and an ethic that present settled norms and procedures for making terrifying decisions. The individualistic empowerment paradigm is consonant with dominant themes in U.S. culture, such as liberty, privacy, and the integrity of one's own body against outside intrusion without consent, including medical intervention. Principles of right are well-ordered; but life near the end (and perhaps at all times) is messy. We have learned in the past three decades much more about the experiential complexity of living while dying, and what we have learned does not fit the order of the individualistic paradigm. The test must be how well the governing principles of an end-of-life care ethic and system of services actually facilitate human flourishing (Morrissey and Jennings, 2006). Several elements of the individualistic paradigm are failing that test. These elements are advance care planning and advance directives, surrogate decision making, and the nature of the doctor-patient relationship. Each turns out to be undermined in practice and self-defeating when understood individualistically, and all of these key components of end-of-life care will likely prove much more successful when approached ecologically and relationally. Simply put, empowerment backfires when it isolates people rather than bringing them together in communion/communication. Rights are undermined in practice unless they are exercised in the context of dialogue and relationships of shared experience and meaning. The individualistic paradigm sees dying patients' rights as claims of noninterference by others; the ecological paradigm sees rights as bonds of interpersonal respect and support.

Let me illustrate the ecological turn in end-of-life care in reference to each of these crucial elements: advance planning, surrogate decision making, and the physician-patient relationship.

From advance directives to advance care planning

End-of-life care decision making is greatly facilitated and led toward good outcomes if people plan ahead for their terminal illness. Most Americans find that exceedingly hard to do. Even when individuals manage to reflect on their own personal beliefs and wishes and then prepare advance directives, these documents do not always prevent conflict within the family at the time end-of-life decisions have to be made. Thus advance directives are most impotent at precisely the time they are most crucial. That paradox can only be solved if the advance directive resides in a broader context of communication and dialogue with family members and one's physician. We set ourselves up for conflict and failure when we see an advance directive as an expression of a detached individual, rather than as a manifestation of values built in relationships and lived interactions and experiences that have grown over time. Because we have not conceptualized advance directives in this relational, ecological way, we have not done much to design mechanisms to facilitate and support the family dynamic of good communication. Our focus on the voice of the patient has not adequately confronted what it means for a family to stand by as death approaches and to walk with a relative into its shadow.

It is essential to move beyond the notion of an advance directive as a legal document that represents a unilateral claim or demand by the individual patient (a "directive") and toward the broader notion of advance care planning as a collective process of dialogue, interpretation, speaking, and listening; a process that produces a common understanding within a family and a sense of common aim concerning the patient's end-of-life care (American Health Decisions, 1997). This move is referred to by one leading commentator as a shift from a "transactional" approach to a "communications" approach in advance care planning (Sabatino, 2010).

From health care proxies to family decision making

Approximately 40 states, most recently New York in 2010, have enacted legislation to authorize family members (or other close friends) to make end-of-life care decisions for dying persons who have lost decision-making capacity and who have not named a health care agent or proxy. This supplement to earlier statutes that authorized the naming of proxies through durable powers of attorney for health care was prompted by the fact that a large majority of individuals had not completed formal advance directives, and therefore health care facilities were forced to rely on family decisions at the end of life *faute de mieux*. It also has arisen to provide guidance in those frequent cases when the patient's wishes are not actually known, and, even if there is a proxy decision maker designated by the patient in place, the person making the treatment decisions must fall back on ethical and legal standards of "substituted judgment" (an inference of what the patient would have wanted) or "best interests" (a judgment about what objectively would be the most reasonable and humane decision for the dying person under the specific circumstances). In these cases it is particularly important that evaluative judgment and decision making in end-of-life care reflect open communication and consensus building within the family unit and between the family and the health care team.

Recognizing the institutional ecology of the doctor-patient relationship

A final self-defeating aspect of the individual empowerment strategy involves the limitations in the way this perspective has focused on the perceived and (sometimes, but not always) real dyadic power struggle between the attending physician and the patient, proxy, or family as a whole. This focus puts adversarialism and conflict in place of collaboration and cooperation. This emphasis is reversed in an ethic of palliative care and a "covenantal" notion of the doctor-patient relationship, an innovative way of thinking that has contributed to the ecological turn in end-of-life care (Fins, 2006).

Moreover, a conception of the doctor-patient relationship as a power dyad tends to exaggerate the agency of both the individual physician and the patient, and it decontextualizes end-of-life decision making from its institutional and technological setting (Kaufman, 2005). From the beginning, the individualistic empowerment strategy has been based on the belief that inappropriately aggressive and unwanted treatment at the end of life is fundamentally a problem within the physician-patient dyad, and in particular a problem caused by prognostic uncertainty and poor physician understanding of the patient's preferences and wishes. According to the empowerment strategy, physicians would follow patient preferences if those preferences (a thin word standing for an exceedingly dense psycho-social condition) were clear and reasonable.

As the SUPPORT (The Study to Understand Prognoses and Preferences for Outcomes and Risks of Treatments) study demonstrated nearly 20 years ago, this is an inadequate account of the problem. The experimental portion of this study showed that physician behavior is not altered significantly by addressing uncertainty and poor communication alone (SUPPORT Principal Investigators, 1995; Lynn et al., 1997). These factors appear to have great importance because the physician-patient relationship is conceptualized as a personal interaction or a transaction. By contrast, the ecological perspective would see the causes of the high incidence of unwanted and ineffective technological overtreatment near the end of life as structural and institutional in nature (Farber-Post, Blustein, and Dubler, 1999). In the modern acute care hospital virtually everything is oriented toward the use of life-sustaining equipment and techniques, not toward forgoing their usage (DelVecchio Good et al., 2004). The informal culture of specialty medicine, the reward system, the institutional pressures faced by family members, the range of choices people in extremis are being asked to make—each of these factors and more make up a system that is remarkably resistant to change (Kaufman, 2005).

SUPPORT was a sobering moment in the history of the end-of-life care reform effort. Its disturbing findings led its sponsor, The Robert Wood Johnson Foundation, to undertake a large-scale follow-up initiative in the 1990s. The Last Acts Campaign launched the contemporary palliative care movement and was an important crucible for the intellectual reorientation that has produced the ecological turn. Even as the Clinton health reform plan was faltering and going down to political defeat, a quiet, almost invisible, but real revolution was taking place around the last lap, so to speak, of the health care system.

FACILITATING THE ECOLOGICAL TURN
The ecological turn in end-of-life care is composed of a number of reasonable, pragmatic responses to the conceptual blind spots and the practical conundrums of the individualistic empowerment paradigm. It draws on basic approaches long inherent in the systems design paradigm of hospice and palliative care,

but applies those insights "upstream," as it were, before a palliative care plan for dying with comfort and dignity has been chosen and while various other care plans, including those involving life-prolonging and disease-modifying interventions, are still being considered. However, our discussion of the ecological turn in end-of-life care would be incomplete if we were to consider merely its logic and conceptual structure alone. After all, a primary insight of the ecological perspective is that theory cannot be divorced from practice, and any reform ideal needs to be rooted in an institutional context and embodied in actual care delivery. Hence in closing we must ask what kind of institutional changes will foster a space conducive to the relationality and communication patterns envisioned by the ecological turn? I believe that this can be done by concentrating on the following three large opportunities and taking steps toward systems and practices to take advantage of them (Murray and Jennings, 2005).

The first opportunity pertains to health policy broadly defined. We must educate and motivate health professionals, adapt institutions, and realign financial incentives so that the right services will be in place and just about the right things will happen for patients, because they are "built into the system" (Lynn, 2005, S17). Our society has devoted considerable effort to protecting patient choice, but we have overlooked the costs of choice. Having too much medical choice can be as burdensome to dying patients and their families as having too little.

If the hospital was once a place of too little choice, lack of transparency, and bald paternalism, in recent years the pendulum has swung to the other extreme, and patients and families are now presented with an excessive menu of complex—always difficult, often bewildering—clinical choices. At an extremely vulnerable time, and with little training or support, our system requires people to micromanage a confusing and emotionally explosive set of clinical responses to a recurring series of life-threatening complications within an underlying progressively degenerative and incurable chronic disease (Hawkins et al., 2005). Instead of focusing on how to accommodate the idiosyncratic decisions of each individual patient, one at a time, we should ask what types of needs do dying persons generally have, and how can we design a health care delivery system that will meet most of those needs for most people, most of the time. It is imperative that we do this for people on the main trajectories of dying.

Distinct trajectories of dying can be distinguished for large populations of patients, each of which poses different sorts of challenges for patients and families, health care institutions, and policy makers. And each of these trajectories requires a specialized type of caregiving system, with different types of medical and psychosocial services offered at different times (Lynn, 2004). An epidemiologically well-grounded approach to the design of end-of-life care systems would help to avoid the burdensome medical micromanagement by dying patients or surrogates mentioned above. And we could still honor the special autonomy of a few who, for whatever personal, religious, or cultural reasons, might opt out of a default system in favor of something more tailor-made to fit their preferences. For instance, if patients very near the end of life were seamlessly transitioned into hospice care, rather than having to struggle to get into it because it requires such an explicit decision, then particular individuals could still be at liberty to opt for a more life-prolonging type of care plan. This is not a matter of rationing or denying individuals the freedom to request certain types of medical care—we shall have to deal with those problems too, but not here. Rather, it is a matter of shifting the systemic presumption and the flow, as it were, of dying individuals through the channels or pathways of the health care system. The philosopher John Locke said that it does not deny someone freedom if he is led away from bogs and precipices. Today we put enormous effort into directing people to the quagmire and to the edge of the cliff. Our health care system puts patients on pathways that lead to technological interventions that are neither benign nor medically appropriate given their underlying biological condition. There is no ethical imperative to do that, and no ethical prohibition against building an end-of-life care system that does that much less frequently.

The second opportunity offered by the ecological turn is to reach across color, class, disability, and moral convictions to create a new consensus on the goals of care at the end of life; a consensus that takes into account feelings of mistrust and lived experiences of unequal treatment. This will not be an easy task, but one imperative is clear: The circle of people engaged in forging the consensus must be enlarged. People living with disabilities, people with strong religious beliefs about the sacredness of life, and people who feel left out by mainstream medicine have a crucial and constructive role to play in this conversation. But it must be a conversation and not a shouting match. There is also reason for hope. Ideological differences are likely to dwindle in significance when people confront the lived realities of suffering patients, grieving families, and compassionate care givers. As I write this I am painfully aware that we are in the midst of one of the most polarized and ideological moments in recent American history. Much that is progressive in health care, not only in end-of-life care, hangs in the balance.

The third challenge is to rebuild, reinforce, and reinterpret our existing laws, institutions, and practices around the acknowledgment that dying is interpersonal, not strictly individualistic. Hospice does this, creating space for families and intimate friends to be close to the dying person; hospice also recognizes the emotional needs of those same people. Proxy and family decision makers in hospital and nursing home settings likewise can and should be concerned for both the patient's interests and the well-being of those whose lives are deeply affected by the patient's medical care and manner of dying. Our default assumption should be that patient autonomy and empowerment are fulfilled, not negated, by a dying process that is minimally destructive to the flourishing of those who love and are loved by the dying person—those who remain behind and must cope with their own grief and conflict, and move on with their lives. We must learn to honor and nurture the solidarity of dying rather than always accommodating its narcissism.

The reinterpretation of surrogacy in the direction of the ecological turn is much closer to the moral common sense of most patients and families today than is the patient versus family suspicion implicit in the individualistic empowerment paradigm, but it will not happen spontaneously and will require institutional support. Surrogates named in advance directives and other family members should be given adequate information, counseling, and support so that they can more effectively position their decision-making responsibility within the dynamics of their family system and its web of interpersonal relationships, tensions, and psychological history (Vermont Ethics Network, 1997). Proxies named in advance by the patient are thought to be preferable to treatment instructions (written or verbal "living wills") precisely because an individual on the scene has the flexibility to exercise judgment and to interpret the patient's wishes and values in light of specific (and sometimes rapidly changing) medical information about the patient's condition, treatment options, and prognosis. Prior instructions cannot have these qualities of flexibility and judgment. But while we seem to expect these skills in agents and surrogates, we have done little or nothing to study the environmental conditions in the health care setting that are most conducive to them, nor have we developed protocols of education, counseling, and support aimed at enabling surrogates to engage in good decision making.

The decisions a surrogate makes redound to affect the surrogate himself or herself (and the entire family) as well. Families and surrogates need to have a framework within which that information has meaning and validates their own past relationship with the patient and their own sense of self-identity as a loving, caring, responsible person faced with life-and-death decisions in the midst of shock, loss, possibly guilt, and grief (Teno and Lynn, 1996). To see surrogacy as simply an information-processing task is to miss most of its human angst and drama. And yet that is the approach that many health care facilities have taken, implicitly or explicitly, by the resources they provide to agents and surrogates, by the nature and style of communication offered to them, and by the low priority most institutions give to multidisciplinary counseling and support. In short, we have thus far focused almost exclusively on how to *empower* agents to make decisions; we now must also begin to address how to *enable* them to make *good* decisions.

Moreover, hospitals and other health care facilities have an institutional and systemic responsibility and role to play in enhancing proxy decision making. This is not to say that individuals and families do not have a responsibility to prepare for these decisions on their own initiative. They do. But up to now, the institutional side of the equation has been relatively neglected. More research and assessment tools are needed to evaluate current institutional practices in this regard, and to improve them in the future. Health care professionals must become more knowledgeable about, and sensitive to, the special needs of surrogates and the special burdens of the role of surrogacy. An appropriate interdisciplinary response should be brought to bear on improving the counseling and support agents and surrogates receive, including medicine and nursing, but also ethics, pastoral counseling, social work, and other sources of expertise about the full range of cognitive and emotional work surrogate decision making entails.

CONCLUSION

This chapter has described the general trajectory of improving the ethics of end-of-life care in the past three decades and has attempted to indicate some new directions for this unfinished work. However, where we have been and where we should go are not the only matters of ethical and social importance. Equally important is how we should get there. In closing then, perhaps a general observation about the type of discourse that will lead in the right direction is in order. I believe it is essential that the movement to improve end-of-life care remain dynamic, flexible, and open to new ideas and to conversation with new voices. The voice of reasoned discourse, pragmatic improvement, and respect for civil rights and human dignity must be the hallmarks of end-of-life care reform in the years ahead. Advocacy must ground its *ethical* norms in *ethnographic* understanding. Moral principle and communicative practice must join together in the hard work of interpreting, sustaining, and achieving humanity in the final chapters of our lives.

Bruce Jennings is director of bioethics at the Center for Humans and Nature and senior consultant at The Hastings Center. He has been active in the end-of-life care arena and has published widely on ethical issues in hospital treatment decision making, palliative care, and hospice. He has served on the Board of Directors of the National Hospice and Palliative Care Organization and the Board of Trustees of the Hospice and Palliative Care Association of New York State. He is coauthor of the Hastings Center Guidelines on the Termination of Life-Sustaining Treatment and the Care of the Dying *(1987) and was cofounder of the* "Decisions Near the End of Life" *program, an educational and practice change program that was conducted in over 200 hospitals in 20 states from 1990 to 1996.*

REFERENCES

American Health Decisions. (1997). *The quest to die with dignity*. Appleton, WI: American Health Decisions.

Asch, A. (2001). Disability, Bioethics and Human Rights. In G. Albrecht, K. Seelman, and M. Buty (Eds.), *Handbook of Disability Studies*. Thousand Oaks, CA: Sage Publications.

Browning, D., & Solomon, M. Z. (2006). Relational Learning in Pediatric Palliative Care: Transformative Education and the Culture of Medicine. *Child and Adolescent Psychiatric Clinics of North America, 15*, 795–815.

Callahan, D., (2000). *The troubled dream of life: In search of a peaceful death* (2nd ed.). Washington, DC: Georgetown University Press.

Cassel, C., & Foley, K. (1999). *Principles for care of patients at the end of life: An emerging consensus among the specialties of medicine*. New York: Milbank Memorial Fund.

Code, L. (2006). *Ecological thinking: The politics of epistemic location*. New York: Y: Oxford University Press.

Corless, I. B., & Foster, Z. (Eds.). (1999). *The hospice heritage: Celebrating our Future*. Binghamton, NY: Haworth Press.

DelVecchio Good, M. J., Gadmer, N. M., Ruopp, P., Lakoma, M., Sullivan, A. M., Redinbaugh, E., ..., Block, S.D. (2004). Narrative nuances on good and bad deaths: Internists' tales from high-technology work places. *Social Science & Medicine, 58*, 939–953.

Dubler, N.N., & Liebman, C. B. (1994). *Bioethics mediation: A guide to shaping shared solutions*. New York: United Hospital Fund.

Eisenberg, J. (2005). *Using Terri: The religious right's conspiracy to take away our rights*. New York: Harper Collins.

Farber-Post, L., Blustein, J., & Dubler, N. N. (1999). Introduction: The doctor-proxy relationship: An untapped resource. *Journal of Law, Medicine and Ethics, 27*, 5–12.

Field, M. J., & Cassel, C. K. (Eds.). (1997). *Approaching death: Improving care at the end of life*. Washington, DC: National Academy Press.

Fins, J. J. (2006). *A palliative ethic of care: Clinical wisdom at life's end*. Sudbury, MA: Jones and Bartlett Publishers.

Hawkins, N. A., Ditto, P. H., Danks, J. H., & Smucker, W. D. (2005). Micromanaging death: Process preferences, values, and goals in end-of-life medical decision making. *The Gerontologist 45*, 107–117.

Hoyer, T. (1998). A History of the Medicare Hospice Benefit. In J. K. Harrold, & J. Lynn (Eds.), *A good dying: Shaping health care for the last months of life* (pp. 61–69). Binghamton, NY: Haworth Press.

In re Quinlan. 70 N.J. 10, 355 A.2d 647 (N.J. 1976).

Jennings, B. (2008). Dying at an early age: Ethical issues in palliative pediatric care. In K. J. Doka, & A. Tucci (Eds.), *Living with grief: Children and adolescents* (pp. 99–119). Washington, DC: The Hospice Foundation of America.

Jennings, B., Ryndes, T., D'Onofrio, C., & Baily, M. A. (2003). Access to Hospice Care: Expanding Boundaries, Overcoming Barriers. *Hastings Center Report, Special Supplement, 332*, S1–S60.

Kaufman, S. R. (2005). *And a time to die: How American hospitals shape the end of life*. New York: Scribner.

Koenig, B. A., & Gates-Williams, J. (1995). Understanding cultural difference in caring for dying patients. *Western Journal of Medicine, 1633*, 244–249.

Lynn, J. (2004). *Sick to death and not going to take it anymore!: Reforming health care for the last years of life.* Berkeley, CA: University of California Press.

Lynn, J. (2005). Living long in fragile health: New demographics shape end-of-life care. In B. Jennings, G. Kaebnick, & T. H. Murray (Eds.), *Improving end-of-life care: Why has it been so difficult? Hastings Center special report S356,* S14–18.

Lynn, J., et al. (1997). Ineffectiveness of the SUPPORT intervention: Review of explanations. *Journal of the American Geriatric Society, 48,* S206–S213.

Mackenzie, C., & Stoljar, N. (Eds.). (2000). *Relational autonomy: Feminist perspectives on autonomy, agency, and the social self.* New York: Oxford University Press.

Meier, D. E., Isaacs, S. L., & Hughes, R. G. (Eds.). (2010). *Palliative care: Transforming the care of serious illness.* San Francisco, CA: Jossey Bass.

Meisel, A, & Cerminara, K. L. (2004). *The right to die: The law of end-of life decision making (3rd ed.).* New York: Aspen Law and Business.

Meisel, A. (1993). The legal consensus about forgoing life-sustaining treatment: Its status and its prospects. *Kennedy Institute of Ethics Journal, 2*(4), 309–345.

Morrison, R. S. & Meier, D. E. (2011). *America's care of serious illness: A state-by-state report card on access to palliative care in our nation's hospitals.* New York: Center to Advance Palliative Care.

Morrissey, M. B. (2011). Phenomenology of pain and suffering: A humanistic perspective in gerontological health and social work. *Journal of Social Work in End-of-Life and Palliative Care, 7*(1), 14–38.

Morrissey, M. B., & Jennings, B. (2006, Winter). A social ecology of health model in end of life decision making: Is the law therapeutic? *New York State Bar Association Health Law Journal, 11*(1), 51–60.

Murray T. H., & Jennings, B. (2005). The quest to reform end of life care: Rethinking assumptions and setting new directions. In B. Jennings, G. Kaebnick, & T. H. Murray (Eds.), *Improving end of life care: Why has it been so difficult? Hastings Center Report, Special Supplement, 35* (6), S52–S57.

National Center for State Courts, Coordinating Council on Life-Sustaining Medical Treatment Decision Making by the Courts. (1993). *Guidelines for State Court Decision Making in Life-Sustaining Medical Treatment Cases.* Revised Second Edition. St. Paul, MN: West Publishing Co.

Nelson, J. L. (1992). Taking families seriously. *Hastings Center Report* 22 (4), 6–12.

Nelson, J. L., & Nelson, H. L. (1995). *The patient in the family: An ethics of medicine and the family.* New York: Routledge.

Ramsey, P. (1970). *The patient as person.* New Haven, CT: Yale University Press.

Sabatino, C. P. (1999). The legal and functional status of the medical proxy: Suggestions for statutory reform. *Journal of Law, Medicine and Ethics, 27,* 52–68.

Sabatino, C. P. (2010). The evolution of health care advance planning law and policy. *Milbank Quarterly, 88,* 2, 211–239.

Schneider, C. (1998). *The practice of autonomy: Patients, doctors, and medical decisions.* New York: Oxford University Press.

Smith. W. J. (2000). *Culture of death: The assault on medical ethics in America.* San Francisco, CA: Encounter Books.

SUPPORT Principal Investigators. (1995). A controlled trial to improve care for seriously ill hospitalized patients: The study to understand prognosis and preferences for outcomes and risks of treatments (SUPPORT). *Journal of the American Medical Association, 274,* 20, 591–598.

Teno, J. M., & Lynn, J. (1996). Putting advance-care planning into action," *Journal of Clinical Ethics, 7,* 205–213.

Teno, J. M., Clarridge, B., Casey, V., Welch, L. C., Wettle, T., Shield, R., & Mor, V. (2004). Family perspectives on end-of-life care at the last place of care. *Journal of the American Medical Association, 291,* 88–93.

Thomas, L. (1974). *The lives of a cell.* New York: Bantam Books.

Vermont Ethics Network. (1997). *Vermont voices on care of the dying.* Montpelier, VT: Vermont Ethics Network.

Webb, M. (1997). *The good death: The new American search to reshape the end of life.* New York: Bantam.

CHAPTER 2

Sticking With the Sick: Access to Palliative Care and Hospice as an Issue of Justice

Nancy Berlinger

Most individuals in the United States, and other developed nations, die of progressive conditions, such as cancer, diseases of major organ systems, or diseases and conditions associated with frailty and dementia (Kochanak, Xu, Murphy, Minino, and Kung, 2011). Individuals often live with these conditions for some period—months, years, or even decades—before their health care needs are identified in terms of end-of-life care. Long before they are dying of a terminal illness, they are living with a chronic illness, an experience that may include the burdens of the disease itself, burdens associated with treatment, and the continuing effects of past treatment.

The term "end of life" connotes the closeness of death and the experience and needs of the person who is likely to die soon. It is also important for palliative care professionals who care for dying patients to consider the large number of persons living with chronic, progressive, and incurable illness, from which, or from the associated complications of which, they will eventually die. We must address the advance planning, medical treatment decision making, palliative care needs, and the life closure issues of this growing population, including the needs of loved ones. The definition of palliative care is already broad enough to embrace the needs of the chronically ill person who may also be chronically dying, because all such persons deserve relief from preventable suffering. Some have called for reforms in the way hospice care is conceptualized, organized, and financed so that it can move "upstream" to provide a care model for chronic illness in an aging society (Jennings, Ryndes, D'Onofrio, and Baily, 2003).

This raises questions about justice. People who live with progressive, eventually fatal chronic illness are members of our moral community; they are persons deserving of equal concern and respect. But their needs are great and they draw heavily on the common pool of resources in a health care system. What share of social goods do they deserve, relative to other members of society with different health care needs? A chronic illness—understood both as an incurable or recurrent medical condition and as the lived experience with such a condition over a long period of time—is often a "self-managed" illness. The well-established primary care paradigm for the management of certain chronic illnesses, such as diabetes or asthma, is premised on the expectation that a patient can and should self-manage their own health care, if provided with adequate support from health care providers. But how do individuals who live with some form of chronic illness self-manage their palliative care needs when they are neither hospitalized nor receiving specialized care at home from a hospice program or a palliative care service? The lack of adequate and timely access to upstream palliative care for chronically ill patients in the community is a central issue of justice in health policy and in the ethics of palliative care and social justice. What kind of access to what kinds of services and support does justice require in this shadow world of our health care system? Justice is most often discussed in terms of fairness and individual rights. In this chapter I suggest that access to palliative care in the context of chronic progressive illness also requires us to comprehend the ethical demands of justice in relationship to the concept of social solidarity.

CASE STUDY

JB is a 48-year-old woman who is the mother of two children, ages 9 and 14. Seven years ago, she was diagnosed with locally invasive, estrogen-positive breast cancer (Stage II, including progression to lymph nodes). Her initial treatment included lumpectomy, followed by chemotherapy, radiation, hormonal therapy, and physical therapy for lymphedema resulting from the surgical removal of affected lymph nodes under her arm. As a consequence of treatment, JB lost some range of motion in her affected arm, requiring her to make changes in her work life and to give up some activities that had long been meaningful to her. Four years ago, JB's disease recurred as inflammatory breast cancer (Stage IIIb), a rare and extremely aggressive form of this disease. Her treatment included neoadjuvant chemotherapy, a complicated mastectomy that included the removal of affected skin and dermal lymph nodes, radiation, and hormonal therapy. During this course of treatment, JB experienced significant pain as the result of rapid tumor growth, and began to be seen by the pain management service at the cancer center where she received inpatient and outpatient treatment. She experienced multiple side effects and aftereffects of treatment, but was eventually able to resume freelance work and to return to other regular activities. Her marriage ended, and with it her medical insurance. Fortunately, she was able to secure comparable coverage through an insurance program for freelance workers.

Two years ago, JB's disease recurred as metastatic (Stage IV) disease, with mets to the supraclavicular lymph node. Initially, she was treated with further hormonal therapies, switching to chemotherapy following continued progression. JB's disease has tended to be refractory to chemotherapy, a fact noted in her medical record and by her oncology team. The first- and second-line chemotherapy drugs used during the second recurrence were somewhat effective in the medical management of chronic progressive disease over the next year. During this period, however, JB developed further cancer-related health problems, including pleural effusion, which was treated surgically, and other lung problems, which were treated with inhalers and antibiotics. Third–and fourth–line chemotherapy drugs failed to slow disease progression to JB's ribs, spine, and pelvis. Her fatigue, pain, and breathing difficulties increased.

For years, JB has been aware that her cancer cannot be cured and is progressing. When she talks about her prognosis with loved ones, she says, "I know I'm going to die of this some day." She has always been clear with her health care providers about her values and preferences, telling them, "I need to parent my children, to get those life lessons in," and "I want to stay out of the hospital unless it's for a really good reason; it's very disruptive to my family." She and her palliative care team have continued to tailor her symptom management plan to help her do things that are important to her. For example, the use of a psychostimulant to counteract fatigue and the sedating effect of narcotic analgesics allows her to take her children shopping or to the movies. However, she and her oncologist have never explicitly discussed what JB wishes to do when treatment stops working.

JB is scheduled to talk by phone with her oncologist to review her most recent scans, which confirm the failure of fourth-line chemotherapy. Due to JB's extensive treatment history prior to this recurrence there are no standard regimens remaining to which she has not already developed resistance. Treatment options now include off-label chemotherapy (specifically, a drug that is likely to be significantly more toxic than past drugs), or forgoing further oncological interventions and continuing palliative interventions by enrolling in hospice. JB confides to loved ones that hospice is difficult to imagine. She has a clear picture of what treatment is like, but no clear picture of what hospice is like. While she does not think further chemotherapy is likely to help now that several drugs have failed ("they don't save the best for last"), she says, "I don't want to think of myself as a quitter."

ANALYSIS

This case is about living with cancer as a chronic illness, and then as a terminal illness. A 2011 multination report on cancer care in developed nations noted that health economists "now label cancer as a chronic disease" due to its prevalence in aging societies and the reality that many metastatic cancers cannot be cured (Sullivan et al., 2011, p. 944). The report identified justice—by which it meant "a declining degree of fairness for all patients with cancer"— as a major concern in social policy in developed nations due to the rising, potentially unsustainable cost of cancer treatments offering small potential for benefit (Sullivan et al., 2011, p. 933).

Approximately 12 million other individuals in the United States are living with a prior diagnosis of cancer (Centers for Disease Prevention and Control, 2007). This "survivorship" population includes individuals who have completed cancer treatment, but it also includes those who are living with cancer as a chronic illness, because their disease cannot be cured, or is likely to recur, or because they continue to experience the effects of past treatment.

With her chronic cancer, JB is caught between "curing" and "dying." There are no television dramas called "Outpatient Clinic." Apart from documentaries, movies about people with cancer are often about a miraculous recovery or the tragic death. The narrative of chronic cancer, or any chronic illness for that matter—the dailyness of being sick, of negotiating with one's body, one's energy, one's responsibilities, one's hopes—remains all too invisible in the broader society, and even to many clinicians. Living with chronic cancer can be described as a "tedious, grinding labor of Sisyphus" (Jennings, Callahan, and Caplan, 1988, p. 1). Like the boulder that keeps crashing back down on Sisyphus every time he pushes it up the hill, the study of how chronically ill people receive health care is a topic one must keep at, knowing that, like chronic illness, it will always be with us. Because people *live with* chronic illness, the philosopher's question—how ought we to live?—is particularly germane with reference to chronic illness. How do people live *with* chronic cancer; how should they live *in spite of* it?

Returning to the case, what may JB's oncologist be thinking about in preparation for the phone conference with JB? The oncologist would know that there are no data suggesting that the off-label drug she has mentioned to JB will increase JB's overall survival, and further, that data are scant on any potential benefit of off-label chemotherapy after approved drugs have already failed to provide benefit. The oncologist would also know, from previous discussions and the medical record, that this patient has said "yes" to highly burdensome treatment many times over the years. JB clearly wants to stay alive for her children; but of course, most parents would want that. Research suggests that cancer patients who have dependent children suffer significantly greater psychological distress at the end of life as they face the prospect of leaving their children, and may, as a result, find it especially difficult to decide to forgo treatment or to complete advance care planning (Nilsson et al., 2009). These issues are further complicated by the fact that oncologists and other health care professionals may perceive "giving hope" as part of their job, and worry that a frank discussion of benefits and burdens will "take hope away" from a patient with advanced disease. However, research suggests that such patients' ability to hope is not dependent on treatment outcomes (Smith et al., 2010).

This oncologist may or may not know whether JB's insurance will cover the off-label drug. Oncologists are often unsure how to talk about drug costs with patients (Neumann, Palmer, Nadler, Fang, and Ubel, 2010). Should the price of a drug always be mentioned? Does it matter only if a treatment is expensive? Only if it is both expensive and not covered by the patient's insurance? What if it is expensive, unreimbursed, and unlikely to benefit the patient? When, exactly, is the right time to have this difficult conversation? (Keating et al., 2010) And how much should a physician be expected to know about each patient's insurance coverage?

What are the ethical issues at stake in this case? Clearly the well-established ethical goals of honoring autonomy and supporting informed choice require that a physician tell a patient the truth about the patient's own health, as this information is owed to the patient and is fundamental to the patient's ability to make an informed choice among treatment options. How this information is communicated requires sensitivity and compassion, and good communication is integral to ethical practice. Truthful disclosure of medically relevant information and the ethical goal of beneficence (doing good) are not incompatible in general and are not in conflict in this case. It would be wrong for JB's oncologist to present an approved or off-label therapy as "the next treatment to try" without explaining the evidence (or lack of evidence) that this drug will offer some benefit to her at this stage in the illness. It is both

JB's right and in her best interest to be in a position where she can consider whether this benefit would outweigh the burdens of treatment. To this end, the oncologist (or another member of the health care team, such as a social worker) should also be prepared to discuss the financial costs of treatment options, so that a patient does not unknowingly take on financial burdens.

Beyond respecting the patient's right to make an informed choice and avoid harms resulting from poorly informed decision making, the ethical issues at stake in this case include the promotion of justice for a chronically ill patient whose medical needs are changing as the result of disease progression. This case illustrates that at the level of individual treatment planning and decision making, the ethics of autonomy and truth telling and the ethics of justice go hand in hand. For example, for JB one of the treatment options she must be informed about throughout the course of her illness is palliative care, and how it can be integrated into oncological treatment. At this stage in her illness, she is, further, owed clear information about hospice. It is unjust to patients to fail to provide them with timely information about a service that may reasonably offer an effective way of managing their medical needs. Comprehensive palliative care available through hospice may offer a more effective, and cost-effective, way to medically manage advanced cancer than that offered by the use of a highly toxic, often highly expensive drug, when that chemotherapy is unlikely to provide benefit to a patient with progressing and chemo-refractory disease, as it came to be for JB.

While some oncology professionals still find it difficult to view hospice as part of cancer care, current policymaking efforts within the field of clinical oncology aim to expand the professional understanding of cancer care to encompass oncology-hospice collaboration and the full integration of palliative care and oncological treatment (Peppercorn et al., 2011). These efforts to improve cancer care enhance patient autonomy and enhance beneficence, and can also be viewed through the lens of justice. If medical professionals are unprepared to present hospice as an option for the medical management of the advanced cancer that this patient is both living with and dying from, then this is a question of justice, not only a question of informed decision making.

Perceiving the justice dimension of this case gives us an opportunity to reflect as well on the difference between two important ways of thinking about what justice means. Many influential accounts of justice in health care often draw on the concept of justice as "fairness" (Daniels, 1985). Fairness has to do with the distribution of goods or services among individuals: does a given distributive share respect the individual's rights? Is it proportionate to his or her needs? Is it equitable relative to the distributive shares that other individuals receive? Because individuals wrestle with questions of "fair" and "unfair" from childhood onward, defining justice as "fairness" can be a productive way of reflecting on and discussing this topic in health care organizations. However, there is another important way of thinking and talking about justice in the context of chronic illness and terminal illness, and in the delivery of palliative care and hospice to individuals like JB who are living with the illness that is likely to be the cause of their death.

This is justice understood as "solidarity." Solidarity has less to do with the distributive shares a person receives and more to do with the pattern of supportive relationships the individual has with other individuals (like caregivers) and with the community as a whole. To treat people living with cancer justly, then, is both about giving them their fair share and about giving them moral membership and location, recognizing them as people who are living among "us," who are part of "us." In public health justice as solidarity is invoked to convey common interests: "we're all in this together." During a natural disaster or other crisis, we all rely on our public health systems to get us through the crisis. As a principle or value that can sustain a social welfare system, solidarity has long been associated with support for Western European–style universal access to health care, and with the underlying notion of health care as a common good. Even within the fragmented U.S. health care system, there are care systems, such as hospice, in which justice as solidarity (sometimes called "presence" or "witness") with the dying person, the family and loved ones, and indeed with the larger collectivity of those near the end of life, is an integral part of the underlying philosophy of care.

As a concept, solidarity is relational at both the level of interpersonal relationships and at the more civic level of the relationship between the community as a whole and its individual members. As noted in the example of hospice care, solidarity comes into play in the ethics of the interpersonal relationship between an individual who is chronically or terminally ill, and an individual who is relatively healthy (or healthier by comparison). Can a person living with cancer and a person who does not have cancer be "in this together" for as long as "this" (illness, a course of treatment, the sick person's life) lasts, while still acknowledging how the experiences of illness and of caregiving differ? How can a person living with cancer and another person who plays a caregiving role maintain their equality as persons amid the experience of chronic illness and the ethical challenges it raises? (Berlinger, 2011)

Further, members of a community can be "in this together" with respect to how they address cancer and other chronic illnesses as things that are going on in that community all the time, things that some of us live with and that all of us should recognize as part of our common life. Sticking with the sick, living in solidarity with our fellow members of society who are living with chronic illness, requires all of us to live with the tension of an unfinished story. The story of chronic cancer in the case of JB is not the heroic story of the community member who "beats" cancer. However, even when it is clear that a chronic illness like JB's cancer is also a progressive illness and will become a terminal illness, this story is not automatically an "end-of-life" story, either. The person with terminal cancer may still be trying to figure out, as JB tried her best to do, how to live with cancer, and how to remain in solidarity with loved ones for whatever time remains.

DECISION

Following the phone conference with her oncologist, JB decided to start a time-limited trial of the off-label drug. After experiencing significantly more burdensome side effects as compared with previous drugs, and after conferring with loved ones and with other members of her health care team, JB scheduled a meeting with her oncologist. During this meeting, the benefits and burdens of continuing this or any other cytotoxic treatment were discussed in greater detail, and hospice was discussed explicitly. JB decided to forgo further oncological treatment and to enroll in a local hospice program. After enrolling, she expressed feelings of anger and frustration to loved ones: "I could have been in hospice months ago." After three months of hospice care at home, she was admitted to the hospice unit of a local hospital and died a week later of renal failure secondary to metastatic breast cancer.

AFTERWORD

Throughout her seven years of living with cancer, JB would say, "I'm lucky." She felt lucky to have health insurance and access to comprehensive cancer care; lucky to have loved ones, including those able to relieve financial burdens; lucky, above all, to be able to parent her children for longer than she expected, if not nearly long enough. She also knew she had endured great misfortune: to be diagnosed at an early age with an aggressive and hard-to-treat form of cancer; to give up work that she loved; to face the break-up of a marriage; and above all, to be forced to leave her children.

What is the difference between misfortune and injustice? This is another way of thinking about "justice" in the context of chronic illness and terminal illness. Consider now, more briefly, a second case, which is a variation on JB's case.

RS is a 32-year-old woman who is the single mother of two young children, whom she supports through her work as a housecleaner. RS is an uninsured member of the working poor population.

She does have access to primary care at a federally–funded community health center, where pediatric visits are covered by Medicaid's State Children's Health Insurance Program (SCHIP) and where uninsured adults can pay on a sliding scale for their own health care. After experiencing increasingly severe chest pain for several months, RS, whose first language is Spanish and who speaks little English, makes an appointment to see one of the Spanish-speaking internists at the health center. The internist detects a palpable mass in RS's right breast. The internist calls a local oncologist who volunteers at the health center and has been willing to take some referrals for uninsured patients who need routine screening for cancers or, as in RS's case, a full diagnostic work-up. The internist makes more phone calls: to a sympathetic Spanish-speaking patient advocate at the community hospital, and to several nonprofits that offer emergency financial assistance to patients with breast cancer.

When RS's full test results confirm that she has Stage IV breast cancer, metastatic to the lungs, the oncologist calls the internist: "We can't cure this, and it's already affecting her lungs. This patient might get some benefit from chemotherapy or radiation to relieve her symptoms. But to do that, we'll have to send her to the ED, get her admitted, and see if the hospital social workers can get her qualified for emergency Medicaid, or tap into some charity care funds at the hospital or a local hospice. She wants to get back to work so she doesn't lose her job, she's worried about paying the rent, she's worried about her kids. I'm not sure how to explain her situation to her so she can make informed decisions—and, well, I've got other patients. She really needs one of those 'patient navigators' to guide her through the system, but we don't have those at our hospital yet. This seems so unfair. It's bad enough for a parent to be diagnosed with advanced cancer at age 32, but to have so few options . . . ."

Political philosopher Judith Shklar (1990) has described how "passive injustice" can flourish when suffering resulting from or worsened by unjust law, policy, customs, or other social structures is attributed to personal or collective misfortune. Both JB and RS suffered a profound misfortune, in the form of very bad medical news. Both women have a variety of medical needs that include palliative care. As hard as it is for JB—the woman with health insurance, financial resources, and social supports—to confront decisions about life-sustaining treatment, the use of palliative care, enrollment in hospice, and the end of life, RS's situation is in some ways harder, because it has been harder for her to be treated as an equal person in the society in which she lives and works. Cases such as this may be troubling to health care professionals, even when they are able to "work the system" on a patient's behalf. Palliative care and hospice professionals who work in communities with significant numbers of uninsured residents need opportunities to reflect on the challenges of providing good care to these community residents when they are chronically ill or terminally ill, and on the special ethical challenges that may arise in these cases. In the years ahead, if the Affordable Care Act is fully implemented, the plight of some portions of the working poor population will almost certainly be alleviated. Serious challenges will still remain for justice as fairness and justice as solidarity with respect to the health care needs of new immigrants and of undocumented immigrants. The new law does little for them except to call for an expansion of resources for community health centers where persons without insurance can obtain primary care (Starr, 2011). How access to palliative care will be provided remains to be seen.

Conclusion
A chronic care system for individuals who are living with cancer differs from an acute care system: most people do not "live" in the hospital. Such a system also differs from a "survivorship" care system, if "survivorship" is defined principally or exclusively in terms of posttreatment needs. Chronic care also differs from end-of-life-care, although, as discussed, efforts to integrate chronic care with hospice care, or with other palliative care for persons near the end of life, reflect the reality that end-of-life decisions may be considered and made in chronic care settings. Paying attention to the needs of the chronically ill person who is living with cancer in the community requires attention to questions of fairness, of solidarity, and of injustice in this community, because this person is part of "us."

Nancy Berlinger, PhD, MDiv, is a research scholar at The Hastings Center, an independent, nonprofit bioethics research institute in Garrison, New York. Her work focuses on ethical issues in the organization and delivery of health care, including end-of-life care, palliative care, cancer care, patient safety, and ethics education for health care professionals. She has a special interest in the management of cancer as a chronic illness. She is project director of the first revision of The Hastings Center's 1987 ethics guidelines on end-of-life care, forthcoming in 2012. She also codirects a research project on ethical issues in the care of undocumented immigrants in the U.S. health care system, and is writing a book about the ethics of workarounds, turfing, and other avoidance practices in health care. She teaches health care ethics to graduate students at the Yale School of Nursing and lectures frequently in medical schools and health care institutions in the United States and internationally.

REFERENCES

Berlinger, N. (2011). Patients and care partners: Ethical questions about sharing information. *The Hastings Center, 2011,* 1–9. Retrieved from www.thehastingscenter.org/hard-questions

Centers for Disease Prevention and Control. (2007). *A summary of CDC data on cancer survivorship.* Retrieved from www.cdc.gov/cancer/survivorship/basic_info/

Daniels, N. (1985). *Just health care.* Cambridge, MA: Cambridge University Press.

Jennings, B., Callahan, D., & Caplan, A. L. (1988). Ethical challenges of chronic illness. *Hastings Center Report Special Supplement, 33*(2), 1–16.

Jennings, B., Ryndes, T., D'Onofrio, C., & Baily, M. A. (2003). Access to hospice care: Expanding boundaries, overcoming barriers. *Hastings Center Report, Special Supplement, 33*(2), S1–S60.

Keating, N. L., Landrum, M. B., Rogers, S., Baum, S. K., Virnig, B. A., Huskamp, H. A.,…Kahn, K. L. (2010). Physician factors associated with discussions about end-of-life care. *Cancer, 116*(4), 998–1006.

Kochanak, K. D., Xu, J., Murphy, S. L., Minino, A. M., & Kung, H. (2011). Deaths: Preliminary data for 2009. *National Vital Statistics Surveys, 59*(4). Retrieved from http://www.cdc.gov/nchs/

Neumann, P. J., Palmer, J. A., Nadler, E., Fang, C. & Ubel, P. (2010). Cancer therapy costs influence treatment: A national survey of oncologists. *Health Affairs, 29*(1), 196–202.

Nilsson, M. E., Maciejewski, P. K., Zhang, B., Wright, A. A., Trice, E., Muriel, A. C., Friedlander, R. J.,... Prigerson, H. G. (2009). Mental health, treatment preferences, advance care planning, and location and quality of death in advanced cancer patients with dependent children. *Cancer, 115*(2), 399–409.

Peppercorn, J. M., Smith, T. J., Helft, P. R., Debono, D. J., Berry, S. R., Wollins, D. S.,...Schnipper, L. E. (2011). American Society of Clinical Oncology statement: Toward individualized care for patients with advanced cancer. *Journal of Clinical Oncology, 29*(6), 755–760.

Shklar, J. N. (1990). *The faces of injustice.* New Haven, CT and London: Yale University Press.

Smith, T, J., Dow, L., Virago, E., Khatcheressian, J., Lyckholm, L. J., & Matsuyama, R. (2010). Giving honest information to patients with advanced cancer maintains hope. *Oncology, 24*(6), 521–525.

Starr, P. (2011). *Remedy and reaction: The peculiar American struggle over health care reform.* New Haven, CT: Yale University Press.

Sullivan, R., Peppercorn, J., Sikora, K., Zalcberg, J., Meropol, N. J., Amir, E.,...Aapro, M. (2011). Delivering affordable cancer care in high-income countries. *The Lancet Oncology, 12,* 933–980.

Ethical Dilemmas in Palliative and Hospice Care

This section considers the ethical dilemmas that often occur in end-of-life care. Erin Talati and Lainie Friedman Ross begin the section with a fascinating case that explores the issue of confidentiality. Here, and in many similar cases, confidentiality poses an authentic ethical dilemma. How can a surrogate truly offer informed consent if critical information is withheld at the client's request? Talati and Ross's analysis of the case offers a process for confronting such situations.

Richard Cohen's chapter further deals with the complexity of communication. For informed consent, it is essential that patients understand the factors relevant to their condition. Yet, as Cohen notes, insensitive communication, "truth-dumping" in Cohen's words, can overwhelm a patient's ability to cope. Cohen echoes Jennings's call for a balance between beneficence and autonomy. In some ways, the pendulum shift from a paternalistic protective perspective that shielded patients to a perspective that all truths should be shared as soon as available may have gone too far. Again, there must be a balance between the information that patients need and the information they want to have and are willing to hear. In open communication, a patient's questions are honestly answered in ways that both extend the dialogue and clarify the patient's underlying concerns. As Cohen notes, this is best done in a context where there is a trusting relationship between patient and physician. The *right to know* is balanced with the *right to choose not to know*.

Mary Beth Morrissey's chapter on surrogacy reinforces an ecological framework from which to consider ethical issues. Surrogacy is a complicated concept, as Morrissey notes. Building on a relationship of trust, guided by advance directives and prior communication, the surrogate is expected to make decisions on behalf of an incapacitated patient. As Morrissey understands, these decisions cannot ignore the surrogate's own wishes and preferences. These are not impassioned decisions of an outsider but likely decisions made by someone the patient both loved and trusted—someone the surrogate likely loves in turn. Moreover, these decisions are made in a crisis atmosphere where surrogates are torn not only between their wishes and the patient's goals but also the surrogate's own ambivalence over whether to end a stressful situation, live in the moment, or hope, however unrealistically, for a cure. The surrogate's decisions may not only affect the patient but also the surrogate's relationship with others in the patient's family and intimate network. Morrissey makes clear that health care professionals need to acknowledge this complexity and offer surrogates information and support as well as time both to consult and reach consensus within community.

Nessa Coyle and Vidette Todaro-Franceschi's chapter on artificial nutrition and hydration further illustrates the complexity of surrogacy. In their case, the patient's daughter is offered both the time and information to reach a consensus with her family on the best mode of treatment. In this chapter, Coyle and Todaro-Franceschi offer an excellent overview of the possibilities and limits of artificial nutrition and hydration. Coyle and Todaro-Franceschi remind readers of the cultural, social, and spiritual sensitivities inherent in withdrawing or withholding artificial nutrition and hydration, reinforcing the importance of providing patients, their families, and the surrogates with education about what artificial nutrition and hydration entail and what occurs as life ebbs. Especially valuable in their chapter is their careful, model analysis of how biomedical ethical principles frame end-of-life decisions.

Terry Altilio and Russell Portenoy affirm that effective palliation is itself an ethical responsibility in end-of-life care. Mostly, that responsibility is discharged in ways that cause little conflict. However, as their case illustrates, this does not always occur. The case of Ms. H demonstrates how a variety of factors—surrogacy, cultural issues and mistrust, family conflict, pain management, communication, and differing goals of treatment—can conspire to create profound ethical dilemmas. Altilio and Portenoy also raise other sensitive issues. How can clinicians navigate between ethical mandates to be culturally sensitive and to provide effective pain relief when there is conflict? Finally, Altilio and Portenoy reaffirm the ecological perspective. Ethical decisions not only affect patients and their families but also can generate moral distress within the care team.

Daniel Sulmasy and Nessa Coyle also address the issue of pain management in their chapter on palliative sedation. Sulmasy and Coyle emphasize that palliative sedation can be ethical when death is imminent, the patient is in intractable pain, and other methods of pain management have been ineffective. Using the rule of *double effect*, Sulmasy and Coyle offer a careful analysis of the ethical principles that should guide the use of palliative sedation.

Charles Corr concludes this section with a discussion of an emerging ethical issue, physician-assisted suicide, legal now in three states—Oregon, Washington, and Montana. In many ways, physician-assisted suicide might be seen as the natural result of a social trend emphasizing the value of autonomy in end-of-life care. Certainly there is a generational perspective as well. The Baby Boom generation has always prized autonomy, individuality, and an ethos of noninterference. Corr offers a history of the Death with Dignity Act in Oregon, an examination of the ways it has been implemented as well as its effects, and most important, a sensitivity to the resultant ethical dilemmas posed to hospice programs and individuals involved in end-of-life care.

CHAPTER 3

Limits to Confidentiality: Ethical Issues in End-of-Life Care

Erin Talati and Lainie Friedman Ross

Central to the concept of autonomy that guides decision making for adult patients is the concept of privacy. Ultimately rooted in a right to be left alone, the concept of privacy arguably extends not only to physical intrusion on a person but also to maintaining confidential information that a person does not want shared. Questions surrounding end-of-life care present challenges to maintaining confidentiality. Decision making for incapacitated adult patients generally rests on a surrogate who ought to make decisions with a person's expressed interests or known values in mind. When one person holds information that may make these interests clear but that individual is not the surrogate, disclosure may be in the best interests of the patient if it would lead to decisions more consistent with the patient's interests. However, this disclosure risks violating confidentiality. A case example based on an actual situation will better illustrate these concerns (Jansen and Ross, 2000).

CASE STUDY

MT is a 50-year-old HIV+ man with chronic pancreatitis who now presents with severe bilateral pneumonia consistent with progression to AIDS given his low CD4+ count and severe illness, although no organisms were cultured that would definitely identify this illness as an AIDS-defining infection. Respiratory failure ensues and MT is placed on noninvasive ventilation, but his prognosis is guarded as other organ systems begin to fail and his respiratory status worsens. MT has been estranged from his sons for the past decade but both are at his bedside since his girlfriend notified them of his serious condition. Neither son is aware of MT's HIV+ status and MT has expressed clearly to his physicians in the past that he does not want this information revealed. He has also expressed that he does not want to be on life support if his illness progressed. MT's girlfriend, who is not the mother of his children, has been his caregiver since he became sick five years ago. She knows about

MT's HIV+ status and his desire not to be maintained on life support, but had promised MT in the past that she would not share the information about his HIV status with his sons and that she would not create conflict at the end of his life. The doctors have tried to explain the irreversibility of MT's illness to his sons without breaking his confidentiality, but the children insist that he be intubated although they believe that MT would not want to be on life support. The doctors are not sure what to do since they know that the children are making a decision against MT's wishes, without all of the information that might help to guide this decision.

ANALYSIS

The doctors face ethical and legal questions. The following questions may help to guide the approach to the case.

1. Who is the appropriate surrogate for MT?
2. What ethical principles should guide the surrogate?
3. What is the legal and ethical basis of the patient's wish to keep this information confidential?
4. What are the limits of confidentiality and what is the scope of the surrogate's right to know?
5. How should the health care team handle documentation that may disclose information the patient wished to keep confidential?

Before discussing the approach taken in the case above, we will first work through an analysis guided by the questions above.

Who is the appropriate surrogate for MT?

Following some of the prominent cases involving limitation and withdrawal of life-sustaining measures at the end of life, in 1991 the federal government passed the Patient Self-Determination Act (PSDA) to reinforce the individual's ability to participate in end-of-life decisions. Among other requirements under the act, hospitals must inform patients about their individual state laws governing health care decision making at the end of life (Federal Patient Self-Determination Act Final Regulations, 1995). These laws indicate a priority order for surrogate decision makers when the individual has not named a specific surrogate in an advance directive. The hierarchy of surrogate decision makers usually begins with individual(s) named in an advance directive, then legal guardians, followed by spouses, adult children, siblings, and other family members or close friends. If a state does not have a particular process by which a surrogate decision maker should be identified, these same parties would be potential decision makers.

In MT's case, the pertinent state law turned first to individuals named in advance directives, then legal guardians, followed by spouses and then adult children. According to this hierarchy, the spouse would be the preferred legal surrogate. However, in this case, MT is not legally married to his girlfriend and they live in a state that does not recognize common-law marriages. Therefore she would not qualify as his spouse. His adult children, then, are the legal surrogates. This is true despite two pieces of empirical data that may lead one to think MT may have chosen otherwise had he written an advance directive. First, his girlfriend is his caregiver and has knowledge both of MT's medical condition and of his desire not to have aggressive measures taken at the end of life. Second, he has been estranged from his children and does not want them to know about his HIV status.

What ethical principles should guide the surrogate?

Autonomy is the fundamental principle underlying medical decision making for adults with decisional capacity, which prioritizes the individual's expression of personal preferences. When adults lack decisional capacity, medical decision making is best guided by advance directives created by the patient, because these may most closely reflect what the patient would have chosen for himself. Advance directives may also indicate who the patient would prefer to make decisions if he lacks capacity. In the case above, although MT had clearly expressed his wishes verbally to both his girlfriend and to his health care providers, he did not execute an advance directive that formally stated his choice of surrogate or his wishes not to be placed on life support at the end of life. Without such a document, his children are his legal surrogates.

Surrogates are instructed to make decisions for incapacitated patients that respect patient preferences whenever possible. Surrogates are first asked to refer to any advance directives to identify the preferences of the patient. If no advance directive is present, surrogates are asked to use substituted judgment. Under this standard, the surrogate determines what the patient would decide for himself if he were able to choose, placing patient preferences at the center of decision making. When the preferences of a patient cannot be identified, the surrogate is asked to make decisions based on what he or she believes the best interests of the patient would be (Brudney, 2009; Buchanan and Brock, 1990).

A number of commentators have critiqued the substituted judgment standard for incompletely capturing the true preferences of the patient. Surrogates often do not know the true preferences of the individual for whom they are making decisions (Fagerlin, Ditto, Danks, Houts, and Smucker, 2001; Seckler, Meier,

Mulvihill, and Paris, 1991; Ouslander, Tymchuk, and Rahbar, 1989), although research has shown that surrogates are better at predicting these preferences than health care providers or other potential deciders (Fagerlin et al., 2001; Seckler et al., 1991; Ouslander et al., 1989; Zweibel and Cassel, 1989). Even when preferences are known, surrogates may advocate decisions that are not consistent with these preferences, and health care providers then must navigate this ethical challenge (Sulmasy and Snyder, 2010; Vig, Sudore, Berg, Fromme, and Arnold, 2011).

Because MT's sons are his legal surrogates, the team must confront the sons' decision to request treatment known to be contrary to his preferences. The medical team has two options. First, the team may want to have an alternative surrogate named. This would require a court order since state law clearly indicates that MT's children are the legal surrogates. Alternatively, the team could disclose MT's HIV status to his adult children, which the health care team believes might influence the children to refuse treatment in accordance with MT's expressed wishes. To pursue the second option, the team must decide that it is appropriate to disclose this information to MT's sons.

What is the legal and ethical basis of the patient's wish to keep this information confidential?

Confidentiality, grounded in the right to privacy, is an integral component of the physician-patient relationship (Perez-Carceles, Pereniguez, Osuna, and Luna, 2005). The right to individual privacy is broad and encompasses the physical privacy of the individual, informational privacy, and decisional privacy regarding personal choices. The doctrine of informed consent protects the physical privacy of the individual by requiring permission prior to any diagnostic or therapeutic intervention. Similarly, the Health Insurance Portability and Accountability Act (HIPAA) maintains informational privacy by not allowing personal medical information to be shared outside of the patient-physician relationship unless specific exceptions are present (United States Department of Health & Human Services, 2003). Finally, advance directives and the naming of health care proxies give weight to the concept of decisional privacy, particularly at the end of life.

From both an ethical and legal standpoint, the individual's right to privacy and respect for patient autonomy would indicate that information about MT's HIV status ought to be kept confidential. MT has clearly expressed his wishes not to have this information shared with his sons and has managed his condition without disclosing this information since his diagnosis. Certainly, prior to the patient's incapacity, it would have been both ethically and legally inappropriate for the physicians to disclose this information to his sons. The physicians in MT's case face a greater ethical and legal challenge when MT loses his capacity; they believe that maintaining confidentiality about his HIV+ status may unintentionally support his sons' decisions to make health care decisions against MT's expressed interests. The health care team must consider whether it is ethically and legally appropriate to disclose MT's HIV+ status despite knowing that it would be a breach of confidentiality. This issue raises questions about the limits of confidentiality and the scope of the surrogate's right to know.

What are the limits of confidentiality and what is the scope of the surrogate's right to know?

There are some circumstances under which the physician is not obligated by the duty of confidentiality. For example, when a patient discloses information to a health care provider that indicates risk of harm to the patient or to a third party, the physician is not only absolved of the duty of confidentiality, but also is obligated by a new duty to warn or to protect the patient or the third party at risk (*Tarasoff v. Regents of the University of California*, 1976). In addition, HIPAA allows for disclosure of confidential information to family members that is relevant to that individual's involvement in the medical care of the patient, with the informal permission of the patient (United States Department of Health & Human Services, 2003).

In addition to the general exceptions to the duty of confidentiality, a surrogate may have a separate right to information about the patient. If the surrogate is tasked with making decisions consistent with the expressed preferences of a patient and these preferences are known by a third party, or a third party has information that may help the surrogate infer what the patient would want for themselves, the surrogate has a right to know this information so that he or she can make decisions under the appropriate standard that best reflects the preferences of the patient.

Given the stigmatization of HIV in medicine and society at large, disclosure requires special consideration (Miller, Grover, Bunn, and Solomon, 2011; Thomas and Gostin, 2009; Zarocostas, 2010). Some have argued that disclosure of HIV status is appropriate when the disclosure is necessary for the surrogate to make decisions that promote the patient's preferences or when failure to disclose would result in foreseeable future risk of harm to the surrogate (Lott, 2007; Vernillo, Wolpe, and Halpern, 2007). Others have argued that disclosure of HIV status alone does not equip surrogates with more information about a patient's wishes than they had previous to the disclosure, while honoring the wishes of the patient to keep information confidential does advance patient preferences and therefore ought to be the default position (Jansen and Ross, 2000; Jones, McCullough, and Richman, 2003).

The issue of disclosure to at-risk third parties is relevant to HIV status in particular but disclosure for assistance in surrogate decision making is not unique to this status. While it is likely true that disclosure of a patient's HIV status alone does not necessarily reveal any particular value or interest of the patient, it is reasonable to believe that this information may help the surrogate to interpret how the patient may make a decision based on other known values or preferences. For example, if the patient had a known preference not to be maintained on life support in the setting of a terminal illness, and the patient presented with pneumonia related to end-stage AIDS, knowledge of the individual's HIV status might impact the surrogate's decision whether or not to allow intubation of the patient. In these circumstances, it might be ethically justifiable to disclose the information if it will ultimately allow the patient's preferences to be advanced. However, extreme care must be exercised when disclosure is allowed for this purpose as it is important to consider whether such disclosure is truly *essential* to advancing the surrogate's understanding. We propose that only when the surrogate cannot otherwise be made to understand the gravity of a patient's condition or the expected prognosis, should disclosure be contemplated. If the medical team believes that the surrogate understands the patient's critical status, and there is nothing particular to the disclosure of the confidential information that will advance the surrogate's understanding of the patient's preferences, the health care team should not disclose.

Balancing the duty of confidentiality and the surrogate's right to know is difficult in the case of MT. MT has clearly expressed two relevant preferences. First, he has indicated that he does not want his HIV status disclosed to his family. He has behaved consistent with this expressed interest by asking his girlfriend not to share the information and by his nondisclosure of this information to his legal next-of-kin prior to losing decisional capacity due to illness. Second, MT has indicated to his providers that he would not want life- sustaining measures if he were dying. Without any indication of which of these preferences MT values more, the health care team faces a difficult decision about disclosure. Disclosure of his HIV+ status may help the sons decide that his underlying condition is irreversible and may help them to make the decision not to place him on a ventilator, which the health care team knows to be MT's preference. However, in this case, it is not clear that the team would *need* to disclose this information to help the sons come to this decision. It is clear that MT is facing a terminal state given the rapid decline of multiple organ systems. The sons have indicated that they do not believe MT would want intubation if his condition were terminal, and the health care team might first try to explore whether they can help the surrogates understand that a decision to intubate would really go against their father's interests without disclosing his HIV status.

How should the health care team handle documentation that may disclose information the patient wished to keep confidential?

When a physician is asked to maintain certain information as confidential at the end of life, the physician must contemplate whether accurate and complete documentation of the patient's care would compromise confidentiality and whether it is appropriate to compromise confidentiality for this purpose. For end-of-life care, documentation on the death certificate will present the biggest challenge.

In documenting the proximate and contributing causes of death on the death certificate, the physician must decide whether to include any diagnoses that might implicate the information the patient wished to keep confidential. The physician ought to consider whether documenting the confidential information is essential to accurate completion of the record of death, which is a legal document. In most cases, it is likely that the physician would be able to accurately document the cause of death, while maintaining the confidentiality of specific information about the cause of death. For example, if a patient died from respiratory failure that was not clearly AIDS-related, it would be appropriate to document that the patient died from pneumonia and respiratory failure, without disclosing the patient's HIV status, since it does not clearly relate directly to the cause of death. However, if truthful completion of the record of death requires the inclusion of confidential information, the physician should do so, regardless of whether the information was disclosed prior to the completion of the record of death. For example, if a patient had pneumonia with respiratory failure and the patient would not have pneumonia *but for* also having AIDS, it would be appropriate to document AIDS as a contributing cause of death. If the physician believes that respiratory failure is a sufficient explanation for the cause of death, the physician should not feel compelled to document the confidential information about the patient's AIDS status. This is particularly true in jurisdictions where the record of death is a public record, such that documentation on a record of death can unintentionally lead to public disclosure of confidential information.

In the case above, the patient has an illness that cannot be clearly connected to his HIV status. Under these circumstances, if the patient dies and the physician has not disclosed information to the family about the patient's HIV status prior to the patient's death, the physician arguably should not include this information on the certificate of death. Instead, the physician should document diagnoses that are directly related to the cause of death, such as any organ system failure that is present.

DECISION

Although the health care team believed that the sons' request to proceed with life-sustaining measures were contrary to MT's wishes, they chose not to seek appointment of an alternative legal surrogate because the most appropriate surrogate—MT's girlfriend—stated that she would not cooperate with any plan that would create conflict with MT's children, based on her prior promise to MT.

The health care team elected not to disclose information related to MT's HIV status to his surrogates. The health care team believed nondisclosure was justified because MT was rapidly progressing toward death from multisystem organ failure, and they did not believe that knowledge of MT's HIV status was essential given how sick MT had become. The health care team was understandably concerned that MT's sons, who were his legal surrogates, knew MT would not want certain interventions but were requesting these interventions regardless of that knowledge. Ultimately, the team did not feel that disclosure of MT's HIV status would change the surrogates' perspective on what MT would have wanted and therefore believed that if disclosure of this information prompted a different decision, this change might be motivated by the surrogates' personal prejudices about HIV rather than on an improved understanding of MT's preferences. Therefore, the team maintained MT's confidentiality regarding his HIV+ status, which resulted in interventions on MT's behalf that the health care team suspected strongly MT would not want.

CONCLUSION

Despite the health care team's worry that MT's surrogates were acting in bad faith—that is, electing to pursue interventions they believed MT would not want—MT's progressive multisystem organ failure quickly resulted in his death. MT's sons remained his surrogate decision makers and MT died without any conflict occurring between his girlfriend and his sons.

What did we learn?

This case demonstrated that respect for patient autonomy can come into conflict with the physician's duty to disclose information to a surrogate that will allow the surrogate to make truly informed choices for the patient. When this occurs, at a minimum, the health care team must consider whether the surrogate is acting in good faith and whether disclosure of confidential information really serves to augment the surrogate's ability to make informed decisions for the patient. In this particular case, the health care team was troubled by knowledge that the surrogates were requesting interventions that they believed their father would not want. The issue therefore was whether disclosure of confidential information would change their mind. Ultimately, the team believed that disclosure would not change the circumstances of MT's condition or the surrogates' understanding of MT's preferences and elected not to disclose. We support this decision on the grounds that respect for the patient's autonomy requires that disclosure of information the individual wishes to remain confidential should occur only in specific circumstances, such as when there is a risk to a third party if the information is not disclosed, or when disclosure is essential for the surrogate decision maker to fully understand the patient's condition in order to make a truly informed decision. It is important to note that when disclosure is believed to be appropriate, respect for the patient's autonomy and wish to maintain confidentiality demands that we encourage limits on the disclosure only to individuals who need the information to make a decision that is consistent with the patient's values, preferences, or expressed interests. When disclosure occurs, the health care team should also stress the importance of maintaining confidentiality and avoiding additional disclosure.

The case also raised the issue of how to deal with families or surrogates who appear to be acting in bad faith. One solution would be to go to court to request an alternative surrogate. This option was not available in this case because MT's girlfriend clearly stated that she would not cooperate with any action that would generate potential conflict. Furthermore, it is not clear that the court would appoint MT's girlfriend as his legal guardian over his biological sons. A second solution is to consider if there is anything the health care team might do to help surrogates who feel unable to make a decision consistent with what they believe the patient's preferences to be. It is important for health care teams to recognize the significant burden placed on surrogates to make end-of-life decisions (Anderson, Arnold, Angus, and Bryce, 2008; Larsen, 1999), and sometimes surrogates may be unable to commit to a decision that they believe is in line with patient preferences if this decision will ultimately lead to the patient's death. Health care teams should recognize that care at the end of life often relies on understanding the patient in the context of a family unit and respect for this patient-family unit should remain a prominent consideration throughout end-of-life discussions. This approach may allow the health care team to take steps to remove burden from the family in making a difficult decision rather than pursuing legal alternatives when it appears that the surrogate is acting contrary to patient's preferences. Some have advanced the notion that the physician and health care team might instead approach this situation by allowing the surrogate to express knowledge and perceptions of the patient's values and preferences; the team could then use this information to inform a best judgment about the appropriate course of action consistent with these interests (Sulmasy and Snyder, 2010; Vig et al., 2011). We agree that preservation of the family unit is an important part of providing compassionate care at the end of life, and to the extent that family or surrogate burden can be respectfully reduced, health care teams should strive to do so.

What will we do differently in the future as a result of our experience?

Much of the distress around MT's case centered around important communication between MT and his primary care providers. While MT clearly expressed an interest not to have his HIV status disclosed, the providers failed to address other important issues that nondisclosure would present. In the future, a wider array of end-of-life care issues must be clarified including identifying and documenting who the patient would want to make decisions when the patient might no longer be able to decide for himself. Encouraging the patient to complete a durable power of attorney for health care is useful even when one's chosen durable power of attorney is the same as the individual who would be chosen by statute because, at least in some jurisdictions, it empowers the surrogate with greater discretion about decisions regarding end-of-life care (Derse, 2005).

What are the larger implications for end-of-life care?

MT's case highlighted many of the difficulties physicians face when dealing with end-of-life care for patients who may have complicated preferences not only regarding their care, but also about who should be involved in that care and what information those individuals should have access to in making health care decisions.

Even without considering the specific issues of confidentiality and nondisclosure, this case has implications that are applicable broadly to end-of-life care. In having discussions with patients about their wishes for end-of-life care, it is not enough to learn about what they want and what they might want to maintain confidential. Physicians must also address the importance of identifying a surrogate with whom the patient is comfortable communicating freely. Sharing information with the patient about who the default surrogate would be if no surrogate is named may help the patient to consider whether they would prefer a different person to make decisions for them. In this discussion, the health care provider should encourage the patient to share all relevant information with the identified surrogate proactively so that if the need arises, the surrogate is well-situated to make the decisions that the patient would have made had he been able to speak for himself. This is particularly relevant in states in which surrogacy law does not recognize certain relationships such as domestic partnerships or common-law marriages that may be most important to patients. Helping the patient to identify a surrogate may protect the value placed on such relationships as well as ensure that the individual who is best situated to identify patient preferences is allowed to participate in that patient's care at the end of life. When a patient does identify a surrogate to a physician, the physician should also take the opportunity to address other preferences about end-of-life care and should encourage the patient to document these preferences in a written advance directive.

Erin Talati, MD, JD, MBE, is a fellow in pediatric critical care medicine with an interest in the ethics of end-of-life care. Dr. Talati completed undergraduate training at Northwestern University, followed by a multidisciplinary graduate level program at the University of Pennsylvania, earning degrees in medicine, law, and bioethics. After finishing a pediatrics residency at the University of Chicago, Dr. Talati is now a critical care fellow and serves on the Ethics Advisory Committee at Children's Hospital Boston. Dr. Talati has previously studied decision making in the setting of treatment refusals in pediatrics and has also investigated the comfort and competency of pediatric residents in providing end-of-life care. While her current research focuses on how children and their parents make decisions regarding research participation, she frequently encounters end-

of-life decision making and the ethics surrounding end-of-life care in the clinical setting and as a member of the Ethics Advisory Committee.

Lainie Friedman Ross, *MD, PhD, is the Carolyn and Matthew Bucksbaum Professor of Clinical Ethics at the University of Chicago, where she has appointments in the departments of pediatrics, medicine, surgery, and the College. Dr. Ross is also the associate director of the MacLean Center for Clinical Medical Ethics and directs the ethics consultation services. Dr. Ross currently serves on the HHS Secretary's Advisory Committee on Human Research Protections (SACHRP) which provides guidance to the Office of Human Research Protections (OHRP). She is also the chair of the American Academy of Pediatrics Section on Bioethics. Dr. Ross has published widely in diverse areas of medical ethics. She has published two books,* Children, Families and Health Care Decision Making *(Oxford University Press, 1998),* Children in Medical Research: Access versus Protection *(Oxford University Press, 2006), and over 100 peer-reviewed articles in medical ethics.*

REFERENCES:

Anderson, W. G., Arnold, R. M., Angus, D. C., & Bryce, C. L. (2008). Posttraumatic stress and complicated grief in family members of patients in the intensive care unit. *Journal of General Internal Medicine, 23,* 1871–1876.

Brudney, D. (2009). Choosing for another: Beyond autonomy and best interests. *Hastings Center Report, 39,* 31–37.

Buchanan, A. E., & Brock, D. W. (1990). *Deciding for others: The ethics of surrogate decision making.* New York: Cambridge University Press.

Derse, A. R. (2005). Limitation of treatment at the end-of-life: withholding and withdrawal. *Clinics in Geriatric Medicine, 21,* 223–238.

Fagerlin, A., Ditto, P. H., Danks, J. H., Houts, R. M., & Smucker, W. D. (2001). Projection in surrogate decisions about life-sustaining medical treatments. *Health Psychology, 20,* 166–175.

Federal Patient Self-Determination Act Final Regulations. (1995). *Federal Register, 60,* 33294.

Jansen, L. A., and Ross, L. F. (2000). Patient confidentiality and the surrogate's right to know. *Journal of Law, Medicine & Ethics, 28,* 137–143.

Jones J. W., McCullough, L. B., & Richman, B. W. (2003). Limits of confidentiality: Disclosure of HIV seropositivity. *Journal of Vascular Surgery, 38*, 1443–1444.

Larsen, G. (1999). Family members' experiences with do-not-resuscitate (DNR). *Journal of Family Issues, 20*, 269–289.

Lott, J. P. (2007). HIV Disclosure to surrogate decision makers: Privacy versus presumption. *Critical Care, 11*, 416.

Miller, C. T., Grover, K. W., Bunn, J. Y., & Solomon, S. E. (2011). Community norms about suppression of AIDS-related prejudice and perceptions of stigma by people with HIV or AIDS. *Psychological Science, 22*, 579–583.

Ouslander, J. G., Tymchuk, A. J., & Rahbar, B. R. (1989). Health care decisions among elderly long-term care residents and their potential proxies. *Archives of Internal Medicine, 149*, 1367–1372.

Perez-Carceles, M. D., Pereniguez, J. E., Osuna, E., & Luna, A. (2005). Balancing confidentiality and the information provided to families of patients in primary care. *Journal of Medical Ethics, 31*, 531–535.

Seckler, A. B, Meier, D. E., Mulvihill, M., & Paris, B. E. C. (1991). Substituted judgment: how accurate are proxy predictions? *Annals of Internal Medicine, 115*, 92–98.

Sulmasy, D. P., & Snyder, L. (2010). Substituted interests and best judgments: An integrated model of surrogate decision making. *JAMA, 304*, 1946–1947.

Tarasoff v. *Regents of the University of California*, 17 Cal. 3d 425, 551 P.2d 334, 131. Cal. Rptr. 14 (Cal. 1976).

Thomas, V. L., & Gostin, L. O. (2009). The Americans with Disabilities Act: Shattered aspirations and new hope. *JAMA, 301*, 95–97.

United States Department of Health & Human Services. OCR Privacy Brief: Summary of the HIPAA Privacy Rule. (2003). Retrieved from: www.hhs.gov/ocr/privacy/hipaa/.../summary/privacysummary.pdf.

Vernillo, A. T., Wolpe, P. R., & Halpern, S. D. (2007). Re-examining ethical obligations in the intensive care unit: HIV disclosure to surrogates. *Critical Care, 11*, 125–127.

Vig, E. K., Sudore, R. L., Berg, K. M., Fromme, E. K., & Arnold, R. M. (2011). Responding to surrogate requests that seem inconsistent with a patient's living will. *Journal of Pain and Symptom Management, 42*, 777–782.

Zarocostas, J. (2010). UN launches commission on HIV to look at discrimination and legal barriers to treatment. *BMJ, 340*, c3507.

Zweibel, N. R., & Cassel, C. K. (1989). Treatment choices at the end of life: A comparison of decisions by older patients and their physician-selected proxies. *Gerontologist, 29*, 615–621.

CHAPTER 4

Ethical Issues in Communication at the End of Life: A View From the Trenches

Richard P. Cohen

CASE STUDY

I was honored to become the primary physician for a professor and mentor of mine, considered by many to be a "physician's physician." A clever diagnostician with superb clinical judgment, this man had been blessed with good health. Nevertheless, a gastrointestinal bleed prompted hospitalization for care of what would soon be diagnosed as widely metastatic gastric cancer. After initial stabilization and diagnostic and therapeutic procedures to remove significant ascites and pleural fluid, plans were made for appropriate care.

Days into the hospitalization, I arrived to make afternoon rounds and quickly found myself confronted by his nurse. She informed me that the patient was very angry at the resident house staff. Sensing that he was likely to be angry at me also, I sheepishly entered his room.

Rage was obvious in his face. "They're not keeping me informed. I need information and results to make decisions," he complained. I sat at his bedside and took his hand in mine. "We can't keep you informed," I replied, "there is too much bad news coming very quickly. You need to trust me to decide the pace at which we keep you informed. It would be mean to just dump the results as they become available." My eyes and his welled with tears, and he squeezed my hand in understanding.

That day, my professor and mentor ceased trying to be a physician and allowed himself to become a patient. His doing so enabled us to provide comfort, dignity, and palliation in a way that was clinically appropriate and empathetic, surely a task larger than simply keeping him informed with facts.

Discussion

This case presents an interesting ethical dilemma—is it always in the patient's best interest to be told the full truth, completely and all at once? Or can a physician, or any health professional communicating with the individual with the illness, acting from the ethical principle of beneficence, based on a long-term trusting relationship, choose to withhold information, at least for a time, "dosing" information, that is gradually exchanging information at a pace acceptable to the patient, so as not to overwhelm a patient's defenses and ability to cope?

The idea that there are ethical issues in talking with patients at the end of life, or even in more mundane medical matters, is obvious. For many, there is the basic ethic that one should simply always tell the truth and that the patient has a right to know. Many individuals would hold that informed consent is a prime ethical directive that is essential to maintain the patient's autonomy. Autonomy itself is enshrined in both law and practice. As early as 1914, the New York Court of Appeals ruled in an oft-cited landmark case, *Scholendorff vs. the Society of New York Hospital,* that patients had the right to consent to any medical procedure. For such consent to be meaningful it has to be informed; the patient has to have the information necessary to make a reasoned decision. Indeed, such notions are outlined in the Patients' Bill of Rights, posted prominently in many hospital lobbies.

Yet, in reality, while the ethical issues in end-of-life communication are obvious, the picture is far more nuanced. Too much information, or information that is only partially available at the time, may not always facilitate effective decision making. It is critical to consider the process of how and when information is communicated.

Talking to patients is an art that is learned by modeling during clinical training. Medical education has typically lagged behind other professions in formally teaching this art. Medical students and residents (unlike clergy, law enforcement officers, or the military) have traditionally not heard lectures entitled "Giving Bad News," nor been given outlines on effective grief counseling. While medical curricula do now include more discussion on end-of-life care, formal grief counseling is not stressed in house staff training. Indeed, medical residents often speak of "getting" a Do Not Resuscitate (DNR) order or permission for autopsy as if they were skills like catching a ball. Observing doctors in training being assigned the task of talking to patients suggests a job that is to be accomplished quickly and efficiently rather than one focused on empathy and compassion. However, talking with patients is surely more than simply telling the truth.

While there is an "art" to be taught in talking to patients at the end of life and specifically in giving bad news, there is a "science" in some of the rules and regulations that define at least the settings for doctor-patient communication. The federal Health Insurance Portability and Accountability Act laws largely define the notions of privacy. While these regulations have been successful in lessening "elevator talk" in hospitals and formulating the appropriate ways of discussing patients with third parties, the laws are not without problems. Some would argue that privacy laws can be used as an excuse to avoid interaction; they may offer a way to avoid coming to the phone that reflects a convenient excuse rather than an interest in privacy. One wonders about the appropriateness of not allowing an emergency room physician to speak by telephone with an inquiring relative concerned about the care that his or her family member is receiving. The caricature of all privacy issues is that after all efforts are made to ensure confidentiality in medical records or communications, most hospitalized patients are still not in private rooms. Any patient's roommates and their visitors can clearly hear doctors talking openly and detailing intimate medical specifics about the patient in the next bed.

Another paradigm that expands the complexity of talking with patients is the regulations regarding translators. For example, in New York, the state mandates that family members may not be used as translators. This mandate reflects an appropriate concern that family members may not translate accurately; they may withhold information they feel their relative would not want to hear or that they do not want the relatives to hear. Further, there is a realistic concern that family members are not subject to the same privacy rules that an approved translator would follow. The complex dynamics of these interactions, particularly in end–of–life situations, is obvious.

A difference exists between talking *with* a patient and talking *to* a patient. The former is typical of history taking or general counseling; the latter is exemplified in the giving of results or treatment recommendations. Whether telling the dry cleaner that one wants their shirts on hangers with starch or reporting to a patient that a breast biopsy reveals cancer, the ability to communicate clearly and efficiently is required and important. What is special and unique about the doctor-patient interaction is that one is communicating about the patient and that patient has an overwhelming interest in what is being said; the dry cleaner is not going to respond to a request for starch in the way that the patient responds to the results of a biopsy. Thus the emotional overtone in doctor-patient communication is different. The intonation of a professional voice and subtle choice of words have a particular meaning. One often hears patients responding to subtle terms that are used, such as "probably" or "if it was my mother," in ways that are not like other interpersonal interactions.

Because of these emotional overtones, a linguistic disconnect can occur. Physicians, as scientists, are used to speaking the language of probability; in science everything is probabilistic. The chance of a remission may be expressed as "very slight," since in the language of science the probability of such an event is low. Yet patients and families, groping for certainty, may hear such a comment as reaffirmation that a remission is possible.

In addition, patients often have *middle knowledge*—drifting in and out of their awareness of prognosis (Weisman, 1972). This concept reaffirms the reality that it is sometimes better to dose information to patients when they are ready to hear it rather than "dump the truth" all at once.

If there is an ethic that guides the current way doctors talk to patients, it is grounded in the notion of the patient's right to know. Autonomy has become an essential aspect of contemporary medical ethics.

It can be argued that, although legal cases such as *Scholendorff vs. the Society of New York Hospital* began to define patient's rights, modern medical ethics really began at the Nuremberg Trials. Despite what is implied in the Hippocratic Oath, the Nazis showed that physicians could indeed commit terrible wrongs as evidenced by well-documented medical atrocities involving human experimentation. While the legal and religious objections to such experiments seem obvious today, the historical response from modern medical ethics can be posited to be focused on the notion of the patient's right to know. It is easy to argue that this, accompanied by the patient's right to refuse a treatment, would have prevented unethical actions such as the Tuskegee syphilis study or those involving troublesome psychological experiments reported in university or prison settings in the past. A formal structure now exists in Institutional Review Boards that looks at safety and ethics involving medical research.

Some health professionals and ethicists lament the absolutism of patient autonomy as reflecting a consumerist notion of health care where the patient is an uninterested observer who is always competent to make complex decisions. Despite all these concerns, the ethical tenet of the patient's right to know, and to decide and to refuse, forms the basis of most ethically driven doctor-patient interactions and determines the way physicians talk to patients. With this understanding, the ethical issue in talking to patients becomes, as previously suggested, simple. Just tell the truth. Yet whether in mundane matters, or at the end of life, it is not so simple.

Always telling patients "the truth" can be, simply put, mean. Many would argue that despite the desire for patient autonomy, it is the physician's role to present the truth in a way that he or she feels is right. How easy it is to truth or fact dump on the patient rather than to make the intellectual effort to decide what, in one's best professional judgment, needs to be said in any given setting. The argument for absolute truth telling disregards the realization that how information is presented cannot be without bias. It is naïve to think that when presenting options to patients that the clinician is presenting "just the facts." Some argue that patients can be given basic data to allow them to make their own decisions, but in reality how data is presented surely prejudices those decisions. An oncologist presenting the options for chemotherapy is as vested as the hospice provider presenting the option of palliative care. Each brings their world view to the situations, whether it be philosophical or, candidly, financial. Factors other than science and statistics influence the way physicians present news. Few would disagree that fear of being accused of not giving all the facts affects interactions. Whether it is concerns about claims of malpractice or, probably more commonly, being subject to subsequent questioning or even scolding, affects the way physicians talk to patients. (This fear of scolding is reflected in the problem of over-testing. The effect of this on medical costs is dramatic and unlikely to be altered by tort reform.)

This paradigm of "truth dumping" warrants examples. Imagine a scenario where a physician receives a disturbing imaging study on a Friday afternoon. Argue that the patient has no expectation that the report is available. Argue that there is absolutely nothing urgent to be done. Is there not a place, despite the patient's right to know, to withhold the results until a call early Monday morning when additional studies can be done to clarify the situation? Is truth dumping on Friday and causing emotional pain all weekend the physician's role? Think of a patient newly diagnosed with metastatic lung cancer that will warrant only, at best, palliative radiation and analgesia. Is the physician obligated to report every area of metastases when such results do not alter prognosis or treatment and are likely to add concern and fear?

Those who argue against the physician's option to withhold facts are, in many ways, guided by a disturbing past. As recently as when today's teachers of medical ethics were themselves students, it was common practice to withhold cancer diagnoses from patients in this country and is actually still the standard in many parts of the world. I dramatically recall from medical school seeing a patient, blinded by a brain tumor at a *cancer* specialty hospital, being told that she was in a different *general* hospital and accepting this as reasonable. The fact that physicians lying to patients was the norm in the past makes understandable the support of many today for complete patient autonomy with its accompanying commitment to full disclosure at all times and discomfort with anything less.

COMMUNICATING THE NEED FOR PALLIATIVE CARE

Particularly at the end of life, when full disclosure becomes the ethic, there is still the potential for inflicting pain and denying hope. In fact, both New York and California state laws mandate that physicians discuss palliative care with appropriate patients. It is still critical that this be done with sensitivity. It is easy to tell a patient with an almost universally fatal disease to "get your affairs in order" when they are told of their prognosis. When such information is given, the conversation needs to be guided by sensitivity and respectfulness.

These discussions warrant an ethic of hope, making clear that palliation and hospice are valuable clinical tools. The truth about palliative care and hospice is special. It is a truth that can allow the doctor to help the patient and family understand the seriousness of his or her illness, particularly when other medical approaches offer uncertain or unlikely benefits and, indeed, prolonged pain and discomfort. The doctor must make clear with empathy and sensitivity what palliation and hospice mean, reassuring all that the goal is not to end life, but to ensure comfort and dignity. Some of this discussion may involve reframing the language. It is not that "there is nothing more we can do"; we can do much to make the patient comfortable. Palliative and hospice care can be redefined as aggressive comfort care!

Undeniably these are not easy conversations to have—for physician, patient, or the patient's intimate network. There are numerous barriers to such honest communication. As stated earlier, middle knowledge implies patients (and their families and intimate networks) move in and out of their willingness to encounter the possibility of death. Physicians may have had little training or practice in the art of communication. Some families are loath to discuss death, or may have cultural beliefs that impede the discussion. Given escalating responsibilities, it may be difficult to set aside the time for such communication, so both physicians and patients may be anxious.

When done well, however, these important conversations can often allow and enable decisions that might make the end of life more meaningful.

There is a paradox—family members often want to preserve hope, yet regret missed opportunities. Engaging in these conversations allows dying persons and their intimate network of family and friends to marshal external and internal resources. Research has indicated that patients want to know realistic information (Baile, Buckman, Lenzi, Glober, Beale, and Kudelke, 2000).

As stated earlier, these conversations about end-of-life care best take place when there is a prior history of open and empathic communication. The assumption is that in this ongoing dialogue, there have been continued conversations about the goals of treatment. If that has occurred, it is possible to ask patients and their families what their goals now are and to gently offer contingencies: *"I too wish we can keep Tom's cancer in check, but if we cannot, what would be important to you?"* Such conversations can introduce the possibilities inherent in palliative care and hospice. One colleague described options to families as "hoping for the best while preparing for the worst." One key is to avoid language that disables (i.e., "giving up," or "nothing more we can do") and instead emphasizing what can be done to maintain the patient's comfort level and quality of life. While ethically the physician has a responsibility to initiate such conversations, it should be recognized that patients and their families may also contribute to the context. I remember one family member who approached me relatively early in his father's final illness. As we addressed contingencies, he explicitly invited me to let him know if and when it would be appropriate to consider hospice care.

Such conversations too are most meaningful when there are a variety of options to offer. For example, there are now open access or bridge programs where hospices or palliative care units can offer services such as pain management, symptom control, and psychosocial and spiritual support while continuing with life-extending treatments. Such options introduce patients to the benefits of such programs, easing eventual transitions as treatment goals and the patient's priorities shift.

Specific protocols have been developed that offer guidance. The SPIKES (Setting, Perception, Invitation, Knowledge, Explore and Empathize, Strategy and Summary) program, for example, offers a six-step strategy for communicating bad news (Baile et al., 2000). This protocol and other similar protocols acknowledge that such communication is not only about medical facts but also has deep emotional undertones. Good communication is a two-way process; it elicits the patient's and family's expectations, hopes, and fears while addressing the primary goal of maintaining as good of a quality of life as possible. It stresses what can be done. Ethical communication implies the promise to assist in the transition from curative to palliative care so the patient and family do not feel abandoned.

The discussions about these options offer hope and allow the physician to be fully candid about the unique services that hospice has to offer. Any suggestion that discussing palliation or hospice is truth dumping misses the entire point that empathy and the relief of discomfort is the goal in every doctor-patient interaction.

Conclusion

An ethic of complete and full disclosure would suggest that in the future, physicians could simply post results on patients' web pages with links to articles about prognosis and expectations. Electronic medical records are not necessarily going to be helpful at the end of life and may actually complicate things further. As electronic medical records become more common, the ability of the individual patient to actually review that record will become more common. The written report of the disturbing imaging study previously posited will be just as available to the patient as the provider. This will only further the role of the physician to interpret findings, rather than simply dumping facts.

In the end, the ethical issue in communication at the end of life emerges as based on empathy rather than simply on patient autonomy or the right to know. It should not fall victim to the easy option of truth dumping. It is an ethic guided by appropriate guarantees of privacy and candor. It is a communication that respects the appropriate value of autonomy over physician paternalism.

In short, what is often neglected is that the right to know also includes the *right to choose not to know*. This is the essence of open communication: where the health professional seeks an ongoing dialogue with the patient, responding to the patient's questions and concerns in a way that maintains the openness of the dialogue. Truth dumping can sometimes close that dialogue in a cruel way. Answering the question: "Am I going to die?' with a simple "yes" may end the dialogue. It may be better to assess what the patient's concerns are, to offer hope of palliation, and to stress that one will not abandon the patient. Open communication means that while the physician never lies or falsifies results, diagnoses, or prognoses, it may not always be in the patient's best interest to face the truth, all at once. This is consistent too with research on patient preferences. While patients differed in when and how they wished to be informed of diagnosis, prognosis, treatment options, and end-of-life preferences, they did want the information dosed and gradual (Deschepper et al., 2008).

This brings us back to the point on the right to refuse as well as the initial case. Had my mentor insisted on the full disclosure of the information relevant to his case, my ethical obligation would be clear. Instead he allowed me to pace the information in a way that he trusted would be in his best interest. He did make a choice—one based on trust.

There is a difference between disease and illness. Diseases are defined by pathology and pathophysiology. Illness couples disease with the individual patient. Similarly, there is a difference between truth dumping and empathetic doctor-patient discussions. It is a focus on empathy that must define the ethic of all doctor-patient communication, particularly at the end of life.

Richard P. Cohen, MD, is clinical professor of medicine at Weill Cornell Medical College and attending physician at New York-Presbyterian Hospital. Dr. Cohen received his undergraduate degree from Clark University and medical degree from Cornell. He is a Fellow of the American College of Physicians. A practicing internist, he has been active in teaching students and residents issues involving the doctor-patient relationship. For many years he has chaired Quality Assurance Committees. He is an active professor in the ethics program at Weill Cornell where he has been honored as an outstanding teacher.

REFERENCES

Baile, W., Buckman, R., Lenzi, R., Glober, G., Beale, E., & Kudelke, A. (2000). SPIKES—A six-step protocol for delivering bad news: Application to the patient with cancer. *The Oncologist, 5,* 302–311.

Deschepper, R., Bernheim, J., Vander Stichele, R., Van den Block, R., Michiels, E., Van Der Kelen, G., ..., Deliens, L. (2008). Truth-telling at the end of life: A pilot study on the perspective of patients and professional caregivers. *Patient Education and Counseling, 71:* 52–56.

Weisman, A. (1972) *Dying and denying.* New York, NY: Behavioral Publications.

CHAPTER 5

Surrogate Decision Making: The Surrogate's Value

Mary Beth Morrissey

Surrogacy is a process and an outcome that has taken on multiple meanings in palliative and end-of-life care today. Public policy has played a major role in shaping surrogacy. Under the U.S. federalist system of government, states have traditionally been the "incubators" of health policy. New York serves as a good example of how such policy developed in the area of health care and surrogate decision making over the last two decades. In 2010, after 17 years of legislative advocacy, New York adopted family decision-making legislation called the Family Health Care Decisions Act (New York Public Health Law [PHL] Art. 29-CC). Prior to June 2010, there was no family surrogate in New York State under the public health law, only a health care agent under New York's 1991 Health Care Proxy Law (New York PHL Art. 29-C) and a type of surrogate decision making under New York's 1987 Do Not Resuscitate (DNR) Law. For incapable patients who had no health care agent or no prior directive, "clear and convincing" evidence of the patient's wishes was legally required pursuant to the U.S. Supreme Court standard in *Cruzan v. Director, MDH* (1990). This evidence standard imposed an unreasonable burden on patients, families, and health care providers.

STATE LAWS AND ADVANCE DIRECTIVES

All 50 states have some form of surrogacy law and advance directive instruments that permit future health care planning, although the legal requirements differ from state to state. Living wills and health care proxies, known in other states sometimes as durable powers of attorney for health care, have been in effect in most states for a number of years. Advance directives are the product of a rational individualistic movement that has prevailed in the United States since the 1980s driven in part by the radical turn to social and economic policies of neoliberalism that began in the Reagan administration, resulting in enactments such as the federal Patient Self-Determination Act in 1990 (Public

Law No. 101-508) and statutes at the state level such as New York's DNR Law and Health Care Proxy Law. This rights-based, contractarian paradigm is rooted in Western notions of autonomy and self-determination, and classical economic liberalism. The values underlying the paradigm are self-interested, rational decision making, efficiency, and a free market.

In more recent history, however, this paradigm has been critiqued as being unduly polarizing across class and culture, unreasonably individualistic and rationalistic, and failing to explain pluralistic American values, choices, and behaviors (Meisel, 2003; Morrissey and Jennings, 2006; Sabatino and Karp, 2011). Nationwide only 30% of Americans have completed advance directives, with certain pockets of the country achieving higher levels of success such as Rochester, NY, where the rate is about 40%. Significant barriers to completion of advance directives have persisted despite massive efforts to convince the American public that they are an effective tool in ensuring that patients' wishes are honored in the health systems. Distrust of the health care system, varying styles of communication, religious values and beliefs, and cultural differences in a diverse society have been identified as some of the numerous factors that have undermined the effectiveness of advance directives (Bullock, 2011; Gutheil and Heyman, 2005).

RESEARCH EVIDENCE

Research evidence has also pointed to outcomes and implementation challenges that run counter to the original policy goals that were formulated to advance autonomy. The SUPPORT Study (Study to Understand Prognoses and Preferences for Outcomes and Risks of Treatment), conducted at five U.S. hospital sites in 1995, examined attitudes toward advance directives and outcomes after an educational intervention by trained health professionals. The study showed poor communication between patients and their physicians, inadequate pain care and heightened patient suffering, little understanding of what patients' advance directives meant and how they could be translated into medical orders in the clinical setting, and continued aggressive interventions at the end of life (SUPPORT Principal Investigators, 1995).

Research in the past year points to regional variations in spending. For example, Nicholas, Langa, Iwashyna, and Weir (2011) reported an economic relationship between use of advance directives that limit treatment and reduced end-of-life Medicare expenditures in high-intensity end-of-life care, in high-spending regions. No such relationship was found in medium- and low-spending regions. This study also showed that there was an association between advance directives and lower probabilities of in-hospital deaths, and higher probabilities of hospice use in high- and medium-spending regions as compared to lower spending regions. These regional variations are consistent with Dartmouth researchers' findings that intensity of care, spending, and utilization of health care vary by region and are influenced by local practice patterns and norms (Wennberg, Fisher, Goodman, and Skinner, 2008; Yasaitis, Fisher, Skinner, and Chandra, 2009). Nicholas and colleagues (2011) also reported that individuals with advance directives were more likely to be white, more highly educated, and wealthy. A study in the ICU of a major oncology center demonstrated that utilization of living wills was higher among individuals who were old or white, and less common among Medicaid beneficiaries (Halpern, Pastores, Chou, Chawla, and Thaler, 2011).

The collective findings of Nicholas et al. (2011), Halpern et al. (2011), and the Dartmouth researchers (Wennberg et al., 2008; Yasaitis et al., 2009) invite consideration of how much end-of-life care and treatment choices at the end of life may be influenced by structural factors such as access to care, economic resources, social capital, and health literacy. While Nicholas and colleagues (2011) acknowledge that the clinical effectiveness of advance directives is context dependent, they go on to reject a global relationship between advance directives and resource use, and explain the differences in expenditures in low- to high-spending regions on the basis of patient treatment preferences that are discrepant from local norms. However, I argue that the collective evidence, including the finding of context dependence, clearly suggests a relationship between advance directives and a constellation of social and economic determinants that influences equitable access to adequate health care. One of such primary determinants is the presence and prevalence of economic differences in a community or region that may be driving health care choices and decisions at the end of life, possibly contributing to broader health disparities among Americans. While the goals of the Patient Self-Determination Act (Public Law No. 101-508, 1990) and state-enabling statutes were in part the outgrowth of economic policy, there was never any intent that advance directives would become a tool for advancing economic inequalities that adversely affect the quality of end-of-life care among the less affluent and less highly educated, an unintended consequence of health care policy making in this area.

PARADIGM SHIFT

A new paradigm that helps to address the unintended consequences of policy making in end-of-life care is taking root in diverse ecological contexts that moves away from a purely rights-based view of the legal, transactional formalities of advance directives toward an ethic of care that focuses on relational processes of communication. This shift toward person-centered care encompasses future-oriented advance care planning that aims to foster process conversations between patients and their physicians. The adoption of a humanistic perspective that is based upon human relationships and human development in relation to meaningful others also conceptualizes autonomy and rights as being essentially relational (Morrissey, 2011a, 2011b). It is in this relational and social context that surrogates assume and carry out their responsibilities to incapable patients.

LEGAL AND ETHICAL FRAMEWORK

The major points of the legal and ethical consensus governing health care decision making that are key to the surrogate decision-making process are the following:

- competent patients (and patients with capacity) have a constitutional right to refuse medical treatment, including life-sustaining treatment (*Cruzan*, 1990; Meisel, 2003; Morrissey and Jennings, 2006);
- incompetent patients (and patients that have not been adjudicated incompetent but who lack capacity) have a constitutionally protected liberty interest in refusing medical treatment, and their rights are exercised by surrogates appointed under state law who make decisions on their behalf; surrogate decisions may be subject to certain evidentiary standards (*Cruzan*, 1990; 42 CFR §483.10(a)(3); Meisel, 2003; Morrissey and Jennings, 2006);
- patients have a right to make advance directives (Patient Self-Determination Act, 1990; 42 CFR §483.10(b)(4));
- the legal authority of the surrogate generally becomes effective upon the determination of the incapacity of the patient (New York PHL Art. 29-C; New York PHL Art 29-CC);
- the legal authority of the surrogate generally is limited to decisions about health care (New York PHL Art. 29-C; New York PHL Art 29-CC);
- artificial nutrition and hydration is a medical treatment and may be withheld and withdrawn pursuant to a patient's constitutionally protected liberty interest (*Cruzan*, 1990; Meisel, 2003; Morrissey and Jennings, 2006); the right to refuse artificial nutrition and hydration may be subject to certain restrictions, especially when the right is exercised by surrogates (New York PHL Art. 29-C); providing nutrition or hydration orally

without reliance on medical treatment is not health care (New York PHL §2994-a(12));

- there is no legal and ethical distinction between withholding and withdrawing life-sustaining treatment (Meisel, 2003; Morrissey and Jennings, 2006); and

- assisted suicide and physician aid-in-dying are legally and ethically distinct from forgoing life-sustaining treatment (Meisel, 2003; Morrissey and Jennings, 2006).

Even in light of this well-established framework, however, surrogates continue to operate in a radically changing pre-paradigmatic environment in seeking to honor the wishes of their loved ones. The evaluation process in which they are called upon to engage in weighing treatment options is complex and has cognitive, social, and emotional dimensions (Morrissey, 2011a). Social and emotional support, as well as provision of critical education to surrogates about their responsibilities, are essential to making the decision-making experience for the relational family or social unit a less burdensome and more meaningful one.

CASE STUDY

The following case study is drawn from a qualitative research study and helps to illustrate the ethical challenges for surrogates in understanding their role and responsibilities to the patients whose care is entrusted to them, especially frail elderly patients who may be struggling with different types of cognitive impairments and disabilities. All information is deidentified. The period described dates from April 2010 through October 2010. During this period, the researcher conducted seven interviews with the study participant. The social and medical profile provides background information about the study participant, who is a nursing home resident. The case findings reported herein reflect the frail elderly resident's subjective lived experiences and life-world meanings in the nursing home.

Social and medical profile M is an 88-year-old woman residing in a nursing home in an urban community in the State of New York. M was admitted to the short-term rehabilitation unit in 2007, and later transferred to the long-term care unit due to her diagnoses and limitations. In the long-term unit, M receives 24-hour skilled nursing care.

Family history and transition to nursing home M was born outside the US, lost her father at an early age, and was raised by her mother, grandmother, and great-grandmother. She came to the US, was married twice, but lost both of her husbands to cancer and supported her family on her own. M has three children, one of whom is very involved with her care. M's adjustment to the nursing home has been somewhat difficult. She is very verbal and makes her needs known to the staff. The staff have made efforts to accommodate her needs and make her feel at home, for example, making her tea.

Medical information and advance directives M has a health care proxy and a Do Not Resuscitate order (DNR). M's health care proxy documents the following: "Do not wish to be on a respirator." Her daughter is her health care agent. M meets clinical criteria for being frail. She requires assistance with activities of daily living and ambulation, and is eating-dependent. She has diagnoses of Parkinson's disease, hypertension, vascular dementia, mild depression, and multi-morbidity, and is receiving psychological services.

Hospice recertification Medical record notes dated April 20, 2010, document that M is receiving comfort care, followed by a May 5, 2010, note that M was recertified for hospice care in this period but might not meet hospice criteria in the next period. (At the initiation of the research, M is already enrolled in hospice.)

Hospice discharge M was discharged from hospice care in July 2010. After discharge from hospice, M was referred to physical therapy to maximize her level of functioning and reduce the burden of care on nursing staff, as documented in the medical record. A physical therapy evaluation in October 2010 documents that M has reached maximum potential. She remains confined to a wheelchair and is unable to stand without assistance.

Decision-making capacity M has decision-making capacity and makes her own decisions. Social Work identified M as a resident with decision-making capacity, and as having task-specific decision-making capacity. There is no documentation in the medical record of a clinical determination of incapacity by a physician.

Care planning meetings M's daughter attended the annual care planning meeting on June 10, 2010. Quarterly meetings are usually held without the resident and family unless there is a particular concern or issue that has to be addressed. M's plan of care is discussed at these meetings. M's social worker reported that M voiced concerns at one meeting that on one or two days she did not have breakfast. The nurse practitioner is the member of the team who is responsible for explaining to M any changes in her medical care or status, such as eligibility for or discharge from hospice.

Patient decision making There is documentation in the medical record that M makes her own medical decisions about her care at care planning meetings. Her social worker reports that her daughters do not make decisions for her. She lets them know that "I am the mother." The social worker also reports that M did participate in discussions about her admission and discharge from hospice. A July 16, 2010 social work note documents that the family was informed of changes in M's plan of care when M was discharged from hospice on July 14, 2010.

Assessment M was assessed as stable at her August 2010 quarterly review. Neither the resident nor the family participated in the quarterly review.

CASE FINDINGS

This case involves a frail elderly woman, whom we shall refer to as "M", who was enrolled and disenrolled from hospice while residing in the long-term care unit of a nursing home. In interviews with M, she describes her relationships with her daughter whom she appointed as her health care agent. She also reveals that she is not comfortable with her participation in the care planning and decision process that led to her enrollment and disenrollment in hospice. She describes her experiences in becoming a hospice patient at the nursing home and the challenges that she met with as a result of this change. One of her primary concerns is her inability to walk and loss of function, and the discontinuation of physical therapy when she becomes a hospice patient. She expresses strong emotion about this change in her care and her consistent failure to be able to access these services that she sees as critical to her health and well-being.

Patient decision making, relational end-of-life planning, and communication

The data show M's engagement in end-of-life planning and the patient decision-making process, and openness to such processes. Patient decision making for M is a life course process that changes over time, and has cognitive, affective, social, spiritual, and cultural dimensions. It includes decisions about health care treatment as well as other decisions about M's person-centered care needs, such as whom she trusts to make decisions for her when she no longer has capacity, and future planning decisions. And it is a process that both involves social systems in which M is embedded such as family and provider, and is self-directed, driven by personal agency, and characterized by a high degree of self-control and perceptions of self-efficacy.

M shares that she has a DNR and a health care proxy. M's engagement in forms of end-of-life planning is a decision process in itself and involves desire and agency. But what distinguishes the end-of-life planning decision process from everyday decision making is the goal toward which M directs her agency—her own end of life. She embraces the horizon structure of suffering in end-of-life decision making and her own end of life in a futural horizon about which she can make decisions in the present.

One of those decisions is the appointment of her daughter as the person she trusts to make decisions for her and "take charge" of everything. She has also had meaningful conversations with her daughter about end-of-life options such as feedings tubes and burial arrangements. The centrality of communication to M's relational meanings and conversations is salient in the end-of-life planning discussions she has with her daughter. The choices and decisions M makes depend on her being able to communicate those choices and decisions effectively to her daughter, whom she has appointed to be her health care agent and to act for her when she no longer has capacity. The trust she has in her daughter and their relational intimacy lay foundations for the type of communication they have—the good conversations. Therefore, there is valuing also involved in patient decision making. M attaches value attributes to her decision process and her decision outcomes.

M describes the experiences she lived through with her two husbands who died of cancer, and her brother, to whom she remained faithful, "foot-to-foot," until his death. In recalling these past experiences, she is expressing her end-of-life wishes about her own future care planning in her current situation in the nursing home, and about the kind of care, attention, and fidelity she expects from her relational caregivers. In discussing her burial arrangements, she discusses freely the hymns she has thought about. She shows no discomfort in having these discussions about her end of life or engaging in the complex thought and decision-making processes involved in forgoing treatment.

M appeals to her caregiver to rub ointment on her back to relieve the soreness and burning she is experiencing. This is an example of M's coping with her suffering condition through palliative decision making about her care, a manifestation of her agency. The example shows that her decision has the meaning of an attempt to restore empathic care and, through it, embodied comfort and security, to eliminate the detrimental aspects of the world, i.e., burning pain.

The decision to forgo cardiopulmonary resuscitation (CPR) in the event of cardiac arrest reflects M's agentic processes at work in end-of-life decision making. Forgoing treatment is a complex decision process because it involves choosing between two or more alternative treatments; weighing the risks, benefits, and burdens of each treatment; deliberating about the alternatives; and making a judgment. In this process, M's end of life becomes thematic for her. M evaluates the burden to herself, the patient, of prolonging life through life-sustaining treatment that is likely to heighten her suffering and be a burden to relational others. She also evaluates the alternative of refusing life-sustaining treatment, choosing to have a natural death that is unassisted by medical technology and that may assure her relief from the burden of suffering in a futural horizon. She gives testimony that she does not wish to be a burden to her family. The concept of burden has complexity in M's end-of-life decision-making process that discloses itself in the data as having social and relational dimensions.

Relationships with health care professionals M's relationships with her health care professionals and direct care staff at the nursing home are part of her situatedness in the nursing home community and environment, and the social context of patient decision making. Overall, M does not have highly developed relationships with the professionals or staff of the nursing home. This is particularly devastating for her given the relational discontinuity she has with family members after her traumatic displacement from her own home. She does not express confidence in her doctor, psychologist, or spiritual care professionals, and cites infrequent conversations with her social worker. The relational problems that she experiences with staff weaken the communication between M and the staff. Her response to her hospice admission and discharge is emblematic of these relational and communication inconsistencies. As a result of these inconsistencies that rupture M's perceptions of self-efficacy, M does not turn to these relationships in the context of decision making.

Types of health care decisions There are three types of treatment decisions in which M is involved in the nursing home: (a) decisions that involve routine health care such as medications for pain; (b) decisions that involve functioning such as physical therapy services; and (c) major treatment decisions such as changes in the goals of care that are related to the trajectory of M's illnesses. M's concern with the various types of health care decisions in her life in the nursing home relate to her sense of health and well-being. One type of decision and self-care is decisions involving everyday choices and deliberations, such as seeking medication for pain or soothing ointment for irritated and raw skin.

While certain areas of everyday decision making could be viewed as routine because they involve regular care needs, the participant's experience of illness or care needs cannot be described as routine. A good example of this is M's experience of pain, such as the pain she describes in her knees and in her hands. While M's pain level is assessed as "none" or "controlled" as documented in the medical record, her communication of her pain experience appears not to be consistent with this assessment. There is a moral claim for relief of pain made by M who presents in pain, showing her pained hands and limbs. In that sense, independent of the intensity and quality of the pain, assessment and treatment of any pain are not routine. Abandonment of the resident in a state of pain heightens the resident's pain and leads to suffering.

Other types of routine decisions in which M is involved are decisions that affect her functional level. M experiences perhaps the most anguish about her health care as that care relates to her functional decline in ambulation. This concern is directly related to the discontinuation of physical therapy by the nursing home staff during the period documented in the medical record prior to discharge from hospice. In view of M's burning desire to walk, and to achieve and maintain mobility, this discontinuation of physical therapy services is greeted by M with terrible frustration and anger. She also expresses persistent unhappiness that she felt she was not made a part of the care planning conversations that led to this decision to terminate her physical therapy services.

This issue has meaning for M in terms of the patient decision-making process and communication. She feels that not only has she suffered relational losses, but these losses have been compounded by communication failures. M experiences a connection between interpersonal relations and communication. For M, relationality founds communication; weak interpersonal relationships appear to limit effective communication between the resident and her health care professionals. In this context, patient decision making and its constitutive processes of deliberation and practical evaluation are revealed as expressions of agency. M draws upon this powerful sense of agency in the process of decision making involving her health care professionals at the nursing home, which she experiences as giving her very little voice in making decisions about her care.

Admission and discharge from hospice A major health care decision for M in the nursing home is both the admission to, and discharge from, hospice. M communicates a weak sense of agency about the decision to be enrolled in hospice, and about the decision to be discharged when she gains weight, begins to flourish, and is no longer eligible for hospice services. This means that she does not seem to comprehend fully the nature of the decisions made and her authorship of the decision process. She suggests that she did not participate fully in the decision process; the decision was presented to her as a *fait d'accompli* or factual state of affairs. However, she is by no means passive or nonagentic. She does share that she was told post facto that she was on hospice and has tried to adjust to this change, and to accept that this is probably the best path for her at this stage of her illness.

Throughout her hospice stay, however, she has struggled to make herself a decision maker by reflecting on and challenging her post-decision state of affairs. M questions why she is not receiving physical therapy services and protests the inability of her hospice aide to assist her with walking, although she acknowledges the basic assistance she receives from her hospice aide. M has a passionate desire to walk and will not allow her desire to be extinguished by her enrollment in hospice. She persists in questioning why she is not receiving physical therapy services and why she did not participate more fully in the decision-making process for her to go on hospice. M does not understand the role of the hospice aide, and experiences a high level of exasperation that her goals to achieve and maintain mobility are not enabled. Communication emerges as a theme in the data with respect to this major decision. In the excerpt below, M describes her "story" of finding out that she has a hospice aide, and what that means to her:

> Excuse me a little…what's her name now, S—[the hospice aide]? So…that's—I told S—to let—S—is the girl that you all paid to sit here with me, right? S—sits with me. Oh, you didn't know about it, too? Well, I don't know. They didn't put it through me. It was after they finished, they tell me that they pick a girl to come in early in the morning and sit with me and if I want anything upstairs, she [S—] could do that.

> My daughter was involved in the decision. I think so. Because I wasn't there. No. So the details, I don't know, but she's [S] supposed to come in and, when I left, she's supposed to make the bed and straighten up the room. So, that's as much as I could tell you about it. So…I haven't spoken to anybody. Anyway.

No, I only heard the name "hospice." But not anybody tell me anything. Because I was even kind of scared to hear the word hospice and—but now I am getting accustomed here...and don't tell anybody that I am around hospice. They say, "Mammy, that's the best—that's the best for you because you know we don't have anybody at home to stay with you and I am afraid when you cook, you might leave the gas on." So that's why I am here. So that's my story.

The decision to be assessed for and enrolled in hospice care is a major change in goals of care for M. But M makes very clear that this was a decision process from which she felt distanced, isolated, and minimally involved. She was told of the decision after she was enrolled in hospice when she is introduced to S, her hospice aide. M also describes the involvement of her daughter, her health care agent, in the decision. In this description of the surrogate's role in the decision process, there arises a tension between ethical principles of autonomy and beneficence.

M no doubt believes that her daughter-surrogate acted in her best interest, as indicated by the story she narrates, but her daughter's assessment of her best interests appears to conflict with M's desire to be autonomous.

M now understands what hospice is, although she confesses that at first she felt frightened and perceived the care transition to hospice as threatening. Even with these insecurities, M attempts to take up the role of the hospice patient and reframe her autonomy in a relational context because her family is meaningful to her. The family instructs her that the decision is in her best interest and she can no longer function independently. However, M does not fully accept the consequences of the change in her goals of care.

S, the hospice aide, does not meet M's expectations in terms of how she understands her goals of care. M had a strong desire to walk, and expected that the hospice aide would assist her in achieving her goals to maintain or improve her functioning. While M received assistance in other areas and care from the hospice program that in all likelihood improved her overall health, her mobility and functioning deteriorated, causing M great distress. This disconnect between M's expectations for the hospice aide and M's care needs reflects a fundamental misunderstanding about hospice care on M's part. It also reflects relational communication breakdown on the part of the health care professionals and the interdisciplinary team, to the extent they failed to help M understand her goals of care and care preferences and how those preferences would be translated into medical orders. M accepted hospice only as far as it meant to her that she was possibly becoming increasingly frail and approaching the end of life, but she did not translate the meaning of hospice on a practical level into the outcome that she would no longer receive assistance with ambulation or range of motion, or might experience a significant decline in functioning. M also makes no disclosures of any thoughts or feelings that would suggest that she makes any connection between her decline in functioning and the natural trajectory of her chronic illnesses.

When hospice is discontinued, similarly M does not feel that she has been sufficiently a part of the conversation about the change in her goals of care. M is not able to exercise any self-determination or control. This surrendering of autonomy in patient decision making and diminution of perceptions of self-efficacy are forms of suffering for M in the nursing home environment.

DISCUSSION AND ANALYSIS

Several key questions emerge from the above case study and findings that relate directly to the role of the surrogate in health care decision making at the end of life, and the value of the surrogate. They are:

- What is the responsibility of the surrogate when a resident has fluctuating capacity?
- Who is the decision maker?
- When does the surrogate have legal responsibility to act?
- What is the ethical relation of the surrogate to the resident and what moral obligations arise in the absence of legal authority to make decisions?
- How does the surrogate negotiate her own values and give life and meaning to the values and preferences of resident? Does this process involve only substituted judgment, or evaluation of suffering?
- What is the role of the nursing home, nursing home staff, and hospice staff?

Capacity issues This case raises very significant issues about the role of surrogates, and the health care professionals who support them, in relation to frail elderly persons who may have fluctuating capacity. This particular case falls under the law of New York State, which is clear in setting forth the requirements for clinical assessment of capacity and determination of incapacity by physicians. Unless there is a determination of incapacity by a physician with a concurrence by a second physician under the New York State Health Care Proxy Law, a patient is presumed under the law to have capacity to make decisions (New York PHL Art. 29-C).

Assessment of capacity is task-specific, and a patient's capacity may fluctuate over time, even short periods of time. A relationship exists between the complexity of the decision and the level of capacity needed to make a decision. For example, the same level of capacity required to make a major medical treatment decision is not needed to appoint a health care agent under the New York State Health Care Proxy law as the decision is not as complex. In the presenting case, there is no documentation of a determination of incapacity in the record. The social work staff of the nursing home communicate that the resident has decision-making capacity. Even more compellingly, the resident's social worker describes the resident's sense of personal empowerment, her reluctance to have family members make any decisions for her, and her strong voice in communicating with staff in order to have her needs met. One example shared is the resident's negotiation with staff about her food choices, and her request to have the staff make tea for her.

While the medical record does document that the resident has vascular dementia, the disease appears to be in its early stages, and based upon all reports and medical record documentation, does not interfere with the resident's ability to make health care decisions. No assumptions can be made that because a resident has a mild cognitive impairment or dementia, the resident does not have decision-making capacity. Residents or patients with dementia can still have task-specific decision-making capacity. However, regular assessment of the resident would be appropriate under such circumstances.

Legal and ethical responsibilities of the surrogate In light of the resident's medical information and medical and social history, it is clear that the resident is the decision maker and exercises autonomy and self-determination about her care choices and decisions. It is the legal and ethical responsibility of the surrogate, in this case the resident's daughter who is the health care agent, to honor the wishes of the resident. The resident describes in some depth the trust she holds in her daughter, how she values this trust deeply, and what it means to her. The surrogate is called upon to treat the trust invested in her with the highest respect.

Ethically, the surrogate also has a moral responsibility to spend time having conversations with the resident whose care has been entrusted to the surrogate, and seek to understand as well as possible what the resident's values and preferences are about her future care. If the surrogate feels it necessary, and with the permission of the resident, the surrogate may also seek the help and support of the nursing home staff in the conversation process. However, it is only when there is a determination of incapacity that the authority of the surrogate is legally effective to make decisions on behalf of the resident who is then incapable of making decisions on her own. A determination of incapacity was never made in this case, and therefore the health care agent had no legal authority to make health care decisions on behalf of the resident.

An important point that emerges from these case findings is that the legal and ethical responsibilities of the surrogate are not co-extensive with each other. In this case, the surrogate is the appointed health care agent who has no legal authority to make health care decisions because there has been no determination of incapacity. However, as an appointed health care agent, even in the absence of such effective legal authority, there arise moral obligations to the resident that exceed any specific legal authority. The health care agent stands in ethical relation to the resident and must take active steps to carry out her fiduciary role and responsibilities. What is the nature of that role and responsibility? Is it contractual?

I would reject the notion that the surrogate's value to the resident is a social contract, or of a transactional nature. Instead, I would argue that the surrogate's value to the resident or patient is fundamentally social and relational. Drawing upon the work and writing of philosopher and phenomenologist Emmanuel Levinas (1969), I would recognize a pre-ontological and pre-theoretical moral claim that the patient makes upon the surrogate that the surrogate cannot deny or refute. Westphal (2008) has described this claim as heteronomous subjectivity. However, I would depart from Levinas in acknowledging the presence of reciprocity in the relationship between the resident and the surrogate. While the presence of such reciprocity is not in the nature of a *quid pro quo* or transactional exchange, and further does not as Levinas feared vitiate the value of the ethical relation, reciprocity that arises in the ethical relation is part of a recovery process for the suffering, seriously ill individual whose capacities and acts of giving to another are an intentional and agentic healing movement (Davidson and Shahar, 2008). Throughout M's interviews, M reveals a capacity to be relational, giving and loving toward her daughter and her family even as she suffers cascading losses.

Honoring wishes, values, and preferences of the resident The critical question presented in this case is how the surrogate ought to have carried out her ethical responsibilities in a way that would have honored the wishes, values, and preferences of the resident. The resident expressed a powerful sense of trust in her daughter, whom she appointed as her health care agent. She turned to her daughter over and over again when she experienced frustration in dealing with the nursing home staff and when she felt her needs were not being met in the way she expected or desired. Yet in the most major decisions of M's serious illness involving her admission and discharge from hospice the evidence seems to indicate that her daughter was not as much of an advocate for her mother's wishes in the decision-making process at the nursing home as her mother would have wanted. Somehow M, who was the decision maker, was marginalized. The surrogate in this case appears to have substituted her own values and judgment for the patient's, without specific legal authority, violating the fiduciary relation. Even if there were a grant of legal authority, the standard of substituted judgment means exactly the opposite—making decisions based upon what the patient would have wanted.

In the absence of legal authority to act, what could or should the surrogate have done to advocate on her mother's behalf? Number one, she should have made it very clear to the nursing home staff that all care planning conversations were to be held with her mother as her mother was the decision maker. She could have taken steps herself and with the help of the social work staff to assure that her mother received the help she needed to understand what her care options were and what those options meant, the risks and the benefits, and the alternatives. It is worthy of note here that physical therapy is a non-core covered service under the federal Medicare hospice regulations (42 CFR §418.72), although under certain circumstances a waiver may be granted (43 CFR §418.74). As part of the care planning conversations, the interdisciplinary team should have evaluated and discussed with M whether palliative physical therapy was appropriate to maintain M's mobility to transfer and assure her safety. If such conversations had occurred employing skilled communication strategies, M would have been in a better position to comprehend and understand her illness trajectory, what the trade-offs were, what she was giving up by going on hospice, and what care she would be receiving that she had not had access to before. After explanation and consideration of all her options, including what physical therapy or range of motion services would be provided under the nursing home hospice program and plan of care, perhaps M would have decided that hospice was not the right option for her in light of her goals of care and that nonhospice palliative care in the nursing home was an acceptable alternative.

Most important, M's surrogate could and should have taken an active role in reducing her mother's illness burden and preventing and relieving her pain and suffering. The ethical responsibility of the surrogate surpasses processes of substitute decision making, and understanding and effectuating to the extent possible the seriously ill individual's wishes, values and preferences. These processes are based primarily upon the ethical principle of autonomy. It is incumbent upon the surrogate, however, to move beyond autonomy in responding to the call of the seriously ill person as a member of the community, and approaching the suffering burden of the resident or patient through relational communications and empathic care. This approach is based upon a humanistic perspective of the human suffering condition, and an understanding that human beings are fundamentally social and relational.

RECOMMENDATIONS AND CONCLUSION

This case provides a very rich understanding of the complexities of decision making for a seriously ill individual at the end of life, and the ethical role and responsibilities of the surrogate who stands in ethical relation to the resident or patient. The case illustrates that the surrogate's relation of trust to the resident is not co-extensive with the grant of legal authority. Moral obligations to the resident arise with the investment of trust in the surrogate. The surrogate is valued because he or she is trusted and is called upon to serve the suffering individual and relieve his or her suffering.

Recommendations for improving end-of-life care based upon the case findings are education for surrogates and interdisciplinary professionals about the role of surrogates and how they can address ethical dilemmas that arise in connection with their responsibilities to seriously ill individuals whose care has been entrusted to them. This area of education in both ethics and end-of-life care has not received sufficient attention. For professionals, education that helps to develop knowledge and skill competencies in care coordination and communication, including assessment and providing social and emotional support to surrogates, is critical.

At the systems level, a heightened focus on improving communication and initiating earlier conversations with seriously ill individuals through shared informed decision-making processes that involve surrogates even before they have a grant of legal authority, with the permission of the resident or patient, will help to avoid conflict at the end of life. Such process conversations and advance care planning can help seriously ill individuals think more deeply and amplify their discussions about goals of care; their wishes, values and preferences; and, as appropriate, have goals of care translated into medical orders.

Social workers have a pivotal role to play in both initiating and advancing these conversations and negotiating conflict that may arise among patients, surrogates, and members of the interdisciplinary team. In their care coordination role, social workers can help to navigate issues about access to services for seriously ill patients such as arose in this case with respect to physical therapy, and for a patient who is transitioned to hospice care, take steps to ensure that the patient is receiving range of motion therapy to prevent loss of function. Providing appropriate social and emotional support to a patient or nursing home resident who is making care transitions, and to the surrogate, is a main pillar of hospice and palliative care.

Finally, in the case discussed herein, a frail seriously ill elderly woman revealed a life-affirming, empathic care-seeking, agentic drive for health and well-being, even while living through illness and suffering burden. Affirming the dignity of the suffering human person in serious illness at the end of life to whom the surrogate stands in ethical relation, and the person's capacity for human agency, human development, and freedom to act, make choices and decisions sometimes even in states of disability and dementia, is a core value of ethics in the exercise of surrogate responsibility.

The author gratefully acknowledges Dr. Fredrick J. Wertz and Dr. Tina Maschi for their support and consultation on research reported in this chapter.

Editor's Note: New York's 1987 DNR Law, referenced above, was formerly New York PHL Art 29-B; prior to 2010, PHL Art. 29-B governed DNR orders in hospitals, nursing homes, and elsewhere; Ch. 8, L. 2010 replaced the DNR Law with the Family Health Care Decisions Act in hospitals and nursing homes, extended to hospice, effective 2011; PHL Art. 29-CCC—Nonhospital Orders Not To Resuscitate, governs DNR in other non-OPWDD settings.

Mary Beth Morrissey, *PhD, MPH, JD, is a postdoctoral researcher for the Hartford Risk and Resilience Project of the Fordham University Graduate School of Social Service. Dr. Morrissey's research interests are devoted to health and mental health policy, public health and community health education, health care decision making, pain and suffering, hospice, palliative and end-of-life care, and vulnerable subgroups of older adults including frail elderly nursing home residents and older adults in prison. Dr. Morrissey has over 20 years of experience as a practicing health care attorney, and concentrates her practice to the intersectionality of* *health law and policy, public health, gerontological social work research, and ethics. Dr. Morrissey is chair of the Policy Committee of the Aging and Public Health Section of the American Public Health Association, Aging Issues chair of the Policy Committee of the Public Health Association of New York City, and a member of the National POLST Paradigm Research Committee. In addition, she is active in legislative advocacy and coalition-building at the state and grassroots levels, currently serving as President of the Westchester End-of-Life Coalition and founder and Chair of the Collaborative for Palliative Care.*

REFERENCES

Bullock, K. (2011). The influence of culture on end-of-life decision making. *Journal of Social Work in End-of-Life and Palliative Care, 7*(1), 83–98.

Code of Federal Regulations, Title 42, Chapter IV, Subchapter G, Part 483; Subpart B, Section 483.10(b)(4); Subchapter B, Part 418; Subpart C, Sections 418.72; 418.74.

Cruzan v. Director, Missouri Department of Health, 497 U.S. 261 (1990).

Davidson, L., & Shahar, G. (2008). From deficit to desire: A philosophical reconsideration of action models of psychopathology. *Philosophy, Psychiatry, and Psychology, 14*(3), 215–232.

Gutheil, I. A., & Heyman, J. C. (2005). Communication between older people and their health care agents: Results of an intervention. *Health & Social Work, 30*(2), 107–116.

Halpern, N. A., Pastores, S. M., Chou, J., Chawla, S. , & Thaler, H. T. (2011). Advance directives in an oncologic intensive care unit: A contemporary analysis of their frequency, type, and impact. *Journal of Palliative Medicine, 14*(4), 483–489.

Hickman, S. E., Nelson, C. A. et al. (2009). Use of the physician orders for life-sustaining treatment (POLST) paradigm program in the hospice setting. *Journal of Palliative Medicine, 12*(2), 133–141.

Hickman, S. E., Nelson, C. A., Perrin, N. A., Moss, A. H., Hammes, B. J., & Tolle, S. W. (2010). A comparison of methods to communicate treatment preferences in nursing facilities: Traditional practices versus the physician orders for life-sustaining treatment program. *Journal of American Geriatrics Society, 58*(7), 1241–1248.

Levinas, E. (1969). *Totality and infinity: An essay on exteriority.* Pittsburgh, PA: Duquesne University Press.

Meisel, A. (2003). The legal consensus about forgoing life-sustaining treatment: Its status and its prospects. *Kennedy Institute of Ethics Journal,* Vol. 2., No. 4, 309–345.

Morrissey, M. B. (2011a). Phenomenology of pain and suffering: A humanistic perspective in gerontological health and social work. *Journal of Social Work in End-of-Life and Palliative Care,* 7(1), 14–38.

Morrissey, M. B. (2011b). Educating ethics review committees in a more humanistic approach to relational decision making. *New York State Bar Association Health Law Journal Special Edition: Implementing the Family Health Care Decisions Act,* 16(1), 65–67.

Morrissey, M. B., & Jennings, B. (Winter 2006). A social ecology of health model in end-of-life decision-making: Is the law therapeutic? *New York State Bar Association. Health Law Journal. Special Edition: Selected Topics in Long-Term Care Law,* 11(1), 51–60.

New York Public Health Law, Art. 29-B.

New York Public Health Law, Art. 29-C.

New York Public Health Law Art. 29-CC.

Nicholas, L. H., Langa, K. M., Iwashyna, T. H., & Weir, D. R. (2011). Regional variation in the association between advance directives and end-of-life Medicare expenditures. *JAMA, 306*(13), 1447–1453.

Patient Self-Determination Act. (1990). United States Public Law No. 101-508. Washington, DC: US Code.

Sabatino, C., & Karp, N. (2011). *Improving advanced illness care: The evolution of state POLST programs.* Washington, DC: AARP Public Policy Institute.

SUPPORT Principal Investigators. (1995). A controlled trial to improve care for seriously ill hospitalized patients: The study to understand prognoses and preferences for outcomes and risks of treatments (SUPPORT). *JAMA,* 274, 1591–1598.

Wennberg, J. E., Fisher, F., Goodman, D. C., & Skinner, E. S. (2008). Tracking the care of patients with severe chronic illness: The Dartmouth Atlas of health care 2008. The Dartmouth Institute for Health Policy and Clinical Practice.

Westphal, M. (2008). *Levinas and Kierkegaard in dialogue*. Indianapolis, IN: Indiana University Press.

Yasaitis, L., Fisher, F., Skinner, E. S., & Chandra, A. (2009). Hospital quality and intensity of spending: Is there an association? *Health Affairs, 28*(4): 566–572.

CHAPTER 6

Artificial Nutrition and Hydration

Nessa Coyle and Vidette Todaro-Franceschi

A 49-year-old male came into the cardiac care unit with an inferior wall myocardial infarction, and shortly thereafter coded. Resuscitation attempts succeeded; however, over the course of a few days he went into multisystem failure. On a respirator, receiving multiple medications to support life, and unable to eat anything by mouth or to tolerate tube feedings, the nursing staff were concerned with his nutritional status. An ongoing debate occurred between the physicians and nurses, with the physicians maintaining that he was not "viable enough" for total parenteral nutrition (TPN) but if his condition were to stabilize he would be a candidate. The nurses argued that without adequate nutrition the patient would never stabilize and heal; they felt that he was being starved to death. The intense emotional response of the nurses led the physicians to rethink their approach to care. After 10 days without food and still in multisystem failure, the patient was started on TPN. Regardless, he died several days later.

Artificial nutrition and hydration (ANH) are medical treatments and imply any form of nutrient intake by an individual beyond assisted oral feeding (American Academy of Hospice and Palliative Medicine, 2006; Geppert, Andrews, and Druyan, 2010). They may be further defined as nutritional and fluid support of an invasive nature requiring placement of a tube into the gastrointestinal tract (enteral tube feedings), or parenteral via the intravenous (central-TPN or peripheral PPN) routes. On occasion, fluids may be administered via subcutaneous (hypodermoclysis) or rectal means.

Food and water are basic human needs, without which we will die. Food and water also symbolize caring and nurturing. To withdraw or withhold food and/or fluids in someone who is at the end of life and is no longer able to spontaneously eat and drink symbolizes for some abandonment and neglect. Because the provision of food and water is so basic to human survival, the role of artificial hydration and nutrition at the end of life remains controversial for many families and clinicians and is frequently fraught with emotions (Diekema, Botkin, and Committee on Bioethics, American Academy of Pediatrics, 2009; Gillick and Volandes, 2008). This is especially the case when a family is struggling to accept that death of a loved one is near, and that ANH will neither prolong life or, for the vast majority, improve comfort.

Although an individual position on artificial nutrition and hydration may be based on religious or moral beliefs, it may also be influenced by misunderstanding of the medical aspects of ANH (Arenella, 2005; Schaffner, Kedziera, and Coyle, 2010). There may be the mistaken perception that forgoing ANH leads to a painful death due to starvation. In addition, there may be a failure to recognize the potential complications and discomfort associated with ANH. The experience of expert hospice and palliative care clinicians, as well as some small studies, indicate that the majority of patients at the end of life do not experience lasting hunger or thirst and that those that do can have their symptoms relieved by meticulous oral care or ingestion of small amounts of fluid (Palecek et al., 2010; Sullivan, 1993).

The provision of food and fluid, in whatever form, is viewed by some religious traditions as ordinary care and obligatory. However, "withdrawing" and "withholding" may be viewed very differently within these religions (Gillick, 2001; Gupta and Mukherjee, 2010). In addition, how the question is framed within the circumstances of the particular patient, including their level of suffering, may also influence the response given. It is important that a belief of a particular religious tradition is not assumed by the clinician or even the family. The framing of the question, with all of the subtleties involved, may influence the answer. The question as posed earlier in the disease process about ANH may have led to one response, but when the patient is close to death, a reframed question about ANH may result in a different answer. The clinician may need to guide the family on how to frame the question or ask permission to ask the question themselves.

As life draws to an end and the body is closing down, it is a natural process that the person will gradually decrease food and fluid intake and eventually stop eating and drinking. This is the usual scenario for someone who dies at home under hospice care. For someone who dies in an acute care setting or long-term care facility, without hospice care, continuing artificial nutrition or hydration is much more common (Teno et al., 2009). In such settings this may be the norm, reflecting an institutional standard of care without careful thought and consideration to the benefits and burdens for a particular individual. However, as hospice and palliative care have begun to move into long-term care facilities, these norms are changing (Lopez, Amella, Strumpf, Teno, and Mitchell, 2010; Teno, Mitchell, Kuo, et al., 2011; Teno, Mitchell, Skinner, et al., 2009).

When advising a patient or surrogate about whether or not to initiate, withhold, or withdraw ANH, it is necessary to have a basic understanding not only of the patient's medical situation, but also of his or her culture, religious beliefs, and traditions, including those concerning nutrition and hydration at the end of life. For example, to a Holocaust survivor, the suggestion that food or fluid be withheld or withdrawn at the end of life may be unthinkable. With this knowledge as a foundation, appropriate information, care, and support can be provided.

It is generally accepted that individuals have a right to voluntarily stop eating and drinking at the end of life. In the United States, the Patient Self-Determination Act (1990) specifies that individuals have the right to refuse any medical treatment, including artificial nutrition and hydration. Withholding and withdrawing such interventions are considered ethically and legally to be the same. Even so, it is not unusual for a clinician to say that it "feels" different to withdraw versus withhold ANH. Some religious and cultural norms also may not accept this ethical and legal position and, as previously noted, consider the provision of food and fluids as ordinary and obligatory care. This reflects a stance that a fundamental difference exists between medical technologies and sustenance technologies that supply nutrition and hydration. The argument is that technologies that supply artificial nutrition and hydration are nonmedical means of maintaining life, unlike optional forms of life-sustaining technologies such as respirators and dialysis machines (Beauchamp and Childress, 2001).

Although every state in the US allows individuals to refuse artificial nutrition and hydration through the use of an advance directive such as a living will or durable power of attorney, state laws vary as to what must be done to make a person's wishes known (Gillick, 2006). Because the provision of food and water is so fundamental to human survival, some state statutes maintain separate and higher legal standards for ANH as compared to other life-sustaining treatments. In some states individuals are required to state specifically whether or not they would want ANH at the end of life. When there is uncertainty or conflict, ANH will usually be continued.

From a strictly medical viewpoint there are indicators and contra-indicators for the provision of artificial nutrition and/or hydration to patients at the end of life (Casarett, Kapo, and Caplan, 2005; National Hospice and Palliative

Care Organization, 2010). An example of a situation where ANH might be of benefit is a patient with a partial gastric outlet obstruction associated with newly diagnosed inoperable gastric cancer, who vomits when attempting to eat or drink, and is complaining of thirst and hunger. Nutrition and hydration may improve these symptoms. Another possible medical indicator for a trial of artificial hydration is in a patient with acute delirium associated with dehydration that may be reversed by rehydration (Bruera et al., 2005).

In contrast, a patient who is dying from end-stage pulmonary, cardiac, or renal disease with normal intestinal function would not benefit from ANH. For the majority of similar patients at the end of life, the burden and risk of ANH far outweigh any potential benefit. Such burdens include fluid overload, edema, ascites, infection, nausea, vomiting, diarrhea, aspiration and pulmonary congestion, among other things (Arenella, 2005; Cervo, Bryan, and Farber, 2006; Ersek, 2010).

CASE STUDY

Mrs. J is an 85-year-old woman with advanced dementia and Stage IV non-small cell lung cancer (NSCLC), being cared for at home. Her daughter was distressed that her mother was no longer able to eat and drink "sufficient quantities to sustain life." Feeding her had become a battle—she spat out her food, turned her head away, and struck out whenever attempts were made to feed her. The daughter asked about placement of a feeding tube so that her mother could be fed "passively" without the "stress" of attempted oral feeding. She expressed that this seemed such a "minor procedure" with the potential for great benefit to her mother. The daughter described her mother as a fiercely independent woman whose husband (her father) had died shortly after her birth. She had never remarried and had worked two minimum wage jobs to support her daughter, as well as attending evening classes in a community college. She was described as a woman who rarely asked for help for herself but had always extended a helping hand to others. The Catholic Church was reported as a place of comfort for her.

This elderly and much-loved woman did not have advance directives and had become increasingly withdrawn and uncommunicative over the past decade. Earlier conversations between the daughter and her mother did not reflect what she would want if she was no longer able to eat and drink independently, although she had expressed throughout her life a dread of being dependent on others. Independence and self-sufficiency were fundamental values for her and ones on which she prided herself. This daughter cared deeply for her mother, acknowledging the sacrifices her mother had made so that she could have a good education and opportunities in life that she herself never had. When Mrs. J was no longer able to care for herself her daughter had taken her into her own home, and had recently taken a leave of absence from work to care for her. Her husband and children were supportive.

ANALYSIS

Clinical ethics are grounded in the narratives of individual patients and their families in the setting of cultural and ethical norms. It is about stories and people, lives interrupted, and suffering. It is difficult if not impossible to apply ethical principles hypothetically; they need to be validated by context on a case-by-case basis. Similar to the medical model, a diagnosis cannot be established until the narrative—the context—is understood. Clinical ethics are not primarily grounded in the medical and science issues. Although those aspects are an extremely important part of the equation, what inevitably comes to the fore, especially when there is conflict or disagreement, are social, legal, religious, and cultural concerns. Many of the concerns, as with the issue of withholding or withdrawing ANH, are emotionally loaded. The ability to acknowledge these emotions, validate them, and then step back to systematically facilitate the conversation, is part of the clinical analysis. Some of these important concerns might be: what would this person want; what is possible; what is consistent with their goals and values and how they have lived their life; and what constitutes good medical care (Gillick, 2006; Gillick and Volandes, 2008).

Tensions may exist between ethical principles, depending on the lens through which the situation is being viewed. For example, beneficence versus maleficence—will withholding or withdrawing ANH in someone close to death prolong or hasten death; increase suffering or prevent unnecessary burden? Intent is a critical aspect in any ethical equation. Sometimes intent may be clouded in the setting of an exhausted family, exhausted clinicians, clumsy communication, and misunderstandings around culture and religious beliefs. Stepping back and again focusing on the individual patient and what that person would want will frequently reground the decision-making process.

The ethical question raised by this case is whether the provision of ANH for Mrs. J, who no longer has capacity to make the decision for herself, reflects her previously expressed goals and values, and whether any benefits of the intervention are disproportionate to the risks. The analysis of the case is grounded in the following: the medical context and goals of care (beneficence, nonmaleficence); her narrative (respect for autonomy with the right to choose); the legal decision maker (who gets to decide); and justice. Each area reflects respect for Mrs. J's dignity and personhood. Within this framework, a series of questions will be posed for the clinician to consider regarding the appropriateness of ANH as a medical intervention in this situation.

The first question is what burdens and benefits is Mrs. J likely to incur?
Mrs. J has Stage 4 NSCLC superimposed on advanced dementia. There are no available medical interventions that will reverse her advanced lung cancer or her end-stage dementia. Artificial nutrition and hydration will not reverse her medical condition and will not prevent aspiration. While in some situations ANH can extend life and improve the person's quality of life, in Mrs. J's situation, ANH may impose significant burden on her dying process with a disproportionate burden-over-benefit ratio. ANH requires the placement of an enteral feeding tube or the use of intravenous access. Depending on the enteral feeding approach selected, associated risks include displacement, bleeding, infection, and burdens such as discomfort, need for repositioning, or replacement.

Studies in people with advanced dementia indicate that ANH does not prolong life, improve function, prevent aspiration, or reduce pressure sores (Cervo et al., 2006; Finucane, Christmas, and Travis, 1999; Kuo, Rhodes, Mitchell, Mor, and Teno, 2009; Meier, Ahronheim, Morris, Baskin-Lyons, and Morrison, 2001). The evidence suggests there is the potential for a decreased quality of life and quality of dying by providing AHN, through increased pulmonary symptoms associated with aspiration, volume overload, pulmonary edema, and dyspnea. In addition there may be gastrointestinal symptoms such as nausea, bloating, and diarrhea. Two ethical principles are appropriate to include in this discussion of benefit versus harm—nonmaleficence and beneficence.

Nonmaleficence: This principle states the obligation not to inflict harm on others. At the end of life, in the discussions around ANH, the distinction between hastening death or killing and letting die come to the fore. Based on the life story of Mrs. J, her medical condition and closeness to death, to initiate ANH is likely to cause her harm without benefit, and therefore cannot be justified. Provision of ANH in this case would be extraordinary and disproportionate to the real burdens it would impose. Invasive procedures such as gastrostomy feeding tube placement are not passive in nature; they are uncomfortable procedures and require the administration of anesthesia, which comes with another set of risks (Arenella, 2005). Tube feedings in and of themselves come with other significant risks for harm such as the possibility of aspiration and fluid overload. There is no obligation, in fact there is quite the reverse, to provide a medical intervention to a patient where there is a disproportionate risk to benefit ratio.

Beneficence: This principle states the obligation to remove harm and to do or promote good. Beneficence implies positive acts. In Mrs. J's case, these acts included offering food but not forcing it, meticulous mouth care, treatment of pain and other symptoms, support for the daughter and family, and sensitive care of Mrs. J as a respected and loved member of the family. It was important that Mrs. J's daughter felt comfortable expressing her unease about not providing ANH for her mother, despite recognition that her mother was dying and the understanding of the harm, rather than benefit, that would likely result from such an intervention. She was encouraged to discuss the situation with her Catholic priest and felt reassured that her decision was supported and was the right one. The medical context does not support recommending ANH for Mrs. J (Ersek, 2003; Good, Cavenagh, Mather, and Ravenscroft, 2008; Kuo et al., 2009; Sorrell, 2010). It is medically contraindicated and there is no obligation for a clinician to provide nonbeneficial medical interventions.

The second question is how much weight should Mrs. J's goals and values be given in advising about the benefit and burden of ANH?

Here the principle of autonomy, recognized through the narrative of Mrs. J, comes into play.

Autonomy: Respect for autonomy recognizes the right of the individual to decide for him or herself according to beliefs, values, and a life plan. The principle of autonomy insists that the rights of those who have lost capacity should have their previously expressed wishes honored. The use of advance directives is encouraged to protect the choice of an individual who has lost decision-making capacity. Mrs. J was determined to lack decision-making capacity. She was unable to understand information and to appreciate her situation. She could not express or communicate a preference or choice. Her advanced dementia and Stage IV lung cancer were irreversible and she was terminally ill. She had not completed an advance directive. However, her previously expressed values, and the way she had lived life, reflected core values of independence and self-sufficiency. There was adequate evidence that she would have found the balance of risks versus potential benefits of ANH as unacceptable.

The third question is who is the decision maker for Mrs. J?

Because Mrs. J has not left an advance directive, is a widow, and has only one child, that child (her daughter) is her legal surrogate and has the authority to make decisions on her mother's behalf. The daughter's role as surrogate is to give voice to and represent what her mother would want in these circumstances, as best as she is able. This role reflects respect for her mother's autonomy. If, however, her mother's narrative did not reflect goals and values applicable to ANH, then the "best interest" standard would apply. Although Mrs. J had not discussed her specific wishes regarding care at the end of life, including the use of ANH, she had expressed a dread of being dependent. The daughter, respecting her mother's Roman Catholic faith, and struggling with whether providing ANH to her mother was basic care rather than a medical intervention, sought the advice of her priest. Based on information about her mother's specific medical situation and terminal state, and after an analysis of her particular case, the daughter was comfortable that withholding ANH was consistent with Catholic views. The daughter was encouraged to offer her mother food, feed her if she accepted the food, but not to try and force her to eat.

Justice: In its simplest form, justice deals with the concept of fairness, especially in the way people are treated or decisions are made. More broadly, *distributive justice* refers to fair, equitable, and appropriate distribution of societal resources. This broader consideration of justice was not considered in Mrs. J's case. For Mrs. J, the concept of fairness implied not imposing the burden of ANH without the likelihood of any benefit to her. It also implied her right to receive respectful, compassionate, attentive, and skilled physical, psychosocial and spiritual care, and for her family to be supported. If considering broader terms of justice, whether or not actions are just from both individual and collective standpoints would be considered.

DECISION

Mrs. J's daughter, supported by her husband and children, decided that it would be in her mother's best interest not to request that ANH be started. Initially this decision was difficult, but through a series of discussions and family meetings, she was able to recognize that her role as surrogate was to represent the wishes of her mother. The daughter recognized that medically the treatment would not make a difference to the course of her mother's disease. More important, she understood that her mother would not have wished to be artificially fed and hydrated. The possible negative impact on the quality of life that her mother continued to experience through the loving care she received from her family also entered into her decision-making equation.

AFTERWORD

Mrs. J continued to be slowly and painstakingly fed by spoon. Sometimes she accepted the food and at other times did not. When she did not eat, her daughter felt frustrated and distressed. Her basic instinct and self-talk was "she must eat or she will die; I am not a good daughter if my mother will not accept the food that I offer." Ongoing reassurance from the home hospice team, supported by factual information about ANH, provided the necessary reinforcement that her mother's inability to eat and drink and her refusal of food and water reflected the natural progression of her disease. Mrs. J died at home under family and hospice care approximately eight weeks after the initial discussion of providing artificial nutrition and hydration was raised.

CONCLUSION

Two fundamental questions are raised in this case. The first is whether the provision of artificial nutrition and/or hydration is a medical treatment. The second and related question is in what situations should artificial nutrition and/or hydration be offered? The commonly held medical view in this society is that these are medical treatments. It is acknowledged, however, that there are strong spiritual, emotional, ethical, cultural, and social overtones in relation to the provision of food and water to someone who is totally dependent on another at the end of life. Compassionate and skillful communication around these issues is, therefore, essential. With this as a caveat, decisions about ANH at the end of life should be made in the same way as any other medical decisions at the end of life, on a case-by-case basis.

The medical indications for a trial of artificial nutrition and/or hydration at the end of life have been reviewed earlier. For the vast majority of dying patients evidence shows that burden and risks of ANH at the end of life far outweigh any likely benefit. Early communication between patients, families, and the health care providers about the benefits and burdens of ANH at the end of life is important. Such discussions will help clarify the patient context, including culture and spirituality, often expressed through values, beliefs, goals, and aspirations. These conversations can be especially difficult if held for the first time when a family is struggling to accept that death of a loved one is near, and that ANH will neither prolong life nor improve comfort. One lesson learned through this particular case— where the patient's loss of decisional capacity was progressive and expected—was that conversations and guidance in completing an advance directive would in all likelihood have been helpful in reassuring her daughter that the decision regarding ANH was indeed her mother's decision, as well as a medical one.

Organizations such as the American Academy of Hospice and Palliative Medicine (2006), the Hospice and Palliative Nurses Association (2003), and the National Hospice and Palliative Care Organization (2010), among others, have developed and published position statements on ANH at the end of life. These tools can be very valuable in helping to guide the clinician, both in framing the issues and holding the conversation.

Nessa Coyle, PhD, ACHPN, FAAN, is a member of the Pain and Palliative Care Service at the Memorial Sloan-Kettering Cancer Center in New York. Her focus is on continuity of care, community education, and the effects of poorly controlled pain and other symptoms on the patient and family living with advanced disease. Dr. Coyle is on the editorial boards of several oncology and palliative care journals. She is a member of the Oncology Nursing Society, the American Pain Society, and the Hospice and Palliative Nurses Association. She has lectured extensively both nationally and internationally on palliative care and end-of-life care. Dr. Coyle is co-editor of the Oxford Textbook of Palliative Nursing *(3rd ed.) (2010) and co-author of* The Nature of Suffering and the Goals of Nursing *(2008). She was elected as a Fellow of the American Academy of Nursing and was awarded the Distinguished Career Achievement Award by the Hospice and Palliative Nurses Association.*

Vidette Todaro-Franceschi, RN, PhD, FT, has been a nurse for 30 years and has worked in a variety of acute and long term care settings. She has been an End-of-Life Nursing Education Consortium (ELNEC) trainer since 2001 and is a fellow in Thanatology (Association for Death Education and Counseling). She is a tenured associate professor at Hunter College and the Graduate Center, both of the City University of New York, coordinates death education and the Clinical Nurse Leader graduate program in the Hunter-Bellevue School of Nursing, and teaches end-of-life care, bioethics, and clinical leadership. She has authored over 30 articles, chapters, and a book. Her internally funded research includes exploring synchronicity related to dead loved ones as a healing modality for the bereaved, the first formal study in this area; a number of studies on death education in nursing; and a pilot intervention study to promote completion of advance directives with older adults in the community.

REFERENCES

American Academy of Hospice and Palliative Medicine. (2006). *Statement on artificial nutrition and hydration near the end of life.* Retrieved from http://www.aahpm.org/positions/default/nutrition.html

Annas, G. J. (1990). Nancy Cruzan and the right to die. *New England Journal of Medicine, 323,670–673.*

Arenella, C. (2005). *Artificial nutrition and hydration: Beneficial or harmful?* Retrieved from http://www.americanhospice.org/articles-mainmenu-8/caregiving-mainmenu-10/48-artificial-nutrition-and-hydration-beneficial-or-harmful

Attig, T. (1995). Can we talk: On the elusiveness of dialogue. *Death Studies, 19,* 1–19.

Beauchamp T. L., & Childress, J. E. (2001). Principles of biomedical ethics (5th ed.). Oxford: Oxford University Press.

Bruera, E., Sala, R., Rico, M. A., Moyano, J., Willey, J., & Palmer, J. L. (2005). Effects of parenteral hydration in terminally ill patients: A preliminary study. *Journal of Clinical Oncology, 23,* 2366–2371.

Casarett, D., Kapo, J., & Caplan, A. (2005). Appropriate use of artificial nutrition and hydration–fundamental principles and recommendations. *New England Journal of Medicine, 353*(24): 2607–2612.

Cervo, F., Bryan, L., & Farber, S. (2006). To PEG or not to PEG: A review of evidence for placing feeding tubes in advanced dementia and the decision-making process. *Geriatrics 61* (6),30–35.

Diekema, D. S., Botkin J. R., & Committee on Bioethics, American Academy of Pediatrics. (2009). Forgoing medically provided nutrition and hydration in children. *Pediatrics 124* (2); 813–822.

Ersek, M. (2010). Artificial nutrition and hydration. In P. Nelson (Ed.), *Withdrawal of life-sustaining therapies* (pp. 59–68). Pittsburgh, PA: Hospice and Palliative Nurses Association.

Ersek, M. (2003). Artificial nutrition and hydration: Clinical issues. *Journal of Hospice and Palliative Nursing, 5,* 221–230.

Finucane, T. E., Christmas, C., & Travis, K. (1999). Tube feeding in patients with advanced dementia. *Journal American Medical Association, 282* (14),1365–1370.

Geppert, C. M., Andrews, M. R., & Druyan, M. E. (2010). Ethical issues in artificial nutrition and hydration: A review. *Journal of Parenteral and Enteral Nutrition, 34*, 79–88.

Gillick, M. (2006). The use of advance care planning to guide decisions about artificial nutrition and hydration. *Nutrition in Clinical Practice, 21* (2), 126–133.

Gillick, M. (2001). Artificial nutrition and hydration in the patient with advanced dementia: is withholding treatment compatible with traditional Judaism? *Journal of Medical Ethics, 27*(1), 12–15.

Gillick, M., & Volandes, A. (2008). The standard of caring: Why do we still use feeding tubes in patients with advanced dementia? *Journal of the American Medical Directors Association, 9* (5), 364–367.

Good, P., Cavenagh, J., Mather, M., & Ravenscroft, P. (2008). Medically assisted nutrition for palliative care in adult patients. *Cochrane Database of Systemic Review 2008, Issue 4.* (DO1:10.1002/14651858.CD006274.pub2).

Gostin, L. O. (2005). Ethics, the constitution and the dying process: The case of Theresa Marie Schiavo. *Journal of the American Medical Association, 293*, 2403.

Gupta, V., & Mukherjee, D. (2010). Conflicting beliefs. *Hastings Center Report, 40* (4), 14–15.

Hospice and Palliative Nurses Association Position Statement on artificial nutrition and hydration in end-of-life care. (2003). Retrieved from http://www.hpna.org/pdf/Artifical_Nutrition_and_Hydration_PDF.pdf

Kelly, G. The duty to preserve life. (1951). *Theological Studies 12 (December)*:550

Kuo, S., Rhodes, R. L., Mitchell, S. L., Mor, V., & Teno, J. M. (2009). Natural history of feeding-tube use in nursing home residents with advanced dementia. *Journal of the American Medical Director's Association, 10*(4), 264–270.

Lopez, R., Amella, E., Strumpf, N., Teno, J., & Mitchell, S. (2010). The influence of nursing home culture on the use of feeding tubes. *Archives of*

Internal Medicine, 170 (1), 83–88

Meier, D. E., Ahronheim, J. C., Morris, J., Baskin-Lyons, S., & Morrison, R. S. (2001). High short term mortality in hospitalized patients with advanced dementia: Lack of benefit of tube feeding. *Archives of Internal Medicine, 161*, 594.

National Hospice and Palliative Care Organization. (2010). *Commentary and position statement on artificial nutrition and hydration.* Retrieved from http://www.nhpco.org/files/public/ANH_Statement_Commentary.pdf

Palecek, E., Teno, J., Casarett D., Hanson, L., Rhodes R., & Mitchell, S. (2010). Comfort feeding only: a proposal to bring clarity to decision-making regarding difficulty with eating from persons with advanced dementia. *Journal of the American Geriatrics Society, 58* (3), 580–584.

Patient Self-Determination Act. (1990). United States Public Law No. 101-508. Washington, DC: US Code.

Schaffner, M., Kedziera, P., & Coyle, N. (2010). Hydration, thirst and nutrition. In B.F. Ferrell & N. Coyle (Eds.). *Oxford Textbook of Palliative Nursing* (pp. 291–303). Oxford: Oxford University Press.

Sorrell, J. M. (2010). Use of feeding tubes in patients with advanced dementia: Are we doing harm? *Journal of Psychosocial Nursing and Mental Health Services, 48*(5), 15-18

Sullivan, R. J. (1993). Accepting death without artificial nutrition and hydration. *Journal of General Internal Medicine, 8*, 220–224.

Teno, J., Mitchell, S., Skinner, J., Kuo, S., Fisher, E., Intrator, O., ... & Mor, V. (2009). Churning: The association between health care transitions and feeding tube insertion for nursing home residents with advanced cognitive impairment. *Journal of Palliative Medicine 12* (4), 359–362.

Teno, J., Mitchell, S., Kuo, P., Gozalo, R., Lima, J., & Mor, V. (2011). Decision-making and outcomes of feeding tube insertion: A five-state study. *Journal of the American Geriatrics Society, 59* (5), 881–886.

CHAPTER 7

Pain Management: When Barriers Exist

Terry Altilio and Russell K. Portenoy

linicians who provide care to patients with life-threatening illnesses and their families enter a profound chapter in the lives of these individuals. They have the potential to inform a developing plot, meaningfully affecting the patient's legacy and the family's remembrances and adaptation. Particularly when the patient has advanced illness, and death is anticipated in the near-term, competent palliative care requires that clinicians grasp the iterative process of the illness experience and its meaning both for the patient and his or her intimate network.

Specialists in hospice and palliative care see the relief of suffering as a moral imperative and perceive their clinical work within an ethical framework intended to support, comfort, avoid unnecessary harm, and maintain trustworthy standards of care (Emanuel, 2001). This ethical framework obligates clinicians to seek the knowledge and skills necessary to offer options for treatments that are effective and targeted to the unique and evolving experience of the patient. Increasingly, clinicians who choose to work with patients and families coping with advanced illness are recognizing the need to obtain special competencies that together support the identification and management of the varied components of suffering. The interdisciplinary team addresses the biomedical, psychological, social, cultural, moral, and spiritual processes that may be important in the experience of illness.

Specialists in hospice and palliative care routinely offer therapies that promote physical comfort, such as opioids for those who have pain. They understand the favorable balance of benefit-to-burden that characterizes these treatments, when administered appropriately, even in the context of far-advanced illness. They incorporate these and other medical approaches into a broader plan of care, and promote both communication and coordination with other professional caregivers to support a system that targets the unique and evolving experience of the patient and has the potential to reduce suffering across time, venues, and treatments.

Although opioid therapy for severe pain at the end of life usually proceeds without issue, it is a major event for some families and can be an exemplar of the complexity that may be encountered by a palliative care team working in a complicated medical system to address the needs of the patient. The potential for variation in knowledge, attitudes, and values within the family, or between the patient and members of the staff, can increase the challenge in care planning and goal setting within a specialty that posits patient and family as the unit of care. Beliefs and values about pain and suffering, and fears or misconceptions about medications, may be expressed: Will opioids hasten death, create addiction, or cloud consciousness so that a perceived redemptive value of suffering is not realized? Will it lead to a new family conflict, or become the justification for a renewal of anger or misunderstanding that has pervaded relationships for years and becomes poignantly visible at the end of life?

The narrative that follows discusses the care of a dying woman whose pain and agitation became a focal point for family and staff disagreement, distress, and frustration. While the care occurred in an inpatient hospice unit, the struggles are not specific to either hospice or facility-based care. The case illuminates the kaleidoscope of values, principles, feelings, and behaviors that inform the complex and shifting interface of ethics and pain management when caring for dying patients, no matter what the setting.

Case Study
Ms. H, a 46-year-old Chinese woman with metastatic renal cell cancer, was admitted to an inpatient hospice unit for the management of poorly controlled pain and other symptoms, and a likely pneumonia. She died 11 days after admission.

History of the Illness
The cancer was diagnosed four years prior to admission. Treatments included surgery, chemotherapy, and radiation; these disease-modifying therapies were believed to have extended her life. Recently, after her last surgery, she became paraplegic and required an indwelling urinary catheter. Although the case manager at the referring institution had spoken with Ms. H about the possibility of sub-acute rehabilitation, symptom distress and progressive fatigue led instead to a referral to hospice. No further treatment for the cancer was planned.

Pain related to bone metastases had been present for months. For most of this time, pain control had been adequate with a relatively low dose of long-acting oxycodone. The patient had no side effects on this dose. Pain increased after a spinal cord injury occurred and the opioid was increased. She had periods of somnolence, during which presumptive aspiration occurred. An antibiotic was administered for possible pneumonia. Despite the opioid, she reported pain at multiple sites. She had severe fatigue and was intermittently lethargic or agitated.

Past History

There was no other relevant medical history. A history of anxiety and depressed mood related to the recent period of disease progression and paraplegia was noted in the records from the referring institution. There was no history of psychiatric disorder.

Born in China, Ms. H was bilingual and spent most of her life in the United States. She worked in business until the present illness began. She was divorced and had two daughters, Lia, age 18, and Melissa, age 25. She was Christian and visits from members of her congregation had been a consistent source of comfort.

Ms. H's father was deceased. Her mother, aunt and uncle, younger sister, Lily, and brother, Paul, were involved in her care since her diagnosis. They took many weeks off from work to be available to Ms. H, and most recently were at her side continuously. Her daughters were encouraged to pursue their respective educations while being kept informed and supported by extended family members. At the time of admission, the extent to which the daughters understood the serious nature of their mother's illness was unknown.

Inpatient Course

Advance directives were clarified on arriving at the hospice unit. Ms. H had told her oncologist that she did not want to be resuscitated in the event of cardiac arrest, and this was confirmed. Her sister, Lily, self-identified as the health care agent. Although there was no legal health care proxy, it soon became clear that the patient and family deferred to Lily and the hospice staff accepted her role as primary surrogate decision maker.

On evaluation by hospice staff, Ms. H appeared frightened and demoralized. It was noted that, while fluent in English, the family often conversed in Mandarin. While this may have created an environment of privacy and comfort for the patient and family, it also had the potential to generate a sense of exclusion for some of the care team. Although the family was present almost continuously, the physician had an opportunity to speak with Ms. H alone. During this brief meeting, she described the experience of a relative's death in an intensive care unit, and this memory appeared to inform her fears about what may lie ahead. Importantly, she attributed her paraplegia to staff who handled her carelessly after surgery, rather than to the surgery or to the cancer itself. There was no evidence from the referring institution to support this belief. However, this perception infused patient and family fears with the result that family was always present, both to protect and to advocate, as Ms. H became increasingly dependent and vulnerable.

A joint meeting was arranged with Ms. H and her family to discuss the goals of care. All agreed that symptom relief was the main goal with a primary focus on unrelieved pain. Ms. H expressed the wish, repeated by the family, that her pain be controlled as the first priority.

The plan of care for pain control almost immediately became contentious. Lily advocated for symptom relief and preserved consciousness, which she stated had been the patient's goal in the past. The physicians and nurses on the unit accepted this, but explicitly stated that pain control in someone so ill is often accomplished only at the cost of consciousness. As the opioid dose was increased, Ms. H quickly became more confused and unable to direct her care. Lily spoke with the hospice chaplain, sharing her belief that the medical team was insensitive to the patient's and family's goals. The chaplain's interventions did not alter Lily's conviction that Ms. H would choose pain and agitation rather than risk consciousness, nor was he able to bridge the growing disharmony with medical and nursing staff. Lily disagreed with decisions to provide any extra doses of the opioid when Ms. H moaned in pain. She repeatedly asked that the dose be further lowered, and demanded that the drug be changed. The extended family deferred to Lily and mirrored her mistrust of the intentions and expertise of the clinical team.

At the same time that medical and nursing interventions were challenged, Ms. H and her family's experience was enriched by visits from a spiritual support community. Ms. H appeared to be comforted by family singing and joining in prayer. The music therapist was able to create a therapeutic relationship, which was a most positive element of the care plan.

The team attempted to address Lily's perceptions directly. Social work and psychologist outreach was met with ambivalence, and the hospice chaplain continued efforts to improve communication. The team validated the demands and isolation implicit in the ongoing role of decision maker, inviting Lily to share the weight of these responsibilities. Lily disclosed that she experienced a profound guilt for the decision to encourage the surgery that resulted in paraplegia. The team hypothesized that Lily's efforts to maintain Ms. H's consciousness may be related to the need to preserve a window of opportunity to seek forgiveness. In a meeting with Lily, this was gently suggested, and rebuffed.

Lily continued to request changes in the opioid dose and drug. She consulted a Chinese physician in the community, who did not see Ms. H but called the physicians to offer "curbside" suggestions. The staff perceived Lily's involvement as an impediment to effective care. Staff distress fluctuated with the degree of pain perceived to be experienced by Ms. H. When awake, she reported pain, and when lethargic, the staff saw behavioral evidence of pain, particularly when she was turned in bed.

Decision

Tension escalated as Ms. H became increasingly obtunded and was perceived to be approaching death. Lily requested diagnostic studies, consultations from medicine and critical care, and full resuscitative efforts despite the patient's prior wish to not be resuscitated in the event of cardiac arrest.

The hospice team told Lily that the Do Not Resuscitate (DNR) status would not be reversed because it reflected Ms. H's stated wish to be actualized in the very situation that was then occurring. She was told that Ms. H appeared to be proceeding into the period of active dying, that a return to consciousness would not occur, and that medication to reduce pain and stop agitation would be given. Lily indicated that she wanted to revoke hospice. She spoke of finding another hospital to accept the care of Ms. H.

Ms. H became hypotensive and Lily demanded that something be done. The hospital's rapid response team was called. They assessed the situation, noted that the patient remained DNR, and informed the hospice staff and Lily that the patient was not a candidate for any critical care involvement.

As death became imminent, the suggestion was made to Lily that she share this information with others in the family in order to allow them the opportunity to participate as they needed. It was suggested that daughters Lia and Melissa be advised of the changing medical condition. This guidance was misconstrued as a challenge to the supremacy of God's will, as "only God knows when someone will die." The tension between the staff and Lily increased.

Ms. H was actively dying and the physician ordered an increase in the dose of the opioid to address restlessness perceived to be related to pain, and a pattern of breathing that may have been experienced as breathlessness. Ms. H's daughters were present, requesting that the staff not allow their mother to suffer. Lily again resisted, stating that Ms. H had wanted a "natural death," which the medications would prevent. The medication was given.

ANALYSIS

Palliative care at the end of life is replete with concepts and phrases that often go unexamined until a case like Ms. H's forces a critical examination of assumptions, decisions, and outcomes. Routinely, the patient and family are described as the "unit of care," as if a unified care plan can always address the needs of all. Caregivers are engaged as "part of the team," as if there is never a need to protect the patient from a family member on the wrong track. Those who advocate for competent and compassionate management of pain speak of "barriers" but the usual list of concerns may be remote from the individual context of a family in crisis. In an effort to respect culture, patient autonomy and the consent process may be delegated without question and scrutiny. The challenging case of a dying woman with pain whose care was compromised by a loving sister invites a critical review of these assumptions.

The patient and family gave Lily decision-making authority and the clinical team expected Lily to guide care in a manner that was consistent with the patient's previously expressed wishes or best interests. Under the best of circumstances, Lily would have developed confidence in the clinical team. Their support and guidance would be invaluable as she became able to share decision making and diminish her continuing distress, isolation, and sense of responsibility. Instead, she expressed deep mistrust of the team, and pursued goals that appeared to diverge from those that the patient had previously expressed, were not consistent with the medical facts, and led to pain control that was less effective than it could have been.

Lily perceived Ms. H's cognitive decline to be the result of the medication for pain, in spite of the medical team's ongoing efforts to explain the multiple factors that converge in advanced illness and cause cognitive deficits. Just as the patient (and presumably Lily as well) attributed paraplegia to a preventable professional error, Lily was unable to accept that cognitive decline reflected the advanced nature of the disease rather than a problem that was under the control of the medical team. The team's reluctance to withhold the opioid from a patient with pain was then perceived as inappropriate care, or worse.

For specialists in palliative care, clear communication and consistency across team members may help to mitigate this type of mistrust and vulnerability.

With time, the patient and family may learn to trust that the team brings to the therapeutic approach a profound respect for the patient's and family's values, preferences, culture, and relationships. This respect may serve to mitigate the anxiety and hyper-vigilance in the patient and family.

The present case, however, demonstrates the limitations within which every team operates. The time during which the events occurred was compressed, just 11 days, and this was insufficient for the building of trust with a family who brought four years of illness history and lifelong family relationships. The challenges posed by late involvement of the specialist team are well known.

Concurrent with the challenges is the ethical obligation to provide care consistent with current standards. Clinicians have an obligation to judge whether the decisions made by a surrogate carry the potential to undermine optimal care or violate the patient's prior expressed wishes. The desire to respond to the family's distress must not eventuate in suboptimal care for the patient. If it is unethical to allow a patient to experience unbearable pain at the end of life, then clinicians who bend to the will of a family compromised by mistrust or other problems may unintentionally fail in their moral obligation to do all within the limits of medical knowledge and available resources to relieve pain. In this setting, the ethical mandate may be to challenge conditions hostile to good patient care (Rich, 2000). This was the course ultimately selected by the team caring for Ms. H when Lily was told that the DNR status would not be reversed and medicines would not be withheld.

This ethical obligation applies to all disciplines on the team. For example, it is core to physician practice, embodied in the Hippocratic Oath. As a nursing code of ethics has evolved, the focus has shifted from an obligation to carry out the orders of physicians to an obligation to safeguard patients from incompetent, unethical, or illegal practice. Social work commitment to social justice, respect for persons, integrity, and self-determination similarly creates professional distress that should drive an effort to engage a discussion about conditions hostile to good patient care.

It is interesting to consider whether some of the conflict between Lily and the palliative care team would not have existed had the family not been Chinese-American. Clinicians may accept the concept of a waiver of informed consent because it reflects culture, and as a result, be less likely to probe a patient like Ms. H for her wishes regarding care. Yet, unquestioning acceptance of traditions that lead to care that adversely affects the most vulnerable patients need not be condoned (Hyun, 2002). Although clinicians must accept a patient's decision to defer to family, this acceptance is contingent on an assessment that excludes coercion or similar factors. The desire to respect cultural diversity does not preclude reasonable efforts to ensure that the patient who chooses to suffer or delegate autonomy to benefit the good of family is acting authentically from their own values—values that do not emanate from deprivations, oppression, or an alliance with those who have had the power to deprive (Hyun, 2002). In the present case, Ms. H's decision to defer to Lily was accepted by the clinicians, who had no reason initially to raise doubts.

Consideration of patient autonomy and the clinicians' responsibility to Ms. H raises other poignant considerations. Was Ms. H choosing to suffer to expiate Lily's guilt? Did she accept that her suffering had redemptive value or did Lily sanction her suffering in a misguided belief that suffering imposed by another was a path to redemption? Was Ms. H unable to assert a preference for relief but expected this as a patient right, with the concurrent expectation that health care staff would not allow Lily's influence to prevail if it was not consistent with the goal of symptom relief?

This case may have ended differently had Ms. H been cared for at home. In the inpatient hospice setting, one might expect staff to have more influence given their direct responsibility for assessment and treatment of pain. As opposed to home care clinicians, unit staff was consistently and personally exposed to Ms. H's undertreated symptoms and the power of the family dynamics. The opportunity for staff splitting and disagreement was ever-present, as was the frustration of clinicians who believed that care was being compromised. Actions taken by the team were also perceived by some clinicians as risking professional or institutional liability, which has the potential to create additional stress. In the home care setting, the outcome may have been different because the patient and family members would have responsibility for medication management and would therefore be the agents of behaviors that did or did not relieve suffering. Most likely, there would be fewer clinicians and perhaps more coherence of message and messenger.

It is important in analyzing this case to focus on the voice of Ms. H, who unfortunately became less and less able to advocate for herself during the time in the unit. Early in the admission, it seems clear that Ms. H and her family brought to the hospice staff a compilation of experiences, values and beliefs, fears, and assumptions that might never be transparent but would challenge the ability of clinicians to practice pain management within standards of care, free and distant from ulterior motives (Emanuel, 2001). Lily quickly intervened to control and contain the medical management of pain and agitation as the advocate for consciousness over comfort. Whether mediated by profound guilt, psychiatric illness, cultural mandate, or anticipatory grief, Lily's efforts could not prevent death, but could modify the path in a direction that was felt to be incongruous with Ms. H's best interests. Interpreting Ms. H's values and preferences for care by reviewing past decisions might have provided guidance to the staff, helping them mediate disagreements, contain Lily's unchecked authority, and assuage any unspoken fears of further blame for medical decision making. Resurrecting Ms. H's voice and considering whether Lily had become so overwhelmed that she was unable to serve the patient might have helped counter staff demoralization.

Framing the events that compromised care in this case as an ethical conundrum also may have helped the staff cope. It would lead to an inquiry that might address issues of social justice, respect for persons, beneficence, and the moral implications of a perceived failure to meet accepted medical standards. The objective process of an ethics consultation might have protected Lily from continuing in a role that had become untenable and provided a method for resetting the balance of beneficence, autonomy, and the unchecked authority of a surrogate decision maker. The process would signal a respect for the suffering of patient and family, as well as respect for a staff that felt helpless to actualize their professional moral and ethical responsibilities to a most vulnerable dying patient.

CONCLUSION

Pain management with opioid medications in those with advanced illness usually is a straightforward intervention, which is highly effective and widely accepted. Rarely, the process becomes the fulcrum for dynamics that are highly complex and have the potential to highlight the challenging interfaces among clinical practice, ethics, and culture. Curiously, the care of Ms. H ended with both a staff and a grieving family experiencing similar emotions—anger, guilt, and mutual criticism. It is uncertain that any change in care plan would have improved these outcomes, but some of the lessons may help in future cases. Although respect for culture and for patient autonomy within the cultural framework is a core principle of palliative care, should surrogate decisions worsen pain and suffering, reexamination of the plan from additional frameworks, including medical appropriateness and professional ethics, may be needed to interrupt a clinical stalemate.

Terry Altilio, LCSW, *is social work coordinator in the Department of Pain Medicine and Palliative Care at Beth Israel Medical Center. She is a recipient of a Mayday Pain and Society Fellowship Award and a Social Work Leadership Award from the Open Society Institute's Project on Death in America. In addition to direct clinical work, she lectures nationally and internationally on topics such as pain management, ethics, palliative care, and psychosocial aspects of end-of-life care. She lectures in the post masters End-of-Life Care Programs at New York University School of Social Work and Smith College School of Social Work, teaching pain and symptom management and ethics. She is on the editorial board of the* Journal of Social Work and End-of-Life & Palliative Care *and has co-authored publications on pain and symptom management, psychosocial issues in end-of-life, and caregiver advocacy. She is co-editor with Shirley Otis-Green of the inaugural* Oxford Textbook of Palliative Social Work.

Russell K. Portenoy, MD, *is chairman of the Department of Pain Medicine and Palliative Care and the Gerald J. Friedman Chair in Pain Medicine and Palliative Care at Beth Israel Medical Center, New York. He is the chief medical officer of MJHS Hospice and Palliative Care and professor of neurology and anesthesiology at the Albert Einstein College of Medicine. Dr. Portenoy is past-president of both the American Academy of Hospice and Palliative Medicine (AAHPM) and the American Pain Society (APS). He is a recipient of the AAHPM's National Leadership Award and has received both the Wilbert Fordyce Award for Lifetime Excellence in Clinical Investigation and the Distinguished Service Award from the APS. He is editor-in-chief of the* Journal of Pain and Symptom Management, *co-edits the* Oxford Textbook of Palliative Medicine, *and has written, co-authored, or edited 19 other books and more than 500 papers and book chapters on topics in pain and palliative care.*

REFERENCES

Emanuel, L. (2001). Ethics and pain management: An introductory overview. *Pain Medicine, 2*(2), 112–116.

Hyun, I. (2002). Waiver of informed consent, cultural sensitivity and the problem of unjust families and traditions. *Hastings Center Report,* September-October, 14–22.

Rich, B. A. (2000). An ethical analysis of the barriers to effective pain management. *Cambridge Quarterly of Healthcare Ethics, 9,* 54–70.

CHAPTER 8

Palliative Sedation and the Rule of Double Effect

Daniel P. Sulmasy and Nessa Coyle

WHAT IS PALLIATIVE SEDATION?

Palliative sedation is a medical therapy that is sometimes used for the imminently dying (those with a life expectancy of from hours to days). It involves pharmacologically induced, controlled sedation intended to relieve intractable pain or other symptoms. A reduced level of consciousness is anticipated and accepted as a necessary part of therapy. The goal of palliation changes from the control of symptoms with the patient maintaining an awake status, to a joint acceptance by the clinicians and the patient that the only available means of controlling the symptom(s) will likely require that the patient be asleep as life draws to a close. The overall goal is not to hasten death but to relieve and prevent unnecessary suffering in those whose death is imminent. The level of sedation required to relieve symptoms varies from patient to patient. The goals of sedation and end points to be monitored must be clear for the patient (where feasible), family, and staff. Clinical vigilance is needed to ensure continued relief of suffering and rapid adjustment of therapy if needed.

A variety of drugs can be used for palliative sedation, depending on the symptom being targeted; sometimes a combination of agents is selected. Commonly used agents include benzodiazepines, barbiturates, neuroleptics, and anesthetics. Frequently one or more of these drugs may be added to the patient's background of around-the-clock opioids already prescribed for the management of pain and/or dyspnea.

For the purposes of discussion in this chapter, the phrase *palliative sedation* will not be used to refer to the use of low doses of sedative-hypnotic drugs in clinical situations to treat neuro-excitatory states such as anxiety, or to alleviate symptoms of insomnia, or as the temporary administration of complete sedation during a medical procedure.

WHY PALLIATIVE SEDATION?

Since the earliest days of hospice care, as explicated by the late Dame Cicely Saunders, the aim of pain relief has been restorative—to decrease pain and other symptoms without excess sedation, with the aim of returning the patient as closely as possible to his or her normal state (Saunders and Baines, 1983). Saunders insisted on this point in order to combat the common misunderstanding that opioids and other potent analgesic drugs always sedated patients into a state of oblivion. Although the vast majority of patients can have their symptoms adequately controlled without excessive sedation, even Saunders recognized that a small minority of patients will, despite all available interventions (both pharmacological and nonpharmacological), suffer intolerably from intractable pain and/or other symptoms at the end of life. Palliative sedation is offered to this population as an aspect of an overall moral commitment of providing compassionate, whole-person care at the end of life (Saunders, 1989).

CASE STUDY

Eddie is a 30-year-old man with end-stage osteogenic sarcoma. Cure is no longer possible after years of struggle with surgery, radiation, and chemotherapy. Five months ago he enrolled in hospice and has a Do Not Resuscitate (DNR) order in place. Over the last two months he has required increasing doses of morphine for pain relief. He has now developed very bothersome myoclonus as a side effect of protracted high-dose opioids. He has become bed-bound and is dyspneic and near death. The myoclonus has persisted despite several opioid rotations, including fentanyl, hydromorphone, and methadone. He is not a candidate for an epidural or intrathecal route of drug administration. Moreover, despite adjuvant treatment with tricyclics and non-steroidal anti-inflammatory drugs, and pharmacotherapy aimed specifically at dampening the myoclonus without excessive sedation, his pain is increasing and responds only to increasing opioids, exacerbating his myoclonus. Trial of a stimulant only increased his distress. He is groggy but alert, and suffering intensely. At a team meeting, it is suggested that Eddie is a candidate for palliative sedation. The social worker on the team expresses concern that this is just a euphemism for euthanasia and a discussion ensues.

PHILOSOPHICAL JUSTIFICATION AND THE RULE OF DOUBLE EFFECT

Intention and transparency are critical issues when palliative sedation is offered as a medical intervention for the suffering associated with intractable symptoms in the imminently dying. The intention of the clinician distinguishes palliative sedation at the end of life from assisted suicide and euthanasia. Classically, in palliative sedation, the intention is to relieve symptoms that are causing great suffering, not to hasten death. In assisted suicide and euthanasia, by contrast, the aim is to induce death as the intended means of relieving suffering (Boyle, 2004).

Intentions matter in the moral evaluation of human actions (Jansen, 2010). One of the earliest moral judgments a child might reach regarding the actions of a sibling is, "You did that on purpose." Juries are asked regularly to make judgments that distinguish manslaughter from murder in its various degrees, based upon their assessments of the intentions of the accused. Differences in intention have concrete and observable behavioral manifestations, and intentions distinguish palliative sedation from euthanasia. Classically, ethicists have argued that palliative sedation is justified as an application of the rule of double effect, a moral rule that depends heavily on the moral evaluation of intentions. The rule of double effect has been proposed to help moral agents mediate the difficult situation one faces when one's duty to do something good appears to conflict with a duty to avoid doing wrong (Cavanaugh, 2006; Sulmasy, 2007). The rule states that an action is morally permissible, even if it results in something one would deem wrong if done intentionally, if the following conditions have been met:

- all other means have been exhausted;
- the action is not intrinsically wrong;
- one foresees a bad effect as a direct result of one's action, but only intends the good effect;
- the bad effect is not the means by which the good effect is brought about; and
- one has a proportionate reason for acting—i.e., the good to be done significantly outweighs the bad that one foresees as a possibility.

Sedation is sometimes an anticipated (foreseen) but unintended side effect of administering certain drugs. Ordinarily, even in palliative care (at least as conceived of by Saunders), one aims to restore a patient by relieving symptoms and avoiding (not intending) this side effect. Typically, one is able to administer drugs that have a sedating side effect in doses that do not result in sedation but restore the patient more closely to the person he or she normally is (e.g., by relieving anxiety with 5 mg of diazepam, or pain with 30 mg of codeine).

Double-effect sedation

In some situations, as in the case of Eddie, the aims of relieving symptoms and avoiding sedation can come into conflict. It is precisely such circumstances in which the rule of double effect can be useful and it is precisely the rule of double effect that justifies palliative sedation in such cases, at least for those who are morally opposed to euthanasia and assisted suicide (Sulmasy and Pellegrino, 1999). The case described fulfills all the requirements necessary to justify the action under the rule of double effect. Suppose that the hospice physician was morally opposed to euthanasia and assisted suicide. She also worried that by increasing the morphine to control the patient's pain, and concomitantly administering a benzodiazepine such as valium, she would thereby be very likely to render the patient unconscious and thereby hasten the patient's death. The rule of double effect provides guidance and support for such a morally careful physician by providing classical ethical grounds to justify the use of these drugs. As described, all other means of treating the pain with lower doses of opioid or by the addition of adjuvant treatment have been exhausted; there is no other treatment available for myoclonus that does not have sedating side effects. It is not intrinsically wrong to prescribe diazepam. In administering the diazepam, the physician would be using a drug that is indicated to treat the specific symptom of myoclonus, but has the foreseeable side effect of sedation. Under the rule of double effect, the conscientious hospice physician would foresee the sedation, but not intend it; she would not be *aiming* at sedation. She would titrate up the dose of the drug until the symptom (myoclonus) is relieved. The cessation of myoclonus would be her intention, even though she recognizes that achieving this goal will likely also result in sedation. The bad effect (sedation) is not the cause of the good effect (relief of myoclonus). And she would have a proportionate reason for acting—the patient is close to death, the pain and the myoclonus are severe, and the short period of sedation (humanely) should not be considered too high a price to pay for the relief of the patient's suffering. Thus, all the conditions of the rule of double effect would be fulfilled and the physician could reassure the social worker that this was not euthanasia.

This type of "double-effect sedation" ought to be justifiable even for clinicians who are morally opposed to euthanasia and assisted suicide. In double-effect sedation, death occurs from the underlying disease, perhaps hastened by the sedation. In contrast to euthanasia, death is not the aim, nor is sedation itself the aim. The aim is the relief of a symptom, using a drug appropriate for treating that symptom that has sedating effects. If the symptom is relieved without sedation, the dose is not increased. In the case described, were the pain and the myoclonus to be controlled but the patient still awake, there would be no further justification for increasing the diazepam dose. The clinician's aim would be fulfilled by the relief of the symptom regardless of the degree of sedation; sedation is not the aim.

The vast majority of ethicists and clinicians agree that if this is what palliative sedation means—double-effect sedation—then palliative sedation is morally permissible.

Under what circumstances? (Timing in relation to prognosis and closeness to death)

Some ethicists have argued that proximity to death is an irrelevant consideration in deciding whether palliative sedation is appropriate (Jansen, 2003). However, the mainstream view is that palliative sedation is acceptable as a medical intervention only for patients (a) who are close to death (within hours to days); (b) whose symptoms are causing intractable suffering; and (c) for whom less dramatic measures have failed (Cherny and Portenoy, 1994). As with any other medical interventions, one needs a clearly articulated rationale and justification for this choice. Patients for whom sedation at the end of life may be an option include patients who have intractable pain and/or other symptoms despite the use of every available intervention, and those who have asked to be removed from life-sustaining therapy and are expected to experience extreme symptoms as a result, such as the respiratory distress that often accompanies withdrawal of ventilatory support. Establishing (justifying) the need for palliative sedation in a particular patient requires the clinician to review the following questions: Are refractory symptoms present and, if so, what are they? Have other pharmacological, psychological, spiritual, and physical measures been used to manage these symptoms, and if so, what were they? Are these interventions and outcomes documented in the patient's chart? Is this a reversible or irreversible situation for the patient? How close is the patient to death? A consensus is reached among the team members that the patient has far-advanced disease and is imminently dying; that the goal of care is no longer to prolong life but to provide comfort; and that this is the informed wish of the patient and/or the patient's surrogate decision maker.

In the case described above, Eddie was very close to death. His suffering was persistent and intense—both pain and myoclonus. Consistent with the rule of double effect, other means such as adjuvant pain modalities with a lower dose of morphine and the substitution of different opioids had been explored and had failed.

Palliative sedation to unconsciousness

Some ethicists and clinicians have argued that a different form of palliative sedation ought to be permitted, one in which the aim is to produce a sedated state as a means of dissociating patients from their symptoms (Quill, Lo, Brock, and Meisel, 2009). Just as one may produce a temporary sedated state in order to allow a patient to undergo a surgical procedure, just so, they argue, when all else fails, one ought to be permitted to dissociate patients from their distressing symptoms until they die. Unlike double-effect sedation, the aim (the intention in acting) is to produce the sedated state. Sedation is directly intended; it is not an unintended side effect. Proponents of this kind of procedure call it *palliative sedation to unconsciousness.*

These ethicists also argue that one may distinguish palliative sedation to unconsciousness from euthanasia because, while death is foreseen, they aver that it is unintended. In euthanasia, the aim is death. In palliative sedation to unconsciousness, they argue, the aim is unconsciousness as a means of dissociating the patient from distressing symptoms. The dose is chosen to achieve a state of unconsciousness short of an independently lethal dose. Thus, in the case above, if Eddie were to say, "I am tired of the myoclonus and the pain. Even if these symptoms can be controlled I just want to sleep until I die. I've had enough. Can't you help me?" A physician who believed in the moral permissibility of palliative sedation to unconsciousness would then agree and would titrate the diazepam infusion until the patient was no longer conscious, but still breathing.

Palliative sedation to unconsciousness cannot be justified under the rule of double effect (Jansen and Sulmasy, 2002a). The two effects invoked in double-effect reasoning (i.e., the good effect and the bad effect) must both follow from the means one is employing, not from the state at which one is aiming. For instance, classically, in justifying the use of morphine in a dying patient with underlying respiratory embarrassment under the rule of double effect, both the good effect at which one is aiming (the relief of pain) and the bad effect (possible further respiratory embarrassment and hastened death) result directly from the administration of the morphine. However, in palliative sedation to unconsciousness, the state at which one is aiming (unconsciousness) is itself the cause of the bad effect (hastened death), and so double effect does not apply. In other words, if one is to employ double-effect reasoning, there need to be two distinct effects. Morphine itself causes both pain relief and decreased respiratory drive, and pain relief does not cause respiratory depression. Thus the rule of double effect can be employed to justify giving morphine to a dying patient with oxygen-dependent chronic obstructive pulmonary disease and severe pain with the understanding that one is aiming at pain control, not respiratory embarrassment. By contrast, if one is using benzodiazepines to induce sedation, one cannot claim that there are two distinct effects that both follow from the administration of the drug, sedation and hastened death. The benzodiazepines would be used to cause unconsciousness, and unconsciousness, in turn, hastens death. This is a causal chain (a causes b which causes c), not a causal fork (a causes both b and c). Accordingly, there is really only *one* effect and so "double" effect does not apply.

Nor can one claim that the practice is justified under double effect by suggesting that one is not aiming at unconsciousness, but only at the relief of suffering. Making the patient unconscious is one's intended means of relieving the patient's suffering, so this would violate the fourth condition of the rule of double effect. Palliative sedation to unconsciousness is not justifiable under the rule of double effect.

To justify palliative sedation to unconsciousness, one would thus have to argue that the permanent loss of consciousness until death is, independently considered, a good at which to aim (Jansen and Sulmasy, 2002b). That view, however, does not seem simple to defend. Autonomy alone, for instance, is not self-justifying. The simple fact that a patient requests something does not make it good. Patients ask for antibiotics for viral upper respiratory infections, for example, but this does not mean it is justified to prescribe them. Thus, one cannot conclude from the simple fact that a patient might request sedation to unconsciousness that it is good. Autonomous consent might be necessary, but it is not sufficient to justify the practice.

Is unconsciousness an unqualified medical good at which a clinician might properly aim? It is certainly not true that unconsciousness until death is a good among those who are not terminally ill. Physicians do not sedate patients to unconsciousness until they are dead upon request if the patients are not terminally ill. Accordingly, one would need to argue that the process of dying makes human beings at the end of life different from the rest of us, and so completely changes the restorative aims of medicine that what is normally considered bad actually becomes good. On close examination, however, it would not seem to be the case that unconsciousness is an unqualified good for those who are terminally ill. Dying people continue to have many interests that require some consciousness, including, among others, opportunities for interpersonal interactions with family and friends, saying goodbye, finding reconciliation, pursuing personal spiritual growth, participating in decision making about their medical care, and fulfilling their social role as teachers for those of us who will survive them (Byock, 1997). Certainly it is not always possible for dying patients to pursue all these interests, but this does not mean that these possibilities are bad for dying persons so that it becomes legitimate to aim at eliminating consciousness. It seems much more justifiable to say that these goods are genuine, but relative, and that one might tolerate the loss of consciousness as a side effect of aiming at the true medical good of symptom relief (as in double-effect sedation), but that one would not consider it something positively good at which a doctor should aim.

The direct aim of all medicine must be something that is good for the patient; that is the meaning of beneficence. To justify palliative sedation to unconsciousness, in which one aims at unconsciousness until death, one would thus be required to argue that it is better for the dying patient to be unconscious than conscious. And if that is the case, it becomes hard to say how the justification for palliative sedation to unconsciousness differs from the justification for euthanasia (Jansen and Sulmasy, 2002b). The justification in both cases must be that it is better for the patient to be rendered permanently unable to speak, think, eat, pray, love, or interact with others, whether this is brought about through induced coma or death. Unsurprisingly, then, there have been reports of those who, failing to see the distinction between the justification for euthanasia and the justification for palliative sedation to unconsciousness, have titrated up the sedating drug far past the dose needed to dissociate the patient from her symptoms, explicitly in order to hasten death. It is a violation of transparency to "cloak" these latter practices deceptively under the guise of palliative sedation. Such deception is hard to achieve if one limits one's practice to double-effect sedation, in which the aim is symptom relief (an unqualified medical good) and unconsciousness is an unintended side effect. Once one has accepted the morality of palliative sedation to unconsciousness, however, the distinction between justifiable and unjustifiable doses becomes easier to blur and the distinction between symptom control and euthanasia becomes more difficult to defend logically. This has led to the charge that palliative sedation to unconsciousness is "slow euthanasia" (Billings and Block, 1996; Tännsjö, 2004).

For these reasons, palliative sedation to unconsciousness remains very controversial while double effect-sedation is widely accepted.

CONSENT

Informed consent is always a process. A patient's symptoms may have been difficult to control over time and may have escalated as the patient's disease has progressed, raising the question of whether palliative sedation might be indicated. Patients (or their surrogates when they cannot speak for themselves) must always be involved in these decisions (Sanft et al., 2009). Palliative sedation involves an important trade-off between symptom control and alertness that different patients will weigh differently. The time immediately before death can be a time of profound personal healing and deep spiritual growth, so that some patients may prefer to be alert even in the face of very significant symptoms. For others, the burden of refractory symptoms may be so great, and the opportunities for personal or spiritual engagement so limited, that the trade-off of symptom relief for consciousness will be worth it. If possible, a discussion of palliative sedation may even be a part of advance care planning: "If your symptoms become difficult to control would you prefer to remain awake and alert? Or would you prefer that your symptoms be completely controlled, even if it requires making you very drowsy or runs the risk that you might slip out of consciousness?" The response provides some guidance to the clinician and to families.

In other situations, however, symptoms may escalate acutely and rapidly and the luxury of time to try various approaches to relieve suffering is not available. The need for sedation may be a palliative care emergency to relieve the distress, and consent would be similar to obtaining consent in other medical emergency situations. A family meeting to discuss the situation would then follow. In some cases, once the severe symptoms of a palliative care emergency have been brought under control, it is even possible to consider titrating down the medication to see if symptoms can be controlled using lower, consciousness-sparing doses. Such trials should be undertaken cautiously in expert hands so as not to cause the patient any unwarranted suffering.

In the case of Eddie, were the patient sufficiently alert, he would need to be included in a discussion with family and the team to obtain informed consent for palliative sedation. His care would thus be compatible with this ethical standard.

Respite Sedation

The foregoing discussion raises the issue of *respite sedation* (Cherny, 2006). Sometimes patients may present with palliative care emergencies when they are not imminently dying and the control of the patient's symptoms may require the use of sedating doses of medication. Perhaps the patient has been unable to sleep for days and this lack of rest is contributing to delirium and exacerbating the experience of chronically uncontrolled symptoms in a vicious cycle. In such cases one may aim directly at a sedated state in order to provide a respite from the symptoms and an opportunity for sleep. While related, this practice should not be confused with palliative sedation. In the case of respite sedation, the patient need not be imminently dying. Also, in contrast with double-effect sedation, the clinician's direct aim is sedation. The intention is that the sedation be temporary, however, not permanent. The reason for the sedation is restorative and consistent with the norms of medical therapy— sleep is restorative; the patient's hyper-excited symptomatic state needs to be restored to a more normal state. Thus, this sedation is a real physiological good at which one may legitimately aim, provided the intention is to use the time to help the patient restore his or her mental reserves through sleep and to design a comprehensive treatment plan that will allow the patient to maximize function through control of symptoms using means that do not require sedation.

Relationship to Withholding and Withdrawing Life-Sustaining Treatment

Some clinicians might worry that while the actual practice of palliative sedation can be distinguished from euthanasia, coupling decisions to withhold or withdraw life-sustaining treatments to the decision to sedate makes the whole package deal tantamount to euthanasia. This is not the case. Decisions to withhold or continue life-sustaining interventions, while made in the context of the decision to engage in palliative sedation, must be justified on independent grounds. Generally speaking, those grounds are that the life-sustaining intervention is either ineffective, or more burdensome than beneficial, as judged by the patient or the appropriate surrogate decision maker (who elects to forgo the intervention on behalf of the patient). As a general rule of thumb, one should ask, were the patient not to undergo palliative sedation, would it be justifiable to withhold or withdraw the intervention? If the answer is yes, one is on very safe moral ground. For example, while it would make little sense to engage in palliative sedation without a DNR order in place, the reason for withholding cardiopulmonary resuscitation (CPR) in such a case is not the relief of intractable symptoms per se, but the inevitability and imminence of death and the fact that CPR would be judged to be far more burdensome than beneficial. In the case of Eddie, for example, the decision to withhold CPR had been made weeks in advance of the discussion regarding palliative sedation and was justified independently of that decision.

Likewise, the withholding of artificial nutrition and hydration (ANH) in a patient who is sedated at the end of life is also justified independently, even though the decision must be made in light of the fact that sedation has been chosen as a treatment option for controlling intractable symptoms. The benefits of ANH in such circumstances are minimal merely prolonging the sedated state before an inevitable and imminent death. Additionally, hydration can worsen distressing signs such as the "death rattle" and make it difficult to handle the patient's secretions. Subsequently, ANH is generally not indicated in a patient who has undergone palliative sedation and families should be counseled against it.

In some cases, the psychological burden of withdrawing ANH from a patient who had previously been receiving this intervention might be sufficiently stressful for a family that one might elect to continue it. Families might become very distressed by the idea of discontinuing ANH, particularly if a feeding tube were already in place. Some might have religious objections. Such families should continue to be counseled about the distinction between euthanasia and allowing a natural death, and about the moral obligation to decide according to the real interests of the patient. However, if the objections are strong and persistent, the potential harm to the patient of continuing ANH might not be sufficient to override duties to care for families, and ANH might be continued. Care must be taken not to over-hydrate such patients, and families should be given any support they need from pastoral care or social work.

The decision to withhold ANH from an imminently dying patient who has undergone palliative sedation for intractable symptoms must be sharply distinguished, however, from proposals that patients who are not imminently dying and have no medical impairment in appetite, swallowing, or digestion be permitted to voluntarily stop eating and drinking and then be sedated and not fed artificially (Quill, Lo, and Brock, 1997). The intention of this practice is death and it is therefore difficult to distinguish this practice from assisted suicide and euthanasia; those who are opposed to euthanasia and assisted suicide could rightfully object to this practice. Consider, for example, a patient recently diagnosed with Alzheimer's disease who is alert, conversant, ambulatory, and fully capable of eating. However, he is experiencing extreme distress due to the onset of memory impairment and the prospect that it will progress, and asks to be sedated after voluntarily deciding not to eat or drink. Clinician participation in this practice should not be confused with the much more common and widely morally accepted practice of withholding or withdrawing of ANH in patients with intractable symptoms who are close to death and have consented to undergo classical double-effect sedation. Terminally ill patients frequently lose their appetites and stop eating and drinking as life draws to a close. This includes patients at the end stages of Alzheimer's disease who have lost their ability to swallow in a coordinated fashion. Such individuals should not receive ANH against their wishes (or the wishes of their surrogates), and any distressing symptoms they might experience should be treated with all indicated palliative care interventions, including, if necessary, palliative sedation.

In the case of Eddie, the man with osteogenic sarcoma and myoclonus described above, death was imminent and inevitable. A feeding tube might only have prolonged his life by hours or days or caused him to experience excessive secretions as he was dying. Even were he not to undergo palliative sedation, ANH could have been considered more burdensome than beneficial and withheld so that he might experience a more natural and comfortable death. The withholding of intravenous fluids and tube feeding would therefore be perfectly justifiable on grounds independent of the justification for double-effect sedation and distinct from euthanasia or assisted suicide.

ROLE OF THE TEAM IN PROVIDING CARE

Clear and ongoing communication about the goals of care, palliative sedation management, monitoring, and patient care are essential among team members and between the team and the family. The support of all involved parties is important. Responsibilities of the various team members are specified, as well as educating the family about what to expect as far as ongoing care for their loved one and for themselves (Pellegrino and Sulmasy, 2009).

Although it is not unusual for patients to experience sedation at the end of life as a consequence of the underlying disease and the dying process itself, treating a patient who was awake and alert previously with doses of drugs that are likely to result in sedation to the point of stupor or unconsciousness is uncommon. Unless meetings with the staff and the family are held, and ongoing, clear, structured communication and support is established, potentially unwarranted moral concerns may arise. Loved ones or staff members may ask, "Is this euthanasia?" "Are we hastening death?" or "Is what we are doing ethical?" Nurses, who have long hours of close contact with the patient and family, are frequent targets for such questions, especially if the dying process is prolonged. Physicians, social workers, and pastoral care team members should also be prepared to answer such questions. Clear documentation can be very helpful to the staff in ensuring transparency and integrity about the goals of care, the symptom(s) being treated, and the endpoint of patient comfort.

In the case of Eddie, the social worker raised questions at a team meeting. A team committed to clear communication would work through the issues together to try to explain the ethics outlined in this chapter and achieve a consensus. The team, in turn, would need not only to speak to the family once to obtain consent for palliative sedation, but would need to continue to communicate with the family over the hours or days that Eddie would remain sedated until his death.

What Are the Appropriate Indications for Palliative Sedation?

Palliative sedation as a means to relieve intractable mental anguish or existential distress at the end of life remains much more controversial than palliative sedation to control physical and neuropsychiatric symptoms such as pain, seizures, or delirium. Some have argued, however, that no matter what the source of patient distress, be it fear, tiredness of waiting for death, despair, profound guilt, alienation, loss of meaning, or distress over loss of control, clinicians have a duty to relieve all suffering patients might experience as they are dying with any means at their disposal (Morita, 2004; Rousseau, 2001). From the discussion above, it should be clear that such treatment could not be justified under the rule of double effect. Sedation would not be an unintended side effect of treating a specific symptom with a specific drug indicated for that symptom but the intended means by which the suffering would be relieved, and therefore would violate the fourth condition of the rule of double effect. Further, critics have argued that palliative sedation for spiritual and existential suffering goes beyond the bounds of medicine, and that the proper interventions for such suffering must be interpersonal or pastoral. Anyone who believes that spiritual or existential suffering would justify euthanasia or assisted suicide would also believe that these states would justify palliative sedation, but those who oppose euthanasia and assisted suicide, as well as the vast majority of clinicians (Curlin, Nwodim, Vance, Chin, and Lantos, 2008), do not believe that these are indications for palliative sedation.

Eddie's symptoms, however, fit squarely within those that are classical indications for palliative sedation. Benzodiazepines are indicated for myoclonus, a neurological state that can be severely stressful. Palliative sedation was not offered because Eddie was lonely or frightened. Thus, his case would fall outside the controversy about whether palliative sedation is ever indicated for spiritual or existential suffering.

Afterword

Eddie's case eventually turned out reasonably well. After a prolonged discussion of the ethics, the team came to a consensus that palliative sedation would be an appropriate option to offer. Following an extensive consent discussion with Eddie and his family about the risk of complete sedation that might ensue if drugs were administered in doses sufficient to control both his pain and his myoclonus, his hospice physician initiated a morphine drip and increased the dose until his pain was controlled, while simultaneously treating the patient with increasing doses of benzodiazepines until the myoclonus was also controlled. The doses of these drugs that were required to control his symptoms combined with his underlying disease to precipitate a coma. A decision made weeks before that the patient not be resuscitated or intubated remained in effect, and during the consent discussion that took place before starting the intravenous morphine and benzodiazepine, a decision was also made that the patient not receive maintenance intravenous fluids or artificial feeding. He died two days later with his family present.

Conclusion

Palliative sedation is widely held to be morally justifiable under the rule of double effect for the treatment of intractable symptoms for patients who are very close to death. The withholding and withdrawing of other treatments is also independently justifiable on the grounds that the treatments are more burdensome than beneficial. Neither double-effect sedation itself nor a composite plan to undertake sedation while simultaneously withholding or withdrawing life-sustaining interventions (such as CPR or tube feeding) ought to be misconstrued as "slow euthanasia." By contrast, directly intending to make a patient fully unconscious until death (palliative sedation to unconsciousness) and sedation for spiritual or existential distress seem more difficult to distinguish from euthanasia and remain much more controversial.

Judiciously applied, double-effect sedation is an important and morally justifiable treatment for palliative care and hospice teams to use in fulfillment of their mission to provide excellent and compassionate care to the dying.

---

*Daniel P. Sulmasy, MD, is the Kilbride-Clinton Professor of Medicine and Ethics in the Department of Medicine and Divinity School at the University of Chicago, where he serves as associate director of the MacLean Center for Clinical Medical Ethics. He received his AB and MD degrees from Cornell, his PhD in philosophy from Georgetown, and his internal medicine training at Johns Hopkins. His research encompasses both theoretical and empirical investigations of the ethics of end-of-life decision making, ethics education, and spirituality in medicine. He has written four books—*The Healer's Calling *(1997),* Methods in Medical Ethics *(2001; 2nd ed. 2010),* The Rebirth of the Clinic *(2006), and* A Balm for Gilead *(2006). He serves as editor-in-chief of* Theoretical Medicine and Bioethics *and was appointed by President Obama to the Presidential Commission for the Study of Bioethical Issues. His numerous articles have appeared in medical, philosophical, and theological journals, and he lectures widely.*

Nessa Coyle, PhD, ACHPN, FAAN, is a member of the Pain and Palliative Care Service at the Memorial Sloan-Kettering Cancer Center in New York. Her focus is on continuity of care, community education, and the effects of poorly controlled pain and other symptoms on the patient and family living with advanced disease. Dr. Coyle is on the editorial boards of several oncology and palliative care journals. She is a member of the Oncology Nursing Society, the American Pain Society, and the Hospice and Palliative Nurses Association. She has lectured extensively both nationally and internationally on palliative care and end-of-life care. Dr. Coyle is co-editor of the Oxford Textbook of Palliative Nursing *(3rd ed., 2010) and co-author of* The Nature of Suffering and the Goals of Nursing *(2008). She was elected as a Fellow of the American Academy of Nursing and was awarded the Distinguished Career Achievement Award by the Hospice and Palliative Nurses Association.*

REFERENCES

Billings, J. A., & Block, S. D. (1996). Slow euthanasia. *Journal of Palliative Care, 12*(4), 21–30.

Boyle, J. (2004). Medical ethics and double effect: The case of terminal sedation. *Theoretical Medicine and Bioethics, 25*(1), 51–60.

Byock, I. (1997). *Dying well: The prospect for growth at the end of life.* New York: Riverhead Books.

Cavanaugh, T. (2006). *Double effect reasoning: Doing good and avoiding evil.* New York: Oxford University Press.

Cherny, N. I. (2006). Sedation for the care of patients with advanced cancer. *Nature Clinical Practice Oncology, 3*(9), 492–500.

Cherny, N. I., & Portenoy, R. K. (1994). Sedation in the management of refractory symptoms: Guidelines for evaluation and treatment. *Journal of Palliative Care, 10*(2), 31–38.

Clark, D. (Ed.). (2006). *Cicely Saunders: Selected writings 1958–2004.* New York: Oxford University Press.

Curlin, F. A., Nwodim, C., Vance, J. L., Chin, M. H., & Lantos, J. D. (2008). To die, to sleep: US physicians' religious and other objections to physician-assisted suicide, terminal sedation, and withdrawal of life support. *American Journal of Hospice and Palliative Care, 25*, 112–120.

Jansen, L. A., & Sulmasy, D. P. (2002a). Sedation, hydration, alimentation, and equivocation: Careful conversation about care at the end of life. *Annals of Internal Medicine, 136*, 845–849.

Jansen, L. A., & Sulmasy, D. P. (2002b). Proportionality, terminal suffering, and the restorative goals of medicine. *Theoretical Medicine and Bioethics, 23*(4-5), 321–337.

Jansen, L. A. (2003). The moral irrelevance of proximity to death. *Journal of Clinical Ethics, 14*(1-2), 49–58.

Jansen, L. A. (2010). Disambiguating clinical intention: The ethics of palliative sedation. *Journal of Medicine and Philosophy, 35*(1), 19–31.

Morita, T. (2004). Palliative sedation to relieve psycho-existential suffering of terminally ill cancer patients. *Journal of Pain and Symptom Management, 28*(5), 445–450.

Pellegrino, E. D., & Sulmasy, D. P. (2009). Ethical issues in palliative care. In W. Breitbart and H. Chochinov (Eds.), *Handbook of Psychiatry in Palliative Medicine*, 2nd ed. (pp. 267–280). New York: Oxford University Press.

Quill, T. E., & Byock, I. (2000). Responding to intractable terminal suffering: The role of voluntary refusal of food and fluids. *Annals of Internal Medicine, 132*, 402–414.

Quill, T. E., Lo, B., & Brock, D. W. (1997). Palliative options of last resort: A comparison of voluntarily stopping eating and drinking, terminal sedation, physician-assisted suicide, and voluntary active euthanasia. *JAMA, 278*, 2099–2104.

Quill, T. E., Lo, B., Brock, D. W., & Meisel, A. (2009). Last-resort options for palliative sedation. *Annals of Internal Medicine, 151*(6), 421–424.

Rousseau, P. (2001). Existential suffering and palliative sedation: A brief commentary with a proposal for clinical guidelines. *American Journal of Hospice and Palliative Care, 18*(3), 151–153.

Sanft, T., Hauser, J., Rosielle, D., Weissman, D., Elsayem, A., Zhukovsky, D. S., & Coyle, N. (2009). Physical pain and emotional suffering: The case for palliative sedation. *Journal of Pain, 10*(3), 238–242.

Saunders, C. M. (1989). Pain and impending death. In P. D. Wall & R. Melzack (Eds.). *Textbook of Pain*, 2nd ed. (pp. 624–631). New York: Churchill-Livingstone.

Saunders, C. M., & Baines, M. (1983). *Living with dying: The management of terminal illness.* New York: Oxford University Press.

Sulmasy, D. P., & Pellegrino, E. D. (1999). The rule of double effect: Clearing up the double talk. *Archives of Internal Medicine, 159*(6), 545–550.

Sulmasy, D. P. (2007). 'Re-inventing' the rule of double effect. In B. Steinbock (Ed.), *The Oxford Handbook of Bioethics* (pp. 114–149). Oxford: Oxford University Press.

Tännsjö, T. (2004). Terminal sedation: a substitute for euthanasia? In T. Tännsjö (Ed.), *Terminal sedation: Euthanasia in disguise?* (pp. 15–29). The Netherlands: Kluwer.

CHAPTER 9

Physician-Assisted Suicide, Aid in Dying, and Hospice

Charles A. Corr

This chapter addresses physician-assisted suicide, aid in dying, and hospice, together with some of the values and principles that govern their interaction. Introductory sections of this chapter explain the key terms under discussion. The chapter then offers a case study and an exploration of the Oregon Death with Dignity Act. Next, the chapter analyzes the ethical issues that arise in the case examples and illustrates alternative responses from hospice providers. Subsequently, the chapter identifies decisions made in the case examples, their consequences, and two lessons that might be learned from this discussion.

PHYSICIAN-ASSISTED SUICIDE

The three central concepts encompassed by the phrase "physician-assisted suicide" (PAS) are: *suicide*; the meaning of *assistance*; and the role of a *physician*. Suicide or "intentional self-harm" in the new international system of classifying causes of death is, by definition, the killing of oneself. The term comes from two Latin roots, "sui" meaning "of oneself" and "caedere" meaning "to kill." In short, suicide is the act of taking one's own life or self-murder. A key point is that suicide is a deliberate or intentional act of self-destruction. Intentions are critical in understanding the concept of suicide, despite the notorious difficulty we often have in determining the intentions of others and perhaps sometimes in divining our own intentions.

It is also important to clarify the meaning of the "assistance" that is relevant to this chapter; here again, intentions are critical. For example, among the many ways to offer help to someone else, merchants who sell guns most often are unaware of the specific, actual intentions of the persons to whom such assistance is provided. To provide the type of assistance involved in physician-assisted suicide, an individual must know that the person receiving the assistance intends to use it to end his or her life and must deliberately act in support of that intention. That is, in assisted suicide the means used to end the life of one person are obtained from and with the cooperation of a second individual who understands that the first person intends to use those means to end his or her life. Whoever the second individual is, the ultimate actor is the individual who uses the means provided to end his or her life. Nevertheless, the person who provides those means has an equally critical role as a witting enabler in the form of deliberate assistance in the ultimate outcome. This distinguishes assisted suicide from active euthanasia in which the ending of the life of one person is accomplished by the direct and deliberate action (often for benign motives) of a second person who does not die.

There may be a wide range of actions involved in assisted suicide, but the three key elements are always the same: one person *intentionally* acts to obtain assistance in ending his or her life from a second individual; the second individual *intentionally* acts to provide the necessary assistance to bring about the death of the first person *with full awareness of how that assistance is to be used*; and the first person *intentionally* uses the assistance provided to carry out his or her own self-destruction (or what some call "self-deliverance").

A special type of assisted suicide occurs in clinical situations when a person asks a physician to help end his or her life—for example, by prescribing medications that only physicians can order. This type of PAS is realized only when the physician *acts in concurrence with the intention of the person who seeks to end his or her life*. In view of the special professional authority accorded to physicians in our society and their access to certain means that can be used in ending a human life, physician-assisted suicide is the type of assisted suicide that has received most public attention in recent years. However, in physician-assisted suicide the physician only provides the means (and perhaps emotional support), but does nothing directly when the person takes action to end his or her life. Again, this absence of participation in the lethal act distinguishes PAS from active euthanasia.

Aid in Dying

"Aid in dying" is a phrase used by proponents to identify a practice that is currently legal only in the states of Oregon, Washington, and Montana. The practice allows mentally competent, terminally ill adults to request a prescription for life-ending medication from their physician and to administer that medication to themselves to end their lives. Although the phrase "aid in dying" has in the past sometimes been used to encompass both PAS and voluntary euthanasia, referenda that would have legalized that double meaning of the phrase failed in the states of Washington and California, apparently because voters were unwilling to legitimize a practice in which death was ultimately brought about not by the person who died but by another agent. Supporters of Oregon's Death with Dignity Act (which will be described in detail later in this chapter), object to describing it as suicide on the grounds that the person's primary objective is not to end a life that would otherwise be open-ended. On this view, aid in dying involves the provision of assistance only to mentally competent adults who already face their imminent and inevitable death. In other words, aid in dying is to be made available as a legal option only to help such individuals who are seeking to find dignity by not having to wait for their underlying condition to kill them. Despite this point of view, however, this meaning of aid in dying is commonly described as a form of PAS in the medical literature and by the majority of hospice programs in Oregon.

HOSPICE

Most readers of this book will be familiar, at least in a general way, with the basic philosophy and principles that define the modern hospice movement as a distinctive mode of end-of-life care. Nevertheless, it may be helpful to identify some characteristic points that will become relevant in later discussions in this chapter (Corr and Corr, 2013).

Hospice, above all, is a philosophy of care, not a facility. The primary focus of this philosophy is on end-of-life care that affirms life, not death. Thus, it is often said that hospice neither seeks to hasten death nor to prolong dying. The key point in this philosophy is to care for and about persons who are coping with dying because they are living human beings and struggling with special pressures and sources of distress in dying. For this reason, the hospice philosophy strives to maximize present quality in living. It does that by offering holistic care, addressing physical, psychological, social, and spiritual tasks. This care is provided to the patient-and-family unit, and that unit may be defined by those who share in it. The hospice philosophy combines the skills of experienced professionals from different disciplinary backgrounds, the human presence symbolized by trained volunteers, and the contributions of both patients and family members, all of whom participate in interdisciplinary teamwork. Services are made available on a 24-hour-a-day, 7-day-a-week basis in a variety of settings, including homes, hospice facilities, hospitals, or long-term care facilities. Continuing care and ongoing support are offered to family members who are coping with dying, death, and loss both before and after the death of someone they love. Hospice services have come to be understood as applying in practice to a variety of individuals who are coping with different types of life-threatening illnesses, dying, death, and bereavement.

CASE STUDY

This case example is a bit unusual since it concerns two men, whom we will call Richard and Robert, who had lived in Oregon for most of their lives. Before they each retired, Richard had been a faculty member at one of the state universities and Robert had been a senior administrator in state government. Now in their early 70s, Richard had never married, while Robert and his ex-wife had divorced many years previously. Both were now afflicted with chronic, life-threatening diseases, Richard with amyotrophic lateral sclerosis (ALS) and Robert with an advanced form of cancer.

Sometime after enrolling in hospice home care programs in the different cities where they lived, Richard and Robert each began to inquire about obtaining the means necessary to end their lives under Oregon's Death with Dignity Act (DWDA). Richard was particularly concerned about the loss of dignity and personal autonomy that was associated with his progressive paralysis. He felt a need to take control of the last chapter of his life before the disease overwhelmed him. By contrast, Robert was concerned about the pain that had at times been associated with his cancer. He was also upset about no longer being able to take part in activities that he had enjoyed over the years and that had been a significant part of his life. Robert was determined not to become a burden on his two adult children who lived in Arizona and Minnesota. Because of the excellent care each was receiving from their hospice interdisciplinary teams, neither Richard nor Robert was currently experiencing any significant pain or other source of distress beyond these psychosocial concerns.

Both Richard and Robert made their desires for aid in dying known to their hospice teams. In Richard's case, his hospice providers explained to him the requirements of the DWDA and explored with him his rationale for pursuing this course of action. After these discussions, members of the team referred him to his primary physician for any further steps he might wish to take.

In Robert's case, however, things proceeded somewhat differently. Representatives of his hospice program informed him that their fundamental convictions did not allow them to help persons for whom they were caring to end their lives. Team members explored with Robert in detail the reasons why he was thinking about wanting to end his life. They also tried to offer what they viewed as other constructive options, such as promising to care for him faithfully and doing their very best to manage any and all sources of distress until his disease brought about a natural death. They even put forward the option of palliative sedation if his pain should become an issue that could not be managed in any other way. Beyond that, they said they could not go.

THE OREGON DEATH WITH DIGNITY ACT

Before we can examine the ethical issues involved in the case examples offered here, we need to consider briefly the context within which they took place. In 1994, the citizens of the state of Oregon approved, by a narrow margin of just 51% to 49%, a ballot initiative establishing a Death with Dignity Act. Efforts by some groups to prevent implementation of the act led in 1997 to a ruling by the U.S. Supreme Court that although there is no "right to die" in the U.S. Constitution, states have the constitutional right to make laws that provide for physician-assisted suicide. Meanwhile, an attempt to repeal the law was placed on the ballot in Oregon in November of 1997, only to be rejected by a vote of 60% to 40%. A subsequent effort in 2001 by the Attorney General of the United States was based on the claim that the DWDA violated federal drug laws, leading him to issue a directive authorizing the government to cancel the federal license of physicians to prescribe controlled substances or "scheduled drugs" if they were used to provide assistance in dying. These efforts were blocked by rulings from federal circuit and appeals courts. Eventually a 6-3 ruling from the U.S. Supreme Court on January 17, 2006, determined that the attorney general did not have the authority to regulate medical practice, a responsibility left to the states, and that the DWDA did not violate the intent of Congress when it passed the 1970 Controlled Substances Act to regulate illicit drug dealing and trafficking.

The provisions of the DWDA stipulate the conditions under which a terminally ill, adult resident of Oregon is permitted to request that a physician provide a prescription for lethal medication that an individual can use to end his or her life (Reagan, 2000). The act only applies to patients with a diagnosed terminal illness and a prognosis of less than six months to live. To comply with the act, several procedures must be followed. These include a requirement that a physician ensure the patient is making this request voluntarily. The patient is required to make two oral requests separated by at least 15 days and to sign a written request in the presence of two witnesses. The prescribing physician must also inform the patient of his or her diagnosis, prognosis, available options (such as comfort care, hospice care, and pain control), and the right to withdraw the request at any time. In addition, the prescribing physician must refer the patient to a consulting physician to confirm the diagnosis and prognosis and to determine that the patient is capable (able to make and communicate health care decisions). Psychiatric illness or depression that might impair judgment must be ruled out. Further, the prescribing physician must request (but may not require) that the patient notify his or her next of kin of the prescription request. Physicians must report all prescriptions for lethal medications to the Oregon Department of Human Services (DHS) and must inform pharmacists of the prescribed medication's intended use.

It is important to be clear that the act only authorizes voluntary self-administration of lethal medications prescribed by a physician for the purpose of ending one's life; euthanasia, or situations in which a physician or other person directly administers a medication to end another's life, is specifically prohibited. Although the DWDA makes clear that physicians and health care systems are under no obligation to participate in its implementation, those physicians and patients who adhere to the requirements of the act are protected from criminal prosecution, and the choice to end one's life in this way cannot affect the status of a patient's health or life insurance policies. The DWDA stipulates that a death under these conditions does not constitute suicide, mercy killing, or homicide under the law.

As already noted, supporters of the DWDA object to the term "suicide" and the phrase "assisted suicide" as applying to actions taken in accord with this law. Nevertheless, in its eighth annual report on this subject, the Oregon Department of Human Services (2006, p. 7) provided the following comment on terminology:

> The Death with Dignity Act allows terminally ill Oregon residents to obtain and use prescriptions from their physicians for self-administered, lethal medications. Under the Act, ending one's life in accordance with the law does not constitute suicide. However, we use the term "physician-assisted suicide" because it is used in medical literature to describe ending life through the voluntary self-administration of lethal medications prescribed by a physician for that purpose. The Death with Dignity Act legalizes PAS, but specifically prohibits euthanasia, where a physician or other person directly administers a medication to end another's life.

Those supporting PAS or aid in dying as public and professional policy have argued that quality in living, personal choice or autonomy, and quality in medical decision making are the important values to be considered in this matter (e.g., Quill and Battin, 2004). Opponents generally maintain that the sanctioning of such practices as public and professional policies is rife with danger, does not possess adequate safeguards, especially those to protect vulnerable patients from coercion of various sorts, and overstates the absoluteness of individual autonomy as if it existed in isolation from all other concerns (e.g., Foley and Hendin, 2002).

During the years since the DWDA first came into effect through 2010, 810 prescriptions were written under the DWDA and 525 individuals ingested lethal medications and died (Oregon Department of Human Services, 2011). In short, only a limited number of persons in Oregon have requested and even fewer have carried out PAS during this period, representing 20.9 of every 10,000 deaths in the state.

Given the relatively small numbers of individuals involved, annual variations among those who have taken advantage of the DWDA in Oregon are unavoidable. Still, it is important to understand the typical characteristics of those who seek out PAS. Those who did so in 2010 have been characterized in the following ways: "Of the 65 patients who died under DWDA in 2010, most (70.8%) were over age 65 years; the median age was 72 years. As in previous years, most were white (100%), well-educated (42.2% had a least a baccalaureate degree), and had cancer (78.5%)" (Oregon DHS, 2011). After cancer, the most prominent underlying illness was amyotrophic lateral sclerosis (10.8%). Further, the vast majority of those who took advantage of PAS in 2010 were enrolled in hospice care (92.6%), died at home (96.9%), and had some form of health insurance (96.7%). Finally, the leading concerns mentioned by these individuals in 2010 were loss of autonomy (93.8%), a decreasing ability to participate in activities that made life enjoyable (93.8%), and loss of dignity (78.5%). Fear of intractable physical pain has not seemed to be a central motivation under the DWDA across the years in which it has been in force. As Campbell and Cox (2010, p. 27) have written: "Patients [in Oregon] do not exercise their legal right to choose physician-assisted death because they are unable to obtain good symptom management."

The Oregon DHS (2005, p. 17) has suggested that the availability of PAS may have led to efforts to improve end-of-life care in Oregon through other modalities.

For example:

> A request for PAS can be an opportunity for a medical provider
> to explore with patients their fears and wishes around end-of-
> life care, and to make patients aware of other options. Often
> once the patient's concerns have been addressed by the provider,
> he or she may choose not to pursue PAS. The availability of PAS
> as an option in Oregon also may have spurred Oregon doctors
> to address other end-of-life care options more effectively. In one
> study, Oregon physicians reported that, since the passage of the
> Death with Dignity Act in 1994, they had made efforts to improve
> their knowledge of the use of pain medications in the terminally
> ill, to improve their recognition of psychiatric disorders such as
> depression, and to refer patients more frequently to hospice.

ANALYSIS

In general, throughout the United States suicide is not illegal, although assisting
in a suicide may be illegal. As a result, in many jurisdictions individuals who
seek to help other persons complete suicide may find themselves in jeopardy
of prosecution—although such prosecutorial efforts are notoriously difficult to
initiate and carry through to conviction with any substantial penalty. Facts are
often unclear, motives are frequently said to be beneficial, and juries have often
appeared reluctant to impose harsh penalties.

The DWDA in Oregon changes all of this within the limits of its specific
provisions, for example by applying only to terminally ill individuals who are
close to death and who do not have a psychiatric illness or depression, and by
authorizing specific practices on the part of physicians to help those individuals
end their lives. At the same time, the DWDA raises a series of ethical issues as to
what behaviors society will countenance at end of life, the scope of acceptable
conduct on the part of those who wish to end their lives, and how physicians
can conduct themselves under the act. In the case of Richard and Robert, like
many others who are receiving hospice care in Oregon, the DWDA also raises
ethical issues for individual hospice providers, hospice programs, and their
sponsoring organizations, if any. For example, on the basis of their survey and
analysis of hospice responses to the DWDA, Campbell and Cox (2010, p. 28)
report that "the policies of a majority of hospice programs contain nuanced
wording that indicates patient requests for physician-assisted death create ten-

sions respecting involvement, legal compliance, and an intent to avoid moral complicity." More specifically, as Campbell and Cox write:

> Hospice programs (1) use different language to describe the act of a hospice patient obtaining a physician's prescription to end life; (2) provide different degrees of information in response to patients' questions or requests regarding physician-assisted death; (3) engage in different levels of notifying the patient's attending physician who will write the prescription (a physician invariably different from the hospice medical director); and (4) present different views of whether hospice staff may be present prior to and during the ingestion of life-ending medication. With respect to a fifth caregiving consideration—whether to provide the patient with the prescribed medication or assist in the patient's act of self-administration—Oregon hospice programs have invariably adopted a posture of nonparticipation. (p. 28)

In this chapter, we can only illustrate through our case examples some of the most prominent implications of what the DWDA has meant for hospice programs in Oregon and what similar situations might mean for hospice programs elsewhere.

Although some hospice programs in Oregon have chosen not to participate in what they understand as physician-assisted suicide, Richard's hospice program was willing under the provisions of the DWDA to have designated staff members provide information about the act and its requirements in a neutral way and to explore with Richard his reasons for seeking to end his life. In this, they sought to confirm that he was not receiving inadequate hospice care and they wanted to ensure that he was acting on his values, even though those values were not consistent with their own philosophy of neither hastening nor postponing death. Although they viewed their commitment to those they served to require that they never abandon a person in their care even at the most extreme moments in his or her life, their practice was to direct Richard to his attending physician and to provide referral information to a patient education and advocacy organization (e.g., Compassion & Choices in Oregon) in order to implement his wishes. They promised to care for Richard both before and after the time when he might exercise his legal rights under the DWDA. Like most Oregon hospice programs, they would not help in obtaining lethal medications, but they indicated that they would permit selected staff (excluding nurses) to be present during ingestion to attend to his "human" but not "medical" needs.

In the case of Robert, his hospice program took the position that their fundamental values did not permit them to take an active part in ending a person's life, either by causing death directly or by assisting an individual to end his or her own life. As a department of a hospital operated by a religious organization, they explained that their official public policy viewed such actions as contrary to their moral obligation to "do no harm," whatever the motivations might be. They made clear to Robert that while he had rights to control medical decisions that affected him, his rights did not extend as far as requiring them to violate their moral and religious convictions as expressed in what they viewed as ultimate respect for human life. Instead, they offered Robert what has been termed "limited participation" with the DWDA. That is, Robert's hospice program was willing to provide scrupulous attention to any sources of distress that might be troubling him and extensive counseling sessions with a social worker and chaplain. They did refer Robert to his attending physician, from whom he might obtain an explanation of the legal provisions of the DWDA and its procedural requirements. However, in order to ensure that physician-assisted death did not become hospice-assisted death, they did not provide that information themselves nor did they refer Robert to an education or advocacy organization for further guidance in these matters. Finally, this hospice did not permit its staff to be present when lethal medications were ingested in order to ensure that they had no direct participation in physician-assisted death, were not involved in any complications that might occur (e.g., regurgitation of the medication), and did not contribute to creating a public perception that they encouraged or endorsed such deaths.

DECISIONS AND CONSEQUENCES

The decisions and consequences that followed in the case of Richard were fairly straightforward. First, as already indicated, the hospice interdisciplinary team that was providing his care took pains to ensure that he complied with the requirements of the Oregon DWDA in every respect. Second, after a thorough exploration of his reasons for wanting to end his life, the team did refer him to other resources for the assistance contemplated under the act. With that assistance, Richard received a prescription from nonhospice sources for medications sufficient to end his life and had that prescription filled. Third, shortly after he had been provided with lethal medications, Richard ingested those medications and died at home.

In the case of Robert, lengthy discussions of his options within the boundaries of what his hospice team specified as appropriate for their program eventually led him to reconsider his decision and to decide to forego further efforts to seek aid in dying. Some outside observers were surprised by this change of course, but members of the hospice team commented that they had seen this type of behavior in some previous cases. They added that they also had experience with individuals who received prescriptions for lethal medications under the DWDA, but who did not actually proceed either to fill those prescriptions or to ingest the medications. In such cases, it appeared to the hospice team that simply having the option of ending their lives was sufficient for some individuals to live on day by day as long as they were enjoying quality in their lives. Robert's symptoms were well-managed; he received expert hospice care, including excellent pain control; he was able to have final conversations with his children; and he lived for several weeks until he died a natural death.

CONCLUSIONS

There are, perhaps, two major lessons to be learned from the cases of Richard and Robert. The first is that however we are to understand the similarities and differences between PAS and aid in dying as they have been described here, the intersection of these activities and hospice care is fraught with ethical and practical decisions and is often subject to the vicissitudes of human choices. Ethical decisions permeate this example, from a society that decides to establish hospice programs as part of its health care system and that makes a decision to offer PAS or aid in dying as a legitimate legal option for its citizens, to the choices made by individuals about the care they wish to receive at the end of their lives, to the ultimate personal and professional decisions made by hospice providers, their programs, and the institutions that sponsor them.

A second important lesson that emerges is that people of good will can come to different conclusions about difficult cases, even when they are acting on similar moral values and principles in what they believe to be thoughtful and reflective ways. We need not think that decisions of this type do little more than reveal that all good is on one side and all bad is on the other side. These are serious matters that deserve serious discussion by all involved. They run to the heart of how we view the value of human life, the principles that should govern our ethical behavior, the ways in which those values and principles should be applied in concrete decision making, the factors that enter into the establishment of public policy, and the scope of legitimate behavior. One might hope that the outcome of responsible discussions of these matters would be the achievement of common conclusions or at least a broadening of common ground within which respect for differences of opinion could be respected and ongoing dialogue might be productive.

Charles A. Corr, PhD, is vice-chair of the Board of Directors for the Suncoast Hospice Institute, an affiliate of Suncoast Hospice. Dr. Corr is also a member of the International Work Group on Death, Dying, and Bereavement (Chairperson, 1989–1993); the Association for Death Education and Counseling; the ChiPPS (Children's Project on Palliative/Hospice Services) Communications Work Group of the National Hospice and Palliative Care Association; and the Executive Committee of the National Donor Family Council. Dr. Corr's publications include more than three dozen books and articles, along with well over 100 chapters and articles in professional journals, in the field of death, dying, and bereavement. His most recent publications include two chapters in Beyond Kübler-Ross: New Perspectives on Death, Dying and Grief *(Hospice Foundation of America, 2011) and the seventh edition of* Death & Dying, Life & Living *(Wadsworth, 2013), co-authored with Donna M. Corr.*

REFERENCES

Campbell, C. S., & Cox, J. E. (2010). Hospice and physician-assisted death: Collaboration, compliance, and complicity. *Hastings Center Report, 40*(5), 26–35.

Corr, C. A., & Corr, D. M. (2013). *Death and dying, life and living* (7th ed.). Belmont, CA: Wadsworth.

Foley, K. M., & Hendin, H. (Eds.). (2002). *The case against assisted suicide: For the right to end-of-life care.* Baltimore, MD: Johns Hopkins University Press.

Oregon Department of Human Services. (2005). *Seventh annual report on Oregon's Death with Dignity Act.* Retrieved from http://egov.oregon.gov/DHS/ph/pas

Oregon Department of Human Services. (2006). *Eighth annual report on Oregon's Death with Dignity Act.* Retrieved from http://egov.oregon.gov/DHS/ph/pas

Oregon Department of Human Services. (2011). *Thirteenth annual report on*

Oregon's Death with Dignity Act. Retrieved from http://public.health.oregon. gov/ProviderPartnerResources/EvaluationResearch/DeathwithDignityAct

Quill, T. E., & Battin, M. P. (2004). *Physician-assisted dying: The case for palliative care and patient choice.* Baltimore, MD: Johns Hopkins University Press.

Reagan, B. (2000). *The Oregon Death with Dignity Act: A guidebook for health care providers.* Portland, OR: Center for Ethics in Health Care, Oregon Health and Science University.

Family and Staff: Ethical Concerns

This section begins by acknowledging the larger ecological perspective: Ethical decisions involve families and institutions. William Scott Long's chapter begins this section with a stark reminder of how issues of cost and viable institutional alternatives can complicate care and create ethical issues. As his case illustrates, the harsh realities of contemporary care can often inhibit the most appropriate forms of care and add to the staff's sense of moral distress. Obviously, there is a need for policy changes that will allow a more seamless provision of care.

This point is reinforced in Eileen Chichin and Jim Palmer's chapter on hospice care within nursing homes. There is an inherent tension between the palliative goals of hospice and the restorative and rehabilitative roles traditionally assumed by nursing homes. Chichin and Palmer note the importance of the need for effective education and communication on all levels if collaboration is to succeed.

The remaining chapters involve the role of family. Mary Beth Morrissey's chapter tackles an issue underlying many of the prior chapters. What can be done when family members insist on care that is futile, that is unlikely to have any medical benefit, possibly incurring increased or unceasing discomfort for the patient, and utilizing needed resources? Morrissey calls for increased professional and community education on advance directives, better care of and communication within the interdisciplinary team, and the use of ethical review policies. Most important, Morrissey also sees some remediation in the shift from an individualistic to a more ecological ethical paradigm.

Family issues are also evident in the chapter by Kelly Komatz and Alissa Hurwitz Swota. Here is another example of family requests for inappropriate care, exacerbated since the patient is a child. As the authors illustrate this case, they reiterate Morrissey's call for improved communication and education about the goals of care.

Komatz and Swota illustrate another point about the need for staff to always be aware of maintaining personal and professional values. Families may make inappropriate requests, not always solely about care demands. In some cases, families may make inappropriate requests that patients not be told they are in hospice care or request that attending staff be or not be of a certain race or ethnicity. In other cases, it may be staff that struggle with inappropriate actions, over-extending their caring to transgress boundaries. For example, one hospice bereavement counselor invited a client to join her family for a Thanksgiving Day dinner, not recognizing the ways that this action blurred professional boundaries. This is another value of ethical committees, clear ethics policies, ethics education, and ethical grand rounds. They provide opportunities for staff to address and explore all the ethical dilemmas that they encounter.

The next three chapters continue to examine ethical issues that arise when the patient is a minor. Brian Carter begins with a complex case involving a newborn infant. The author is sensitive to the contrasting perspectives of health care providers and parents, describing the latter as individuals who "may acknowledge limits, but nonetheless want to live out their parental roles and responsibilities in what is most certainly a different sense of 'normal'—but nonetheless allows them to fulfill their role as 'bearers of hope.'" Drawing on work from researchers in adult situations, his comments on the differences between "hoping for something" and "living in hope" are striking and pose important opportunities for clinical and ethical reflection. Carter urges caution in communications and predictions, in respecting the values and preferences of parents, and in avoiding the need of some professionals to move too quickly to closure in their judgments. That leads to thoughtful comments on "futility," comments that pair nicely with Morrissey's chapter on family requests for futile treatment.

Timothy Arsenault's chapter addresses similar issues. Arsenault poses a challenging case example of a mother bereaved by the prior suicide of her husband who now wants to hang onto her son, her sole remaining family member, at all costs, along with a boy who is willing to accede to his mother's wishes no matter what. The moral distress of the staff caring for this boy is evident and understandable, reaching its height in the well-meaning but misguided intervention of a palliative care social worker who attempts to bypass the mother's instructions and is disciplined for that behavior. Arsenault nicely notes the constructive efforts of a hospice volunteer after the boy's death when both mother and volunteer share stories of their children's deaths. There are numerous interesting dimensions to this chapter, including comments on what a hospice and palliative care team might have done had they not been thwarted by the mother's efforts to block communication with her son and demand full-bore curative interventions. The chapter implicitly raises a very interesting issue. Ethically we affirm that a child, while not legally capable of offering consent to treatment, ought to at least *assent* to that treatment. This case illustrates how difficult that concept can be in practice.

This is further illustrated in Kristin Meade and Sarah Friebert's chapter on informed consent and adolescents. They begin with the paradox that in the transitional period of adolescence, many adolescents have the mental capacity to make decisions even though, under the age of majority, they lack legal capacity. Again the principle of assent—shared decision making—is affirmed even as the case demonstrates difficulty. Meade and Friebert offer sound guidelines to assist families and staff in negotiating this difficult terrain.

Capacity is not just an issue with minors; it arises as well when patients suffer from dementia. Charles Corr, Karen Corr, and Susan Ramsey discuss the ethical dilemmas that arise when a patient has dementia. In a carefully drawn chapter, the authors urge that when writing advance directives, adults clearly consider the possibility of future dementia. Yet, this raises an interesting ethical issue. Are such advance directives still determinative or does the very fact of dementia so dramatically alter prior persona of the person that such earlier choices now have limited meaning? The value of an agent who can speak for the values and wishes of a person who can no longer speak for himself or herself is clear in this case example, as are the challenges that confront such an agent.

Kenneth Doka's chapter ends this section. Again affirming an ecological perspective, Doka notes that the ethical decisions made throughout the illness have implications for survivors after the death. Such decisions can complicate or facilitate the grief of survivors and ease or add to the moral distress of staff.

CHAPTER 10

What Next? A Case Study of Transfer From Hospice to Nursing Home

William Scott Long

The rapid success of the modern hospice movement in America from 1974 forward has depended on two major elements: its goal of caring for the dying and their families, and its means of providing interdisciplinary care, that is attractive to patients, their families, and caregivers. At the time of its inception the goal had been neglected or only partially met in clinical practice, especially in medical practice, and interdisciplinary care was relatively uncommon. Both expanded even in an era when scientific and technological progress was successfully promoting subspecialty medicine. Unfortunately, in addition to obvious benefits, this growing specialization of medical practice led to fragmentation of patients' care and diminished concern for their families. In some sense both the goals and means of hospice have stood in opposition to subspecialty medicine throughout the subsequent decades. In those early years, nurses and social workers, along with some doctors, sought to forward the more interdisciplinary and humanistic approach of hospice in clinical care. As Florence Wald commented: "We caregivers thirsted for ways to give comfort, to restore civility and to be compassionate. Eager as we were, the public was even more so" (Adams, 2008).

The rise of hospice in America was so rapid that in 1982, only eight years after Wald began caring for the first American hospice patient, the U.S. Congress amended Medicare to provide the Medicare Hospice Benefit (MHB) for its recipients facing the end of life. This financially generous coverage imposed on its enrollees two entrance requirements: refusal of further therapy aimed at cure and a prognosis of six months or less. The MHB applies to Americans 65 years old or older, but most insurance programs and most hospices in the United States have adopted these guidelines for younger patients.

To my knowledge, no other nation requires such a clearly defined prognosis before enrolling its citizens into programs for end-of-life care. As a result, few if any other countries create such clear-cut distinctions between supportive care along the entire trajectory of a patient's life-threatening illness and supportive care within six months of a patient's death, designated as hospice care in the US.

These defining requirements give rise to problems for all concerned—patients, families, and caregivers. Patients whose hospice course suggests a prognosis longer than six months may be dropped from the program. The National Hospice and Palliative Care Organization (NHPCO) estimates that for the calendar year 2008, about 15% of patients enrolled were dropped from hospice programs for extended prognosis, further curative therapy, or other reasons (NHPCO, 2009). Many such patients had stabilized or even improved due to effective interdisciplinary care. Patient improvement on hospice programs has been fostered in recent decades not only by interdisciplinary care but also by the expanding interventions available in hospice, as the overlap between curative and palliative care has become more evident. For example, radiation therapy may be used to control the pain of bony metastases in a hospice patient with no intention of cure of the underlying cancer.

However, most patients dropped from hospice programs still live with chronic progressive disease, malignant, nonmalignant, or commonly both. Frail elderly patients with multiple comorbidities constitute a rising demographic in the US, aided in part by the increasing power of scientific and technologic advances and in part by successful programs of public education and health.

As the ranks of the elderly infirm with multiple illnesses rise in the decades ahead, so will the problems of appropriate referral out of hospice programs and into safe and adequate care (Lynn, 2004). Where and under what conditions to transfer those ex-hospice patients within the current American health care system will continue to complicate the lives of patients, families, and their caregivers.

The case below presents the course of such a patient discharged from an inpatient hospice unit with the attendant clinical, administrative, and ethical issues confronting the patient and her caregivers. The account has been extensively adjusted to protect the identity of those involved.

CASE STUDY

On admission to hospice Mrs. H was a 68-year-old divorced female, previously living in her own apartment with some support from her daughter. She was on home oxygen for her chronic obstructive pulmonary disease (COPD). She saw her local physician infrequently but received medication prescriptions through his office and perhaps from others as well. A Medicare recipient on Medicaid, she was admitted to a regional hospital through its emergency room (ER). On admission she was in respiratory crisis and required oxygen at 15 liter/min by non-rebreather mask. In addition to COPD she had a history of depression, anxiety, benzodiazepine dependence, peptic ulcer disease with a recent GI bleed, multiple falls attributed to opiate intoxication, a history of congestive failure, and osteoporosis with compression fractures producing chronic back pain, all documented in her multiple recent admissions and ER visits.

Both in the ER and during her care on the hospice unit, Mrs. H's situation illustrates the difficulty of choosing a single disease by which to characterize her clinical state. When the young (and relatively young) are ill, often a single diagnosis uncomplicated by other disease will guide treatment (e.g., a glioblastoma in a 35-year-old). In the elderly, however, accumulation of illnesses makes choice of a single disease state an inaccurate and misleading guide to care (Tinetti and Fried, 2004). The precipitating cause for Mrs. H's admission to the local hospital and then to our unit was respiratory; but as we discovered, her care was further amplified to treat co-existent psychiatric, musculoskeletal, addiction, and social problems.

Rather than present a chronologic description of Mrs. H's stay in the inpatient unit of our hospice, I present a problem-oriented and somewhat simplified summary.

Social Mrs. H had had four children. The two older children had remained in SE Asia near their father. The two local children had different fathers. The available daughter was a single mother employed in a fast food chain with three children of her own, eight to twelve years old. The other local child was never involved in his mother's care. According to his mother he was "useless" and "never around when I need him." His sister dismissed him as "a creep with a drug habit." Mrs. H had made no advance directives. Her daughter was the only available decision maker whenever the patient was unable to make her own choices, which was the case on her transfer to us.

Throughout her mother's lengthy stay on the hospice unit, her daughter visited only sporadically, in part because of the demands of work and child care, and in part because, as she told a social worker, "She's hard to please and half the time she don't seem glad to see me or the children. They don't want to come anyway."

Respiratory On admission the patient's COPD initially appeared life-threatening. Her emphysema was addressed by use of routine nebulizer therapy, steroids, opioids (also used for her chronic back pain), and oxygen therapy. Benzodiazepines helped with anxiety associated with her dyspnea. She finally became more stable with better control of both dyspnea and anxiety. At this point iron supplements were added to improve her anemia, with good effect. During her final days in the hospice inpatient unit she was receiving oxygen at 3-5 liters per hour per nasal cannula with 92-95% saturations in addition to steroids, nebulizer therapy, and greatly reduced doses of morphine.

Intermittently Mrs. H had what appeared to be life-threatening respiratory crises during which she was poorly aware and lay on her side for oral drainage. Despite prn nebulizer and opioid therapy added to her routine respiratory medications she had an agonal respiratory pattern. Triggers for these episodes were not always evident, sometimes attributed to anxiety, at other times seemingly unprovoked. On such occasions her condition appeared so severe that several times on sign-out one physician reported to another, "She probably won't be here when you arrive tomorrow." Her daughter was called several times for what appeared to be a prognosis of hours but never was, thanks to the concerted and timely efforts of the nursing and medical staff.

Psychiatric Problems identified on admission included longstanding anxiety, depression, and addiction to various substances. During initial assessment our consultant psychiatrist reported that in addition to anxiety Mrs. H showed signs of delirium with occasional visual hallucinations and of delusions in a history of polydrug abuse including alcohol, cocaine, and possibly opiates. She had stopped smoking with her next-to-last admission to the hospital ER. On her first interview with Mrs. H, the psychiatrist found her to be alert and oriented but with limited short- and long-term recall and spotty recent memory. Her affect was appropriate, but she seemed guarded and evasive when asked about previous psychiatric history. The psychiatrist recommended tapering benzodiazepines to zero. To Mrs. H's credit she cooperated with the taper and showed no subsequent benzodiazepine-seeking behavior. She used prn buspirone for anxiety. On a second visit the psychiatrist noted marked improvement in cognition and affect.

Mrs. H at times appeared to lose contact with the rest of the institution and her visiting daughter. She could not be aroused, but vital signs and oxygen saturation were all in her usual range. Her breathing was unlabored with her usual rate and depth and distant breath sounds in clear lung fields on auscultation. One observer felt that she was faking unresponsiveness; on a single occasion when a nurse tried to lift an eyelid, she responded: "Leave me alone." Once or twice more at other times the same maneuver provoked no response.

In our day-to-day contact Mrs. H alternated between being withdrawn and demanding, even belligerent in a vocabulary not heard elsewhere on the service at that time. This routine behavior was sometimes illuminated by frank expressions of gratitude, which became more frequent as her general condition improved. In addition to these welcome moments, her long stay and her effective struggle with some important goals (reduced use of benzodiazepines and opioids) engaged us strongly.

Pain Mrs. H had a history of chronic back pain, considered the primary cause of her long-term use of opioids and benzodiazepines. Earlier in her stay with us, the patient had not only back pain but described pain radiating into her legs suggesting neuropathic pain, possibly as a result of compression fractures or spinal stenosis, for which she received pregabalin. At times she complained of generalized pains in her chest and abdomen, often relieved with more effective bowel care or warm packs to the affected region. Other pains were unexplained, but none was long-lasting.

As her stay on the hospice unit lengthened, her pain control improved. At the same time, with her cooperation, we were able to reduce her use of opioids for pain and dyspnea by two-thirds. We removed her pump for morphine (an obstacle for transfer to local health care institutions) so that for the last weeks of her stay she was comfortable on reduced long-acting morphine with only occasional breakthroughs. Her caregivers and daughter were heartened at her cooperation in reduction of both opioids and benzodiazepines and said so to her. At our instigation Mrs. H appointed her daughter with power of attorney for health care matters.

At this point Mrs. H was receiving from us what we consider to be routine palliative care. The two psychiatric consults were done for her comfort and to guide our choice of therapy. We consulted physical therapy, often used with interested and capable patients for their physical and psychological comfort, even when limited to in-bed exercise. Because of her ongoing bed rest, we encouraged her to spend more time out of bed and increased the tempo of her physical therapy. Her cooperation initially was intermittent and half-hearted but improved with time.

After several weeks with her decreased reliance on medication and improved control of dyspnea, pain, and anxiety, the interdisciplinary team (IDT) raised the question of whether Mrs. H rightfully belonged in hospice.

Here Mrs. H's care entered a new phase. At that moment in her life she belonged to an increasingly important group of patients: the frail elderly with multiple comorbidities. She had been brought back to, and maintained in, a relatively stable condition through intensive interdisciplinary care. Because our institution is an acute care hospital (ACH), not a skilled nursing facility, her enrollment in the MHB meant that we could not keep her only for sustained care if we felt her prognosis was greater than 6 months, difficult as it can be to prognosticate accurately. Not only are we bound to observe the guidelines of the MHB, but we need to consider patients in more acute need of hospice care.

However, we feared that without the interdisciplinary care received with us, Mrs. H's condition would deteriorate with decreasing likelihood of survival. We had to recognize that her hospice eligibility, in particular her prognosis, might depend not only on the pathophysiology of her illness but also on her site of care in the landscape of contemporary American health care. If we were to discharge her from hospice because of her lengthened prognosis in our setting, she might with less intense care move back into the short prognosis, qualifying her again for the hospice care from which we had dismissed her. Worse, we foresaw the risk that in another institution not prepared to meet her needs during respiratory crises, she might die.

In our regular weekly clinical team meeting, the IDT discussed Mrs. H's uneven but overall improving status. During this period she had become more alert, spent more time sitting up in a chair, ate better and fed herself, provided some of her own personal care, and walked with assistance to the bathroom. She described herself as more comfortable and was more accessible, at times even congenial, with some staff. At her request the Arts Department made a small plaque for the wall facing her bed, with the word JAKARTA surrounded by a loose wreath of vividly colored orchids. In counterbalance to this overall improvement, recent respiratory crises were routinely introduced in our discussions as rationale to maintain her on the MHB.

We held weekly sessions for utilization review to determine each patient's status as appropriate for continued care on the hospice unit or as a candidate for discharge to another setting with or without hospice home care. The clinical team continued to feel that Mrs. H was not a candidate for continued hospice coverage based on her prognosis and the regulations of the MHB, and so the clinical and administrative team members began to consider places where she would be safe and receive adequate care. What institutions would accept her and under what conditions? Outside hospice, where would she find the interdisciplinary care that had slowed her deterioration, or even reversed it, as one optimist on the team suggested?

In an ideal situation, we would have readily transferred her into an institution prepared to offer expert pulmonary support during her crises and tailored rehabilitation at other times, all with the goal of strengthening her for a possible return to less demanding care, e.g. at a skilled nursing facility (SNF) or at home with extensive support. In the world we shared, however, we had to consider other immediate options.

Home Like most patients, her desired goal at discharge was to live at home. However, her daughter had closed her mother's apartment. Furthermore, on the hospice unit Mrs. H was not able to get independently in and out of bed for toileting or bathing, and meal preparation would have been impossible without major support. Her daughter was not able to provide either supervision or care needed for the patient's activities of daily living, either in her own home or in another apartment where her mother might live. Most important, skilled caregivers would need to be ready at any hour to help Mrs. H get through the recurrent but unpredictable respiratory crises outlined above. Even devoted in-home help and maybe friends (none had visited) would find themselves stretched beyond their capabilities and set up for failure that afterward might mark their lives.

With obvious regret her daughter quickly acknowledged that she could not care for the patient in her own home. We observed some strengthening of ties between mother and daughter who hoped we would place her mother "some place close to where I live or where I work."

Skilled nursing facility If she could not go home, Mrs. H insisted on being cared for near her daughter. Her daughter wanted to avoid the 30-minute drive between home or work and the hospice, as did her mother who missed the visits from her daughter and grandchildren. This requirement meant considering a local nursing facility.

Skilled nursing facilities are an important site of care in the United States. 20–25% of Americans currently die in nursing homes nationwide, and the figure is expected to rise to 40% in the decades ahead. At least 40% of Americans spend some part of their last month of life in nursing homes (Miller, Teno, and Mor, 2004). Data from Connecticut show 31% of patient deaths occurred in nursing homes, compared to the national average of 24% (Teno, 2002).

Care in nursing homes, including end-of-life care, can be excellent; but variation abounds (Forbes-Thompson and Gesser, 2005; Hodgson and Lehning, 2008; Miller and Han, 2008; Miller, Teno, and Mor, 2004; Waldrop and Kirkendall, 2009). Care is often limited in intensity by the ratio of patients per nursing personnel; by the larger numbers of certified nursing assistants (CNAs) and licensed practical nurses (LPNs) relative to registered nurses (RNs); by the limited training and high turnover of staff; and by administrative goals (Hanson, Sengupta, and Slubicki, 2005; Hodgson and Lehning, 2008; Miller, Teno, and Mor, 2004). In general, compared to inpatient hospice units, most elements of interdisciplinary care in SNFs are understaffed. In providing end-of-life care, specialized training is needed and frequently missing (Miller and Han, 2008). Symptom control of pain and of dyspnea as observed by family members is often inadequate (Reinke et al., 2008). Physicians attached to most skilled nursing facilities do not visit individual patients daily, often not weekly (Wetle, Shield, Teno, Miller, and Welch, 2005).

The clinical team worried about adequate care in a SNF, especially because of her ongoing respiratory crises (Reinke et al., 2008). Patients with non-malignant disease have become the majority of patients cared for by hospice (NHPCO, 2009); and those with end-stage lung or heart disease, wherever they are cared for, typically present with recurrent crises (Lynn, 2001). For SNF patients such care often occurs in the emergency rooms of hospitals (Stefanacci, 2011). For Mrs. H, survival from such crises in our inpatient hospice unit was the result of a trained, informed, and devoted nursing staff present on all three shifts, in consultation with the physicians who visited her every day. We considered that Mrs. H's survival through such crises in her future would require the same sort of inpatient care although she would no longer be a hospice patient.

Long-term acute care hospital (LTACH) These institutions make up a relatively new addition to health care institutions in the US. First appearing in the mid-1980s, such sites provide specialized and intense clinical attention to well-defined medical issues for selected patients (Hotes and Kalman, 2001). Respiratory disease with and without ventilator support constituted nearly a quarter of the case load of LTACHs in 2006 (Muñoz-Price, 2009). Their programs range from close observation units for patients weaning from ventilators to outpatient programs; some long-term residential care is available depending on needs and financial support. Reports of their success vary (Himes, 2008; Kahn, Benson, Appleby, Carson, and Iwashnya, 2010; Votto and Hotes, 2010), but these institutions represent an attractive possibility for patients like Mrs. H Almost all our patients considered for discharge fall outside the purview of these facilities.

This state's single LTACH offers specialty-level respiratory care, both inpatient and outpatient, for patients with Medicaid coverage, which Mrs. H had. Several obstacles blocked the patient's referral there, however. Its distant location made it unacceptable to the patient and her daughter. In addition, admission criteria for patients supported by Medicaid required that she be admitted to the LTACH from a SNF or ACH or that evidence be provided that she had been refused by a SNF or comparable institution. Occasional exceptions are made for this requirement, but in that case the request must be submitted to an independent agency for an ultimate decision.

Mrs. H did not welcome the decision to transfer out of hospice. Her desire to be closer to her daughter and grandchildren counterbalanced her mounting anxiety about her care and safety. Her concerns reflect those found in the literature (Enes, Lucas, Aberdein, and Lucioni, 2004). However, as in her weaning off benzodiazepines and decreasing use of opioids, she made serious efforts to cooperate with us.

Many attempts at placement at last identified a SNF prepared to accept her. I called to review her case with the head of nursing there. In particular, I wanted the institution to realize that Mrs. H was a patient who rewarded care despite her history of substance abuse and of episodic respiratory distress from which she had been rescued with appropriate and timely treatment. Eventual return to a family member's home seemed unlikely but might be possible. I was readily assured by the nursing supervisor that the receiving facility was prepared to meet all those challenges. I also learned the name of the medical director and faxed ahead of time my detailed discharge summary to him, a copy of which accompanied the patient on transfer.

Within a week Mrs. H was dead.

I called the nursing home. My request for details received a careful but limited response. Within a few days of arrival, Mrs. H had gotten out of bed without assistance and fallen. "I think she just wanted to leave. She told me she was tired of living," the nursing supervisor recalled. In addition, her daughter reported that Mrs. H had been confused and was receiving antibiotics for an infection. Work-up in a local emergency room after her fall revealed no fractures, and she was returned to the SNF. The following day when her daughter visited in the late afternoon, her mother was more confused but did appear to recognize her. Later that evening, her daughter received a call to tell her that Mrs. H had died.

Although she was no longer our patient, the clinical team at its next meeting recommended bereavement follow-up for her daughter and grandchildren through the hospice. This was a rather formal response to the general distress felt throughout the team.

What went wrong?

One major threat for patients like Mrs. H is the absence or paucity of local institutions in which appropriate care can be delivered for their complex needs. The population of elderly infirm with multiple morbidities continues to grow with no slowing foreseen. Many if not most will require assistance and protection from the consequences of ill health long before they become eligible for interdisciplinary care on hospice. Some after entering hospice will improve with its intensive care, only to be discharged from the program, as Mrs. H was. LTACHs are uncommon, and nursing homes are often unprepared to treat such complicated patients. The current economic and regulatory climate makes unlikely the implementation of proposals to address end-of-life needs through new education programs, expanded hiring, retention, and training of relevant caregivers. However, some culture changes in the world of nursing homes through education and cooperation with existing hospice programs will help (Miller, Teno, and Mor, 2004; Miller and Han, 2008).

A second major problem concerns cost. As regulations now stand, the patients needing long-term care will not receive outside financial support unless they meet the requirements of Medicaid. Medicare alone does not cover extended stays in long-term care institutions except for a maximum of 100 days following a justifiable three-day admission of a nursing home resident to an ACH. Otherwise, the cost must be borne privately. Some families will and have become impoverished.

In 2010 a group from the Department of Health Care Policy at Harvard University proposed a new benefit for end-of-life care in nursing homes (Huskamp, Stevenson, Chernew, and Newhouse, 2010; Meier, Lim, and Carlson, 2010). Their proposal recognizes that the current MHB does not adequately respond to the changed clinical condition of the elderly infirm with multiple illnesses. Their proposed end-of-life benefit for nursing home residents differs from the current MHB. It is not prognosis-driven but does require designation of end-of-life status; beneficiaries do not have to opt in; and they are not forced to forego further therapy for cure. Such a provision would certainly have served Mrs. H well, although again such a proposal requires that nursing homes be able to provide effective end-of-life care (which is an ongoing problem), and/or able to contract with local hospice programs. This proposal, which has implications for care of elderly patients beyond those in nursing homes, faces the same problems of federal funding that confronts many competing programs in our current economic and political climate.

These system problems are beyond our immediate reach. However, at the local level, in our inpatient unit, additional measures suggest themselves in retrospect as desirable changes to her history.

ANALYSIS

A pronounced change in hospice since its earliest days has been the understanding that promotion of comfortable death may these days involve interventions once considered only curative. Did we overreact in trying to promote this patient's survival? I don't think so. None of our measures, e.g., physical therapy, iron supplements, respiratory support, analgesia, and psychiatric consultations, fell outside routine measures for comfort, and in that context nothing blocked a natural death.

When in response to these basic interventions Mrs. H showed both psychological and physiologic resilience despite serious diagnoses, we understood that she could improve to the point where discharge from hospice and MHB coverage might occur. Would it have been in the bounds of the hospice mission to arrange for a specialist in respiratory disease to enlarge our understanding of her disease and to guide therapy in anticipation of her potential transfer away from our care? Seen only within the context of hospice care many might say, "No, you don't have to do that. She is a hospice patient." But if hospice staff sees as its vocation care for a patient not as an institutional entity but as a whole person in a continuing life, they might construe such an intervention as appropriate support for a safer transfer.

In our consideration of her discharge planning, two other options might have received more vigorous discussion: transfer to the state's LTACH and her continuation on the MHB. Mrs. H and her daughter both stated resistance to any transfer that increased the distance between them. Mrs. H's continuance on the MHB for an additional period on hospice home care in the SNF would have allowed us to provide palliative nurses for consultation, extra care, and surveillance in the SNF. However, it would have concerned us deeply to claim that she needed more time on the MHB when in our estimation she didn't.

A final word about my role as one of the physicians on the team caring for Mrs. H:

Beneath her difficult behavior, sometimes demanding, disagreeable, and ungrateful, sometimes sulking and withdrawn, I sensed in Mrs. H a more solid base built earlier in her life. I admired her struggle to regain some control in her life, her faltering but finally successful attempts to be rid of addiction.

She and our team had formed a bond, working together to enable more—and more enjoyable—days with her family as her condition improved.

However, in our current medical system, her transfer disrupted those bonds and shared goals. Following her out into the SNF with its own staff was not possible beyond social visits. Once she arrived in her nursing home, did she feel abandoned? What happened that she told the nursing supervisor there that she was tired of living, words she didn't use with us? In the transfer did she carry some sense of abandonment, even rejection by those who had spent more time with her than her family had in the last months? (Back et al., 2009; Enes, Lucas, Aberdein and Lucioni, 2004)

We should not try to console or distract ourselves with alternative histories. Instead we must remember that again and again we have opportunities to find ways new and old to serve more patients across institutional borders and bureaucratic categories. Our experience with Mrs. H helps those patients and us.

William Scott Long, MD, has practiced palliative and hospice medicine for the last 20 years and is a member of the clinical faculties of Connecticut's two medical schools. He serves on the advisory committee for the end-of-life section in Yale's Interdisciplinary Bioethics Center and is a member of the Board of Directors of the International Work Group in Death, Dying and Bereavement. He has taught palliative and hospice medicine abroad (Latvia, Uganda) and has helped train inmates to work as volunteers in Connecticut's prison hospice program.

REFERENCES

Adams, C. C. (2008). *Dying with dignity in America: The transformational leadership of Florence Wald* (Doctoral dissertation). University of Hartford, Hartford, CT.

Back, A. L., Young, J. P., McCown, E., Engelberg, R. A., Vig, E. K., Reinke, L. F.,...Curtis, J. R. et al. (2009). Abandonment at the end of life from patient, caregiver, nurse, and physician perspectives: Loss of continuity and lack of closure. *Archives of Internal Medicine, 169,*474–479.

Enes., S. P. D, Lucas, C. F., Aberdein, N., & Lucioni, J. (2004). Discharging patients from hospice to nursing home: A retrospective case note review. *International Journal of Palliative Nursing, 10,*124–130.

Forbes-Thompson, S., & Gesser, C. E. (2005). End of life in nursing homes: Connections between structure, process, and outcomes. *Journal of Palliative Medicine, 8,* 545–555.

Hanson, L. C., Sengupta, S., & Slubicki, M. (2005). Access to nursing home hospice: Perspectives of nursing home and hospice administrators. *Journal of Palliative Medicine 8*,1207–1213.

Himes, D. (2008). Long-term acute care hospitals. One hospital's experience. *Critical Care Nursing Quarterly, 31*, 46–51.

Hodgson, N. A., & Lehning, A. J. (2008). Palliative care in nursing homes: A comparison of high- and low-level providers. *International Journal of Palliative Nursing 14*, 38–44.

Hotes, L. S., & Kalman, E. (2001). The evolution of care for the chronically critically ill patient. *Clinics in Chest Medicine, 22*, 1–11.

Huskamp, H. A., Stevenson, D. G., Chernew, M. E., & Newhouse, J. P. (2010). A new Medicare end-of-life benefit for nursing home residents. *Health Affairs 29*, 130–135.

Kahn, J. M., Benson, N. M., Appleby, N., Carson, S. S, & Iwashnya, T. J. (2010). Long-term acute care hospital utilization after critical illness. *JAMA, 303*, 2253–2259.

Lynn, J. (2001). Serving patients who may die soon and their families: The role of hospice and other services. *JAMA 285*, 925–932.

Lynn, J. (2004). *Sick to death and not going to take it anymore! Reforming health care for the last years of life.* Berkeley, CA: University of California Press.

Meier, D. E., Lim, B. & Carlson, M. D. (2010). Raising the standard: Palliative care in nursing homes. *Health Affairs 29*, 136–140.

Miller, S. C., & Han, B. (2008). End-of-life care in U.S. nursing homes; nursing homes with special programs and trained staff for hospice or palliative/end-of-life care. *Journal of Palliative Medicine 11*, 866–877.

Miller, S. C., Teno, J. M., & Mor, V. (2004). Hospice and palliative care in nursing homes. *Clinical Geriatric Medicine, 20*, 717–734.

Muñoz-Price, L. S. Long-term acute care hospitals. (2009). *Healthcare Epidemiology 49*, 438–443.

National Hospice and Palliative Care Organization. (2009). *NHPCO facts and figures: Hospice care in America.* Alexandria, VA: National Hospice and Palliative Care Organization.

Reinke, L. F., Engelberg R. A., Shannon, S. E., Wenrich, M. D., Vig, E. K., Back, A. L., & Curtis, J. R. (2008). Transitions regarding palliative and end-of-life care in severe chronic obstructive pulmonary disease or advanced cancer: Themes identified by patients, families, and clinicians. *Journal of Palliative Medicine 11*, 601–609.

Stefanacci, R. G. (2011). Urgent care in the nursing home: Aligning the incentives. *Annals of Long Term Care, 19*, 22–24.

Teno, J. (2002). Change over time, Connecticut. Site of death 1989-2001 (Chart). In: *Facts on dying*, maintained by Brown University. Retrieved from www.chcr.brown.edu/dying/brownsodinfo.htm

Tinetti, M. E., & Fried, T. (2004). The end of the disease era. *American Journal of Medicine, 116*, 179–185.

Votto J., & Hotes, L. S. (2010). Critically ill patients and long-term acute care hospitals. *JAMA 304*, 1441–1442.

Waldrop, D. P., & Kirkendall, A. M. (2009). Comfort measures: A qualitative study of nursing home-based end-of-life care. *Journal of Palliative Medicine, 12*, 719–724.

Wetle, T., Shield, R., Teno, J., Miller, S. C., & Welch, L. (2005). Family perspectives on end-of-life care experiences in nursing homes. *The Gerontologist 45*, 642–650.

CHAPTER 11

Ethical Conflicts: Hospice and Nursing Home Care

Eileen R. Chichin and Jim Palmer

A significant number of elders age in place and die at home or in hospitals after an acute event. However, many of the oldest and frailest members of our society spend their final days, months, and years in nursing homes. Most nursing home residents are slowly declining as a result of chronic, life-limiting illnesses. Accordingly, many, if not all of them, are candidates for palliative care, an approach that is driven by the individual's goals of care and maximizes comfort and support for both the patient and the family. When nursing home residents are believed to be within six months of death, hospice is an appropriate consideration. Generally recognized as the gold standard of care for the terminally ill, hospice sees the patient and the family as the unit of care and provides another layer of physical care as well as psychosocial and spiritual support to both the nursing home patient and family. Patient autonomy is an overarching theme in hospice, and achieving goals of care that take the patient's wishes into consideration and maximize comfort is its highest priority. From a philosophical perspective, contrary to the usual nursing home goals of care that emphasize rehabilitation and restoration (Hanson, Henderson and Menon, 2002; Martz and Gerding, 2011), hospice care acknowledges that the patient is experiencing an irreversible decline and develops a care plan that incorporates that understanding. In addition to the many complexities associated with providing optimum care at the end of life, that difference in perspective often challenges relationships between hospice teams and nursing home staff.

Hospice services have been provided in nursing homes for several decades, and more and more nursing homes are developing hospice contracts with long-term care facilities (Stevenson and Bramson, 2009). When nursing home residents are on hospice, the nursing home is considered their home, so hospice services are delivered in the nursing home in the same fashion as in a community home. There are visits from a hospice nurse, social worker, and clergyperson, as well as intermittent care delivered by a home health aide. The nursing home provides room and board.

Hospices and nursing homes, like all of the health care industry, are highly regulated and subject to significant oversight. Thus, both of these programs are careful in their spending, and their reliance on governmental or other funding streams regulates the type of care that can be provided. This reality must be taken into consideration by the care team and explained to the patient and family who may not understand why certain services may not be available to them.

Surprisingly, while about 90% of nursing homes have contracts with hospices, only about 30% actually have nursing home residents on hospice, and generally only a few per facility (Stevenson and Bramson, 2009). Although it seems to follow that referral to hospice will enhance end-of-life care, the position of hospice within nursing home settings is often an uneasy one. The case below illustrates some of the challenges that arise when hospice care is delivered in the nursing home. While some of the issues encountered are a function of these two programs attempting to work together, others might be encountered when hospice services are provided in the patient's home as well.

CASE STUDY

Ms. L is a 75-year-old widowed woman with advanced dementia. The beloved mother of one son and three daughters, Ms. L immigrated to the United States with her late husband in the late 1960s, and all her children were born here. For several years, after her other children married, Ms. L resided in a small apartment with her unmarried daughter, Millie. Ms. L's son, two other daughters, their spouses, and several young grandchildren lived in the same city and were regular visitors, participating in her care as much as they were able. However, all of Ms. L's children worked outside the home. Two of them were involved in running the family's antique business, which was struggling financially and on the verge of bankruptcy. Ms. L's worsening condition prevented them from caring for her adequately. She had become bed-bound and nonverbal. She began to require spoon-feeding, which was accomplished with minimal success. Over time, her oral intake diminished. With the strong encouragement of Ms. L's long-term community physician, but with heavy hearts, Ms. L's children had her admitted to a nursing home in February of 2008. Soon after her admission and evaluation by the nursing home team, Ms. L was referred to the home's palliative care consultant to assist with a plan of care. This consultant felt Ms. L's condition met the dementia criteria for hospice referral (Standards and Accreditation Committee, Medical Guidelines Taskforce, 1996) and contacted Mr. L, the son, to discuss this possibility. Although Ms. L's daughters were part of the discussion, Mr. L, as the eldest son, was the primary decision maker. After hearing medical opinions about Ms. L's declining condition and dismal prognosis, as well as the additional services she would receive through hospice, all of the children agreed that contacting hospice was the best option.

The hospice team met with the L family and explained their services. Ms. L's prognosis was also one of the primary discussion topics, along with the goals of care for someone with such advanced disease. Although the family verbalized their understanding, it was clear that they maintained a degree of hope that their mother would recover to some degree. This was particularly evident with Millie, who appeared to have the closest relationship with her mother. At one point, Millie announced that her dream was to be able to come in at noon each day and feed lunch to her mother.

Hospice services began immediately. A home health aide was assigned to Ms. L for four hours per day. Mary, the hospice nurse, visited weekly, as did Carlos, the social worker, and the hospice chaplain. A hospice physician met regularly with this interdisciplinary team to discuss Ms. L's situation, although the nursing home physician was more involved in her day-to-day care. Ms. L remained nonverbal and spent her days between her bed and a comfortable lounge chair specially fitted to her needs. At mealtime, she was patiently fed, either by her hospice aide or one of the nursing assistants on her unit, although she ate very little. Carlos quickly established a relationship with Millie. While he was available to and supportive of the other children, he quickly recognized that Millie was truly suffering as her mother declined and thus required the most attention. Frequent phone calls took place between Carlos and Millie, and although Ms. L continued her downward slide, Millie was clearly maintaining some hope.

One evening, Millie encountered another resident's physician, Dr. Smith, as he was getting ready to visit his patient. Millie engaged Dr. Smith in conversation about her mother and her mother's failing condition. Dr. Smith commented, "Maybe a feeding tube would perk your mother up."

The next day, the hospice administrator and the palliative care consultant both received a phone call from Ms. L's son, requesting a meeting. The meeting was scheduled for the next day, and Mr. L informed the hospice and nursing home teams that the family had decided they wanted a feeding tube. A lengthy discussion took place, with the clinical teams emphasizing the terminal nature of dementia and Ms. L's significant decline. The hospice and nursing home teams queried the family about their knowledge of Ms. L's wishes in a situation such as this. All the family members stated emphatically that this topic had never been broached, and that members of their culture generally opted for the use of life-sustaining technology (Blackhall, Frank, Murphy, Michel, Palmer, and Azen, 1999). The pros and cons of long-term enteral feeding were discussed, stressing the burdensome nature of this treatment in someone in Ms. L's state. It became obvious that Mr. L and two of his sisters understood all this, and their primary goal for their mother was her comfort. It also became clear that Millie was grasping at any possibility of hope, and the thought of her mother "perking up" was a dream come true. Mr. L also mentioned at the meeting that his wife was in the late stages of pregnancy and experiencing some complications. He mentioned that while traditionally he was the family decision maker, given his own personal situation and Millie's distress, he had decided to defer all decision making to her. He requested that both the hospice team and the nursing home team use Millie as their primary contact, and she could share the content of those communications with him and their two sisters. The sisters were also in agreement.

The procedure to insert Ms. L's feeding tube (a percutaneous endoscopic gastrostomy, or PEG tube) was scheduled, and early one morning she was transferred to the local hospital for placement of the tube. Ms. L returned to the nursing home the same evening, having tolerated the procedure well, and feedings through the tube were begun a few days later. Many of the nursing home nurses and nursing assistants, who pride themselves on their ability to "keep someone going," were very pleased by this outcome since they felt a feeding tube would keep Ms. L alive longer.

Ms. L's return to the nursing home with a feeding tube in place provided another opportunity for the hospice to discuss goals of care with the nursing home staff. Sharing of information and education about good end-of-life care for both families and professionals is an important role for hospices. Although the hospice team had been in place in this nursing home for several years, every patient and family situation provided a new opportunity for their nurse, social worker, and clergyperson to interact with the nursing home staff. Ongoing discussions between the hospice team and the nursing home team about goals of care and the actual specifics of care provided are key to quality patient care in the nursing home setting. This is particularly challenging given the sheer number of team members in the two combined teams, but it is always a high priority.

Ms. L remained stable for several days, but suddenly developed a fever of 102 degrees. A chest x-ray was done at the bedside, and it was determined that Ms. L was suffering from pneumonia. The tube feedings were temporarily discontinued to enhance her comfort. Although not all nursing homes have this capability, Ms. L's nursing home routinely used intravenous antibiotic therapy when needed. Ms. L was started on IV antibiotics and within several days her fever had subsided and the feedings were resumed.

The hospice team used Ms. L's return to a more stable state to reintroduce goals of care to the family. Yes, Millie reiterated; they wanted Ms. L to be comfortable. However, Millie was not going to give blanket permission to avoid treatment should an infection recur. Unfortunately, another bout of pneumonia *did* occur, and the same procedures (stopping feeding and using intravenous antibiotics) were implemented. These medical treatments were ordered by the nursing home physician, often under pressure from Millie.

In the next eight months, Ms. L experienced two additional bouts of pneumonia. In reviewing medication records, the pharmacist involved in her care noted that Ms. L's pharmacy costs were among the highest in the nursing home. The nursing home administrator expressed concern about this. The hospice team was becoming increasingly distressed because the decisions being made seemed to be counter to hospice goals of care and they felt they were witnessing the prolonging of a long, slow dying process. The nursing home team, however, was content. Ms. L was still with them—testament to their ability to keep someone going no matter how advanced the illness.

Carlos, the hospice social worker, had frequent lengthy conversations with Millie, in which she volunteered that she harbored resentment and envy toward her siblings. She felt she lacked the family support from spouses and children that they had to get them through this difficult ordeal. Millie also alluded to her fear of the grieving process that would take place once her mother died. On several occasions, she told Carlos she had neither the time or the wherewithal to deal with her mother's death right now so wanted to postpone it for as long as possible.

It was evident to the hospice team, as well as the nursing home team, that Millie was the family member with the greatest need, and every effort was made to minimize her great psychic distress. The other family members tended to remain in the background, allowing Millie to remain steadfast in her desire to keep her mother going at all costs, despite the burdensome nature of the treatments she was receiving. In addition to the four bouts of pneumonia Ms. L had suffered, she had once experienced a change of mental status and at another time, an apparent intestinal obstruction. Both of these events resulted in hospitalization. Millie became very distressed with every acute illness, but insisted on hospitalization whenever she felt her mother was "slipping."

The hospice team continued to work with Millie, and even the nursing home team, who often opt for the use of mechanisms to delay dying, began to be distressed by the degree of what appeared to be futile treatment being used. Finally, given the family's ongoing preference for pursuing treatment that prolonged Ms. L's dying, the hospice team decided they had no choice. After much angst-ridden deliberation, they informed the family that they would have to disenroll their mother. The family seemed to understand the predicament, but were overwhelmed by their—and especially by Millie's—desire to keep their mother on this earth. Sometime after disenrollment from the hospice, Ms. L was admitted to the hospital one more time and died there a few days later.

ANALYSIS

A number of issues with ethical underpinnings are woven through this case. To begin, respect for patient autonomy is the cornerstone of health care ethics. Thus, Ms. L's plan of care should have taken that into consideration. In the case of a person with end-stage dementia who has left no advance directives, the patient's preferences can only be articulated by those who knew her. With respect to Ms. L, there was apparently no knowledge on the children's part of what Ms. L would want. In this kind of situation, decision makers are generally encouraged to think in terms of substituted judgment. That is, given what we know about Ms. L as a person—her personal philosophy, her religious beliefs, etc.—what decision would she have made with respect to any of the usual treatments that may be offered (Post, Blustein, and Dubler, 2007). However, despite encouragement from the hospice team to think in terms of what Ms. L would want, her children seemed to be focused primarily on themselves and their own needs. If the family had no idea of what Ms. L's decisions might be, they needed to think in terms of what would be in *her* best interest. So, although the hospice team constantly reinforced making decisions in that context, many treatment decisions were made that did not appear to be in Ms. L's best interest and were counter to the standard of care.

End-stage dementia generally has specific manifestations. Persons with dementia (PWD) in the final stages lose the ability to speak, to walk, and to swallow. They are prone to infection, with pneumonia and urinary tract infections the most common. Treatments that may have been offered to this patient population in the past are now thought to be more burdensome than beneficial and surrogate decision makers need to be supported to make choices that maximize comfort. Since the beginning of the 21st century, the standard of care for end-stage dementia patients holds that the use of feeding tubes is contraindicated (Finucane, Christmas, and Travis, 1999; Gillick, 2000). Feeding tubes do not prevent aspiration of fluid into the lungs (Martin and Sabbagh, 2011), which is a significant complication, as was evidenced in Ms. L's case as she experienced multiple bouts of pneumonia. Hospitalization, which is often considered when nursing home patients suffer an acute event, is disorienting to PWD (Martin and Sabbagh, 2011). Hospitals focus on treating the acute event and may unintentionally ignore the basic care that nursing home patients require to maintain skin integrity, such as frequent turning and positioning. Thus, if the PWD does not die during her hospital stay, she usually returns to the nursing home with multiple pressure ulcers, as well as a diminished cognitive status.

The community physician who told Millie that "a feeding tube might perk up" her mother is not unusual in his thinking. Unfortunately, a number of clinicians of various disciplines remain ill-informed about specifics of end-of-life care for a frail, older person. They adhere to ingrained practice patterns that may be inconsistent with the current standard of care. In this physician's case, it would have been wiser for him to reserve comment and refer Millie to Ms. L's own physician or the hospice physician, who were both more familiar with Ms. L's overall diagnosis and prognosis as well as accepted standards of care. Short of that, he could also have discussed the role of substituted judgment in making treatment decisions for others.

Dr. Smith's voiced opinion may have been a function of previously learned practice patterns or older professional attitudes toward care at the end of life. Traditionally, medicine was a paternalistic profession, with patient and family wishes being secondary to the physician's opinion and practice. Not until 1980 did the American Medical Association change its Code of Ethics to acknowledge patients' rights (Veatch, 2003). Nursing, for many decades, deferred to physicians, supporting and defending them, often to the detriment of the patient (Murphy, 1984). Social work, in contrast, founded on the premise of self-determination (Reamer, 2006), historically was out of sync with medicine and nursing. In the past several decades, life-saving technologies have been developed and a very informed lay public has become more knowledgeable and demanded a voice in decision making (Arras and Steinbock, 1999). The views of medicine and nursing changed over time, and all three professions perceive respect for patient autonomy as their highest ethical value. Dr. Smith's opinion, while well-intentioned, was based on a lack of understanding and full knowledge of the medical situation and ethical treatment decision making, and subsequently contributed to Ms. L's prolonged dying process.

There was an assumption on the part of both the hospice team and the nursing home team that many of Ms. L's family's wishes were culturally driven (Ms. L had grown up in South Korea). Over the extended period that the teams spent with the family, particularly Millie, however, the family's culture did not appear to be an issue. The beliefs about filial piety that have traditionally been associated with the Korean culture seem to diminish somewhat as members of that group become increasingly assimilated (Han, Choi, Kim, Lee, and Kim, 2008). Ms. L had lived here for several decades and all her children were born in the United States. Over the prolonged period of their interactions, the hospice team and the nursing home team agreed that Millie's situation was unique to Millie and not necessarily a function of her culture.

Nonetheless, this case brings up an issue that clinicians deal with regularly in this country: multiculturalism and the ethical challenges associated with it (Searight and Gafford, 2005). While the use of nursing homes and hospice is relatively commonplace in mainstream American culture, it may be less so in other cultures. Many new immigrants, in particular, come from cultures where care of elders is a family responsibility, and nursing homes are essentially non-existent. In some cultures, speaking about death is contraindicated (Kwak and Haley, 2005), so the use of hospice may not be the norm. Planning for future illness is frowned upon by some cultural groups (Turner, 2002). Truth-telling, thought of as the norm in this country, is frowned upon in several other cultures (e.g., Surbone, 1992). Preferences for how clinicians should communicate with families vary from one culture to another (Thomas, Wilson, Justice, Birch, and Sheps, 2008). Regulations that we take for granted, such as the Health Insuance Portability and Accountability Act (HIPAA), which limits with whom clinicians may share health information, may be a problem for members of cultures where entire families are an integral part of the decision-making process (Kwak and Haley, 2005). Very patriarchal cultures, where the husband makes all health care decisions, may be difficult for health care professionals in the U.S. to understand, since it seems counter to our ethical perspective on respect for patient autonomy. Pain management in 21st-century medicine has become so prominent that assessing pain has become the fifth vital sign after temperature, pulse, respiration, and blood pressure. Yet in some groups with particular religious beliefs, experiencing pain may be perceived as redemptive in value, with suffering in this life leading to a better afterlife (Doka, 2006).

There is strong encouragement in the health care arena for clinicians to try to familiarize themselves with other cultures to every degree possible. At a minimum, we should have a constant awareness of the need for cultural sensitivity, and encounters with patients and families should include the question, "What do I need to know about you and your culture to be able to give you the best care possible?" Basic knowledge of other cultures is imperative for clinicians to care effectively for those whose ethical practices differ from those in mainstream America.

Another major challenge with the use of hospice in nursing homes is the seemingly opposing goals of the two organizations. As mentioned earlier, nursing homes have traditionally focused on restoration and rehabilitation. Thus, those who are employed in this setting aim for the nursing home resident under their care to get better, if possible, but definitely not to get worse. Work with certified nursing assistants (CNAs) in nursing homes suggests that their primary goal is to "keep their resident going" (Burack and Chichin, 2001). In addition, because the long-term relationships that develop between CNAs and nursing home residents become so emotionally close, the dying and death of residents under their care are quite traumatic to them. They are very proprietary about their residents, and see those for whom they care as "their" patients, believing they know what is best for them. "Turning them over to hospice" represents failure and loss. This view can potentially delay a hospice referral, thereby preventing both the nursing home resident and the family from receiving optimum end-of-life care and survivor support.

This perception, in many nursing homes, goes all the way to the top. Administrators may feel that bringing hospice into their facilities is a clear indication that their own end-of-life care is inadequate. Perhaps even more challenging is that many administrators associate a financial disincentive with Medicare reimbursement. If, for example, a person with a terminal illness and complex medical needs requires nursing home care, the facility will receive a significantly higher rate if the patient is admitted as a subacute patient reimbursed through Medicare Part A. If that same patient is admitted as a hospice patient, under the Medicare Hospice Benefit, the reimbursement to the nursing home will be much lower (Stevenson and Bramson, 2009). Successful nursing home–hospice partnerships generally embody mutual respect, awareness, and accommodation of the respective needs of both programs from administrators and clinical staff (Miller, 2009).

Another ethical issue that was not in the forefront but may be the elephant in the room is allocation of resources. A review of pharmacy records revealed that the cost of Ms. L's antibiotics over the long term outpaced the medication costs of any other long-term care resident. Given Ms. L's advanced disease and terminal prognosis, some may question the wisdom of this approach. Millie had demanded aggressive treatment of her mother's multiple bouts of pneumonia. Accordingly, costly antibiotics were used repeatedly, along with intravenous hydration, which involves personnel expenditures associated with performing an intravenous line insertion and careful monitoring of the infusing fluid. Since Ms. L's comfort was the stated goal, as is the case in hospice care, the symptomatic issues associated with pneumonia could have been managed with opioid medication and nasal oxygen at a much lower cost. The potential for this kind of situation to become a more visible issue at some point is great as the emphasis on minimizing health care costs grows.

DECISION

The clinicians involved in the case of Ms. L felt, for the most part, that her care was not based on a single discrete decision, but was rather a work in progress. The initial family decision (made in collaboration with the nursing home team) to refer Ms. L to hospice was just the beginning. This decision clearly was in Ms. L's best interests, given her terminal prognosis and her evident decline. In view of the fact that Ms. L could not speak for herself and had left no written or oral directives, the best-interest approach is ethically appropriate.

When it came to the feeding tube, as noted earlier, the hospice team strongly disagreed with the family's decision. Their clinical expertise, based on current standards of care, suggested strongly that this treatment was not in Ms. L's best interest. However, in treating the patient and family as the unit of care, as is standard in hospices, both the nursing home and the hospice teams supported the family through and after the decision. Supporting this decision, however, presented an ongoing challenge to the hospice team. As time went on and Ms. L endured repeated bouts of pneumonia, the hospice team felt that this approach had not necessarily resulted in maximum comfort for Ms. L.

Nonetheless, the hospice team worked closely with the nursing home team to manage the symptoms Ms. L manifested, and Carlos was spending increasing amounts of time with Millie, providing outreach and emotional support.

Over many months, as Ms. L continued to experience acute events that were managed by aggressive, somewhat costly treatments, the hospice considered and reconsidered its role. The decision by the hospice team to disenroll Ms. L from hospice was made after much thoughtful discussion. As noted earlier, this decision was influenced by the family's insistence on a plan of care inconsistent with hospice goals, as well as the hospice's concern about regulatory standards. By the time Ms. L was disenrolled from hospice, even the nursing home team began to question the wisdom of decisions involving treating her repeated infections with intravenous antibiotics or sending her to the hospital for various acute events. On one hand, her death in the hospital was surprising to them, since she had survived so many other crises. On the other hand, it was somewhat anticlimactic.

AFTERWORD

Both the hospice team and the nursing home team regarded this experience as one of their most challenging. Perhaps because it was a work in progress until its unfortunate end, or perhaps *because* of its unfortunate end, the case of Ms. L tended to be perceived by both the hospice and nursing home teams as a failure. By the time Ms. L died (and not peacefully in the nursing home, as the hospice would have preferred), both teams saw her dying as having been unnecessarily prolonged by burdensome treatments. Nonetheless, it was a learning experience for all. In the many months after her death, the hospice team and the nursing home team involved in her care still spoke of Ms. L and her family and the difficulties they had all experienced in the time she had been under their care. Although they all questioned themselves and replayed the entire case, no amount of retrospection has brought forth suggestions of other approaches they could have taken with this family. However, the situation provided a number of implications for both education and practice. Indeed, this has proved to be an excellent teaching case for students from a variety of clinical disciplines.

CONCLUSIONS

The use of hospice in the nursing home has proven benefits; there is evidence of enhanced symptom management, greater family satisfaction with care, better end-of-life education for staff, and the availability of bereavement support for survivors (Stevenson and Bramson, 2009). However, the use of hospice in the nursing home is not without its challenges. Among these are turf issues, since the nursing home staff assumes they have ownership of the patient, and the hospice perceives the patient to be their's. This situation requires perhaps more sensitivity on the part of the hospice since they are the outsider in the nursing home setting. In the case of the teams caring for Ms. L and her family, the hospice had had a longstanding collaborative relationship with the nursing home, and their gentleness in approaching the nursing home team was consistent. Nonetheless, subtle differences of opinion continued to emerge from time to time, most notably around the insertion of the feeding tube and the repeated hospitalizations.

The differing (some would say contrasting) philosophies of nursing homes and hospice present significant challenges. As noted earlier, nursing homes have long focused on restoration and rehabilitation. Thus, those who are employed in them see "making people better" as their goal. The prolongation of life, no matter the level of decline or illness, is often paramount to them. Hospice, on the other hand, recognizing the terminal status of those under their care, focuses on maximizing the quality of each remaining day by minimizing pain and discomfort and providing high levels of psychosocial and spiritual support. This approach is viewed by many in the nursing home as an attempt to rush the dying process, at worst; at best, it may be seen as "just letting them die."

All these perceptions strongly suggest the need for ongoing education for nursing home staff with respect to the terminal nature of many of the conditions that afflict the nursing home population. Education is particularly necessary with respect to advanced dementia, which is often not recognized as a terminal illness. Over time, nursing home clinicians regularly see the natural dying process of persons with dementia prolonged by burdensome treatments. This becomes the norm. The inevitability of their deaths remains, but staff often fail to understand that the use of these treatments only serves to make the process of dying more burdensome. Ongoing palliative care education, gently and skillfully provided, can hopefully effect a change in the thinking of many nursing home staff. The move to change the culture in nursing homes to a more homelike and less medicalized environment may also provide fertile ground for this way of thinking to grow.

Lack of education was perhaps most starkly evident in the interaction between the community physician and Ms. L's daughter Millie. Although not technically a part of the nursing home team, Dr. Smith had been seeing patients at the home for well over a decade and was well known to the staff. While no nursing staff in the home actually verbalized his view that "a feeding tube might perk her up," it is likely they were feeling the same thing. Contrary to the high turnover common in many nursing homes, many of the nursing assistants in this facility had been employed there for 15 to 20 years. Thus, they had seen numerous end-stage dementia patients survive for a few years with a feeding tube in place, inserted at a time when such treatment was considered the norm for this population. Dr. Smith, in nursing home practice for about 25 years, had a similar history, and had clearly not updated his thinking to the current standard of care.

Dr. Smith's off-the-cuff suggestion precipitated a cascade of events that included the use of burdensome treatments, return to a lower baseline, use of more treatments, and increased hospitalizations. The many months in which this cycle repeated itself were troubling to the hospice team but only in the final few weeks to the nursing home team. This situation was the impetus for enhanced in-service education for the medical and nursing teams in the nursing home. Since the current standard of care for end-stage dementia patients strongly suggests the avoidance of a number of burdensome technologies (Martin and Sabbagh, 2011), and there is a fair amount of evidence to support this (Finucane, Christmas, and Travis, 1999; Gillick, 2000), the nursing home's clinical leadership hoped to avoid situations similar to this in the future.

A particular challenge for nursing homes with respect to dementia care is determining prognosis. One of the most prevalent diagnoses in the long-term care setting, dementia in its late stages has a very different presentation than the many diseases, such as cancer and end-stage organ illnesses, commonly seen in hospice. Although there are prognostic criteria for dementia (Tsai and Arnold, 2009), often the person with this disease outlives the prognosis. In some cases, the person stabilizes sufficiently enough to be discharged from hospice. Hospice disenrollment in these cases may be more difficult for the family than for the nursing home resident, who is likely unaware of what is happening. From the family's perspective, their loved one is losing the added services (weekly nursing, social work and pastoral care visits, care from a home health aide, etc.) and the family is losing the psychosocial, spiritual, and eventual bereavement support available to them through hospice.

In Ms. L's situation, however, stabilization of her condition was not the reason for discharge. Rather, it was the family's desire not to pursue an appropriate hospice plan of care and instead demand ongoing aggressive treatment intended to prolong her dying. While the need to do this was distressing to the hospice team, they were essentially obligated to discharge her in order to follow the guidelines established by Medicare.

Hospices excel in recognizing and treating symptoms whose manifestations may go unnoticed by clinicians not trained in hospice care. Disenrollment from hospice, with its accompanying decrease in symptom oversight and management, could potentially be associated with increased suffering on the part of the patient. Unfortunately, an accurate assessment of symptoms in end-stage dementia is difficult to achieve. Clinicians only have their best guess and some carefully crafted assessment tools—for example, the Pain Assessment in Advanced Dementia (PainAD) (Warden, Hurley, and Volicer, 2003)—that may not necessarily yield definitive results. Suffering on the part of the family was also a possibility without the added support of the hospice team.

Another major challenge in providing hospice care in nursing homes is the large number of team members involved in care (Chichin and Mezey, 2002). Between the hospice and the nursing home teams, more than ten direct caregivers may be involved in any one case. Other temporary workers may drift in and out, supplementing the regular staff. Accordingly, there are numerous opportunities for communication breakdown. Hospice–nursing home collaborations need to be aware of the need for close communication about all aspects of care, including goals, symptoms, treatments, and psychosocial and spiritual issues affecting both the family and the patient. Failure to do so can have deleterious effects not only on patient care but also on interpersonal relationships among the caregiving staff.

Complex families will always be a challenge for health care providers. In the case of Ms. L, the hospice team was continually troubled by the contrast between what her family was requesting and what seemed to be in Ms. L's best interest. Best interest is a compelling concept. Who should determine what best interest is? Although the unit of care in hospice is the family, Ms. L is the identified patient. Given the family's involvement and the cultural considerations in this case, who is best suited to determine what is in her best interest? Is there any possibility that if Ms. L could speak for herself she would or would not want her care team to use every attempt to maintain her life? As Lo (2009) reminds us, problems with best interest are common and controversial. The individuals involved in this situation might have considered accessing an ethics committee for added support and information (Post,

Blustein, and Dubler, 2007). Although the ethics committee will not issue a mandate, it may provide some expertise and additional dialogue and offer clinicians some peace of mind.

Another possible use for the ethics committee is the discussion of expensive antibiotics (or other costly mechanisms) in the face of end-stage disease when other more modestly-priced comfort-inducing options are available. Again, this may just be an opportunity for further reflection and not a concrete solution, but as budgetary issues become more prominent in health care, allocation of resources is likely to become an even more visible issue.

The use of hospice in nursing homes is clearly a positive. A significant body of literature supports the fact that with hospice referral, we see enhanced symptom management, greater family satisfaction with care, better end-of-life education, and bereavement support for survivors. However, merging hospice care with nursing home care is not without its challenges. If we are to provide the optimum level of patient care, there is an ethical mandate to use the best methods available whenever possible. To achieve that goal, unless and until nursing homes are able to provide superb palliative care on their own, hospice is the answer.

Eileen R. Chichin, PhD, RN, served as codirector of the Greenberg Center on Ethics and Palliative Care at Jewish Home Lifecare. Dr. Chichin's role at the Jewish Home included the implementation of clinical palliative care initiatives at two of the home's nursing home campuses as well as its community service division. In addition to her clinical responsibilities, Dr. Chichin was a member of the Home's Research Institute on Aging and has been the principal investigator and coinvestigator on a number of grant-supported projects focusing on palliative care and end-of-life ethical issues affecting patients and nursing home staff. Her publications and presentations focus on end-of-life issues in the long-term care setting. In addition to numerous journal articles, she is a coauthor of the chapter, Palliative Care in the Nursing Home, in Morrison and Meier's Geriatric Palliative Care (2003, Oxford University Press); the lead author of End-of-Life Ethics and the Nursing Assistant (2000, Springer); and a coeditor of Controversies in Ethics in Long-term Care (1995, Springer).

Jim Palmer, MSW, LCSW, is a clinical social worker with The Lilian and Benjamin Hertzberg Palliative Care Institute at Mount Sinai Medical Center in New York City. The Institute is part of the Brookdale Department of Geriatric and Palliative Medicine. In his role, Mr. Palmer serves as social worker in several hospital settings, including the Palliative Care Consult Service, the Wiener Family Palliative Care Unit (opened in June 2011), and the Palliative Care Outpatient Clinic located in the Martha Stewart Center for Living. Before coming to Mount Sinai, Mr. Palmer's previous clinical work was in the arenas of outpatient oncology, home-based and institutional hospice, and long-term care. Mr. Palmer has many professional affiliations and serves as board member and program committee chair for the West Side Inter-Agency Council for the Aging, New York City's first interagency council.

REFERENCES

Arras, J., & Steinbock, B. (1999). Moral reasoning in the medical context. In J. Arras & B. Steinbock (Eds.). *Ethical issues in modern medicine.* Mountainview, CA: Mayfield.

Blackhall, L. J., Frank, G., Murphy, S. T., Michel, V., Palmer, J. M., & Azen, S. P. (1999). Ethnicity and attitudes toward life-sustaining technology. *Social Science and Medicine, 48*(12), 1779–1789.

Burack, O. R., & Chichin, E. R. (2001). A support group for nursing assistants: Caring for nursing home residents at the end of life. *Geriatric Nursing, 22*(6), 299–305.

Chichin, E. R., & Mezey, M. D. (2002). Professional attitudes toward end-of-life decision-making. In M. D. Mezey, C. K. Cassel, M. M. Bottrell, K. Hyer, J. L. Howe, & T. T. Fulmer (Eds.). *Ethical patient care: A casebook for geriatric health care team* (pp. 67–82). Baltimore, MD: Johns Hopkins University Press.

Doka, K. J. (2006). Social, cultural, spiritual, and psychological barriers to pain management. In K. J. Doka (Ed.). *Pain management at the end of life.* Washington, DC: Hospice Foundation of America.

Finucane, T. E., Christmas, C., & Travis, S. (1999). Tube feeding in patients with advanced dementia: A review of the evidence. *Journal of the American Medical Association, 282*(14), 1365–1370.

Gillick, M. (2000). Rethinking the role of tube feeding in patients with advanced dementia. *New England Journal of Medicine, 342*, 206–210.

Han, H. R, Choi, Y. J, Kim, M. T., Lee, J. E., & Kim, K. B. (2008). Experiences and challenges of informal caregiving for Korean immigrants. *Journal of Advanced Nursing 63*(5), 517–526.

Hanson, L. C., Henderson, M., & Menon, M. (2002). As individual as death itself: A focus group study of terminal care in nursing homes. *Journal of Palliative Medicine, 4*(1), 117–125.

Kwak, J., & Haley, W. E. (2005). Current research findings on end-of-life decision-making among racially or ethnically diverse groups. *Gerontologist, 45*(5), 634–641.

Lo, B. (2009). *Resolving ethical dilemmas: A guide for clinicians* (4th Ed.) New York: Lipincott, Williams & Wilkins.

Martin, G. A., & Sabbagh, M. N. (2011). *Palliative care for advanced Alzheimer's and dementia*. New York: Springer.

Martz, K. & Gerding, A. (2011). Perceptions of coordination of care between hospices and skilled nursing facility care providers. *Journal of Hospice and Palliative Nursing, 13*(4), 210–219.

Miller, S. (2009). A model for successful nursing home-hospice partnerships. *Journal of Palliative Medicine, 13*(5), 525–533.

Murphy, C. P. (1984). The changing role of nurses in making ethical decisions. *Law, Medicine & Health Care, 12,* 173–175, 184.

Post, L. F. Blustein, J., & Dubler, N. N. (2007). *Handbook for healthcare ethics committees*. Baltimore, MD: Johns Hopkins University Press.

Reamer, F., (2006). *Social work values and ethics* (3rd Ed.). New York: Columbia University Press.

Searight, H. R., & Gafford, J. (2005). Cultural diversity at the end of life: Issues and guidelines for family physicians. *American Family Physician, 71*(3), 515–522.

Standards and Accreditation Committee, Medical Guidelines Taskforce. (1996). *National Hospice and Palliative Care Organization*. Alexandria, VA: NHPCO.

Stevenson, D. G., & Bramson, J. S. (2009). Hospice care in the nursing home setting: A review of the literature. *Journal of Pain and Symptom Management, 38*(3), 440–451.

Surbone, A. (1992). Truth-telling to the patient. *Journal of the American Medical Association, 268,* 1661–1662.

Tsai, S., & Arnold, R. (2009). Prognostication in dementia. Fast facts and concepts. Retrieved from www.eperc.mcu/fastfact/ff_150.htm

Turner, L. (2002). Bioethics and end-of-life care in multi-ethnic settings: Cultural diversity in Canada and the USA. *Mortality, 7*(3), 285–301.

Veatch, R. (2003). *The basics of bioethics.* (2nd Ed.) Upper Saddle River, NJ: Prentice Hall.

Warden, V., Hurley, A. C., & Volicer, L. (2003). Development and psychometric evaluation of the pain assessment in advanced dementia (PAINAD) scale. *Journal of the American Medical Directors Association, 4,* 9–15.

CHAPTER 12

Unjust Demands for Futile Treatment: When Treatment Should Cease

Mary Beth Morrissey

This chapter addresses family requests or demands for non-beneficial or futile treatment in light of ethical considerations bearing on when treatment should cease. These issues are examined within the larger social and cultural contexts of what "care" means and how such meanings of care are distinguished from "treatment." The author also recognizes the significance to this discussion of well-established human rights to health and adequate health care under international covenants (Sen, 2008; United Nations, 1948; Wronka, 2008).

One of the biggest challenges today for seriously ill individuals, their loved ones, and their health care professionals is accessing and deepening understanding of lived-through meanings of care. The hospice and palliative care movements have made significant contributions to expanding consciousness of an ethic of care. In the structure of hospice and palliative care, the provision of care remains essential and invariant. While treatment may cease or the intensity of care may vary, care never ceases. Instead of focusing solely on the legal rights of the individual patient, a palliative ethic of care (Fins, 2006) is concerned primarily with moral relationships, the ethical encounter between the provider of care and care recipient, and a moral obligation to provide empathic care in the contexts of relationship and community (Byock, 2002; Zoloth-Dorfman, 1993). At the heart of the transformative philosophy of hospice and palliative care is a therapeutic model that moves away from the conventional medical model of objective disease-diagnosis and treatment. In care ethics having a palliative intent and purpose, a radical turn is made to a person- and family-centered social unit of care, giving primacy to the subjective experiences, wishes, values, and preferences of the patient and family in goal setting, advance care planning, and decision making. This ethical and ecological turn is rooted in core notions of solidarity, mutual aid and full civic participation in global public health (Jennings, 2007; Prainsack and Buyx, 2011).

Escalating costs of health care and regional variations in spending and care utilization have generated heated debate as part of health care reform efforts. Specifically, there is much disagreement over what is adequate care, especially for those who are seriously ill with an advanced life-limiting or life-threatening condition. Ironically, in the policy debates that raged fiercely in the period leading up to the federal health reform legislation in 2010 (Affordable Care Act, 2010), concerns about access to care for the uninsured or underinsured, health disparities, or values of adequacy, equity, and health care justice (Sulmasy, 2003) were subsidiary to concerns about limits on resource use for those who already have health benefits such as those with employment-based health insurance or Medicare benefits. Most Americans have been reluctant to accept any limits on resource use or any form of explicit rationing that might be seen as an infringement upon their liberty. Except for public discourse about implicit and explicit forms of rationing in which Daniel Callahan (2011) has dared to engage us, myths persist among a broad swath of Americans who continue to believe that higher spending and unlimited resource use mean better quality of care. Not surprisingly, new research in the international community indicates that individual differences in educational levels influence access to specialist palliative care services and general end-of-life care (Bossuyt et al., 2011).

How are hospice and palliative care changing this picture? First, evidence continues to mount that both hospice and palliative care are successful health care delivery systems that are effective models in saving costs (Morrison and Meier, 2011). For patients in serious illness or at the end of life, these systems also are associated with good outcomes such as controlling pain and symptoms, optimizing quality of life, providing comfort care including comfort feeding, and in some instances extending survival (Mitchell et al., 2009; Palacek et al., 2010; Temel et al., 2010). The most recent report card from the Center to Advance Palliative Care reports more than a doubling in hospital-based palliative care programs across the country over the last decade due to the growing prevalence of chronic illness (Morrison and Meier, 2011). Overall, hospice utilization has increased dramatically as well. The rate of increase in some health care sectors has drawn the attention of federal regulators (Office of Inspector General, 2011), who continue to demonstrate a somewhat limited understanding of the complexity of the needs of the non-cancer terminally ill population served by hospice. In 2009, over 1 million Medicare beneficiaries received hospice services from approximately 3,500 providers (Medicare Payment Advisory Commission [MedPAC], 2011). The average length of stay for Medicare decedents in 2009 was 86 days, an increase of 32 days from 2000 (MedPAC, 2011). According to MedPAC, this change is related to longer stays among patients with the longest stays reflecting the chronicity of illness in this patient population.

Yet concerns persist about the grounds for withholding and withdrawing life-sustaining treatments for seriously ill individuals who may be subjected to prolonged pain and suffering due to unnecessary or avoidable medical treatments. Although the evaluation of end-of-life options is often associated with hospice and palliative care, evaluation also takes place at the hospital bedside, in nursing homes and assisted living residences, or as part of appropriate advance care planning—sometimes well before the onset of illness. What is common to all these experiences is evaluation, or the decision process of valuing one's care choices. Patients who are living through illness and suffering burden, or anticipate such lived experiences, go through a process of attaching value attributes to their suffering experiences in which their emotions play a strong role (Morrissey, 2011a). Suffering persons may value life-prolonging treatments negatively based upon their emotional responses and states as they discern that these treatments will heighten their suffering burden without providing any benefit such as improving function or quality of life.

There are important distinctions to be made between care that is beneficial, nonbeneficial, or only marginally beneficial (Jennings and Morrissey, 2011). Decisions about beneficial and nonbeneficial care engender less disagreement. However, there may be reasonable disagreement in the marginally beneficial category concerning the medical outcomes for patients, their suffering and illness burden, and how they would value such experiences (Jennings and Morrissey, 2011). These distinctions are made in the context of a decision process implemented in different types of care settings with a range of restrictions. Although it is impossible to provide an exhaustive review of such variations in this chapter, the following brief descriptions of therapeutic care models and care settings are provided to help clarify what patients may face when navigating care transitions and negotiating the evaluation and decision process in serious illness.

Palliative care Palliative care is a therapeutic model of care and a delivery system that can provide both disease-modifying therapy and varying levels of care to the patient, depending upon the patient's medical needs and goals of care. Palliative care can be provided as part of hospice or outside of hospice, i.e., nonhospice palliative care. "Upstream palliative care" is the term used to describe palliative care that targets chronically ill individuals in earlier stages of illness. Typically, as a patient's serious illness progresses, the balance shifts from principally curative to more intensive levels of palliative and comfort care (Fins, 2006). Palliative care can be accessed in the hospital, in the nursing home, or in the community, and generally aims to: (a) strengthen communication among patients, family members, surrogates, and health professionals; (b) improve care coordination; (c) enhance quality of life; and (d) relieve pain and suffering.

Hospice care Hospice care is a comprehensive interdisciplinary care program that provides pain and symptom management as well as psychosocial, emotional, and spiritual support services to patients. While there is sometimes confusion about the relationship between hospice and palliative care, hospice care is a form or subset of palliative care (Jennings, Ryndes, D'Onofrio, and Baily, 2003) that serves patients who have been certified by their physician to have a life expectancy of six months or less. This eligibility criterion is a requirement of the Medicare Hospice Benefit (MHB), the primary financing mechanism for hospice care. As a result of the MHB, access to hospice care is more restrictive than palliative care. Regular Medicare coverage is suspended for beneficiaries who elect the MHB and thereby agree to forgo curative or conventional medical treatment (MedPAC, 2011). Providers are reimbursed only for services that are primarily palliative and have a palliative intent, except for items and services covered by Medicare unrelated to the terminal illness. Nevertheless, as an exception to the general rule, some hospices have "open access" policies that permit certain curative or disease-modifying treatments at the same time as comfort care.

Many hospice patients upon enrollment in hospice consent to a Do Not Resuscitate (DNR) order, which is an order to forgo cardiopulmonary resuscitation (CPR)—a life-sustaining treatment—when there is no pulse or breathing. A DNR order can be evidence of a first type of end-of-life decision making by seriously ill patients or their surrogate decision makers (Fins, 2006), especially in electing a transition to hospice care. Hospice patients or their surrogates may also consent to a written hospice plan of care that provides for the withdrawal or withholding of life-sustaining treatments.

Hospital-based care Increasingly, hospital-based care is providing access to both hospital-based palliative care programs and hospice. Program models may vary from hospital to hospital. Patients or their surrogates will evaluate their palliative and end-of-life options as part of the decision-making process in the hospital. Transfers to acute settings may add additional complexity to the evaluation and decision-making process, especially as such transfers typically involve curative approaches to care and evaluation of more aggressive treatment options.

Nursing home care Nursing homes also provide hospice care and, in many instances, integrate palliative care into the institution's standards of care. Nursing home residents who are nonhospice residents, or their surrogates, evaluate palliative and end-of-life options as part of making medical decisions. Decisions involving the withholding or withdrawal of life-sustaining treatment in nursing homes may be subject to additional restrictions, such as ethics committee review. (This is the case in New York State.)

Community-based care Hospice care is provided to patients in the community. Innovative models of palliative care are also being embedded in the community. Patients in the community must go through the same decision evaluation process as patients in hospitals and nursing homes, and must weigh their palliative and end-of-life options. DNR orders, and to a lesser extent Do Not Intubate (DNI) orders, are typically available in the community. However, in the community, surrogates may be subject to restrictions when it comes to other types of life-sustaining treatment decisions.

It is clear that the available range of treatment options and variety of treatment settings can be confusing to patients and those who are supporting them, including their health care professionals. The structural complexity in health care and health care decision making—in particular, decision making about end-of-life options—requires comprehensive education for professionals and patients. In most cases, education lags behind the implementation curve of new laws and regulations. This complexity and lack of knowledge create fertile ground for conflict when a loved one is sick. Such conflict frequently occurs within the family and if it cannot be resolved through informal processes or ethics committee review, it may escalate and end up in the courts. This is an undesirable outcome for everyone involved. How do physicians and other health care professionals adhere to their professional ethical responsibilities while family members make demands for treatments that may be often nonbeneficial or marginally beneficial, and could be described as "futile"? How can cases that are conflict-laden be kept out of the courts?

FUTILE TREATMENT: HOW IS IT DEFINED?

The term "futility" has more than one meaning when used to describe medical treatment. In its original formulation, futile treatment means an intervention that is not effective or would not be successful. The treatment evaluation is based upon physiologic evidence of treatment failure or ineffectiveness. According to Fins (2006), futility can be understood both quantitatively and qualitatively. Using the narrowest physiologic basis, a determination of futility is tied to failure in the last 100 cases, although application of this measure in the clinical setting poses challenges (Fins, 2006). Fins (2006) explains that "futile" literally means "leaky," or a holding that is physically impossible or unable to be sustained. For example, under New York's prior DNR law (NY PHL Art. 29-B), a DNR order could be entered upon consent by a surrogate to a finding by two physicians that CPR "will be unsuccessful in restoring cardiac and respiratory function or that the patient will experience repeated arrest in a short time period before death occurs." This standard, which is no longer law in New York, established medical futility as a clinical criterion for consent to a DNR order. In practice, in the absence of a DNR order, a physician may make a medically appropriate ethical decision to halt resuscitative efforts that are unsuccessful in restoring cardiac or respiratory function when a patient experiences a cardiac arrest on grounds of physiologic futility (Fins, 2006).

However, futility has taken on a broader meaning of having no benefit for the patient in ways that go beyond physiological evidence, that is, failing to improve quality of life or function, or failing to relieve pain and suffering. Within the penumbras of this multidimensional meaning of futility is the much greater difficulty of navigating decisions about when treatment should cease. Fins (2006) correctly points out that most futility disputes about what constitutes medically and ethically appropriate care arise from communication breakdowns among the patient, family, and physician.

CASE

A recent court decision in New York is illustrative of both the complexity of end-of-life decision making and the role of family conflict. The case of *Matter of Zornow* (2010) involved a 93-year-old woman, Mrs. Joan M. Zornow, who resided in a nursing home and had advanced Alzheimer's disease. This is not an uncommon situation in nursing homes in the United States. The majority of nursing home residents are chronically ill, frail elderly women, many of whom will at some point in their illness trajectory experience some form of cognitive impairment (Bern-Klug, 2010; Mitchell et al., 2009). In a multisite study of nursing home residents with advanced dementia conducted by Mitchell and colleagues (2009), over 85% of the study participants were women, and Alzheimer's disease was found to be the most prevalent type of dementia.

As she approached the end of her life, Mrs. Zornow had a number of things in her favor that might have prevented adverse outcomes. First and foremost, she was blessed with seven children (*Zornow*, 2010). In addition, she had a DNR order in place. Mrs. Zornow also had two MOLST orders, or medical orders for life-sustaining treatment, signed by a physician that documented her wishes to forgo artificial nutrition and hydration.

However, as is also not uncommon, a conflict arose between one daughter and the six other children about Mrs. Zornow's wishes. In response to a petition to the court for the appointment of a guardian, the court made a number of findings, revoked the MOLST orders, and appointed co-guardians for Mrs. Zornow to make decisions based upon Catholic teaching (*Zornow*, 2010). This case was decided under New York's recently enacted and implemented Family Health Care Decisions Act, effective June, 2010 (N.Y. Pub. Health Law [PHL] Art. 29-CC), authorizing public health law surrogates to make decisions for incapable patients who have neither appointed a health care agent nor have any prior directives.

Below is a summary of the court's findings and order as reported by Mental Hygiene Legal Services:

> A guardian of the person was appointed to make major medical and end-of-life medical decisions as the statutory surrogate under the Family Health Care Decision Act (FHCDA) for a ward who was a devout Catholic. Under FHCDA the guardian was obliged to make that decision in accordance with the ward's religious beliefs. The Court observed the irony that with respect to artificial hydration and nutrition, had there been a health care proxy (HCP) executed in favor of a most trusted friend or relative, the statutory presumption would have been in favor of artificial hydration and nutrition, but absent the HCP, under the FHCDA, the presumption is against it because the "quality of life" ethic is paramount under the FHCDA rather than the "sanctity of life" ethic. The court discusses in great detail Catholic

doctrine, and concludes that under the "sanctity of life" doctrine of the Church, in nearly every instance, hydration and nutrition, even when administered artificially, are considered by the Church to be "ordinary" rather than "extraordinary" measures, and that hydration and nutrition must be administered except under certain very rare and narrow exceptions which are also discussed in great detail. The court also holds that with respect to end-of-life decisions, the guardians should consult with and obtain the advice of a priest or someone well trained in Catholic moral theology, as is recommended for in the Catholic Guide to End-of-Life Decisions by the National Catholic Bioethics Center. (Mental Hygiene Legal Service, Second Judicial Department, 2011, p. 98).

As this summary suggests, everything that could have gone awry with this case did so, including the court decision itself. It is also of note that, in the full decision, a very lengthy discussion of Catholic dogma manages to significantly muddy the waters as to what Catholic teaching and moral tradition are in the areas of artificial nutrition and hydration and withholding and withdrawal of life-sustaining treatments (Sulmasy, 2006; Tuohey, 2010; US Conference of Catholic Bishops, 2009). This intense and inappropriate focus on the teaching of a particular faith draws attention away from the central issues in the case, which I discuss more fully below, and their relevance to futile treatments and medically and ethically appropriate care.

ANALYSIS

In light of the complex medical, social, legal, and ethical issues involved in the case selected for discussion, I identify the following questions that are helpful in analyzing the case and guiding the discussion:

- *Who is the resident? What are the resident's known social and medical history, and current clinical diagnoses?*
- *Does the resident have capacity? If not, are there prior directives? Is there an identified surrogate decision maker?*
- *What are the proposed and alternative treatments that are in issue?*
- *What are the goals of care?*
- *Does treatment hold any promise for recovery?*
- *What is the evaluation of the resident's suffering and illness burden?*

- *What values enter into the evaluation of benefits and burdens, and appropriate care?*
- *Is life-sustaining treatment medically and ethically appropriate?*
- *What informal processes are available in the clinical setting to resolve conflict?*
- *What is the role of the institutional ethics committee?*

Description of resident, resident's history, and diagnoses Based upon what is known from the court decision, the resident is of advanced age at 93 years old, and has advanced Alzheimer's disease (*Zornow*, 2010; Makofsky, 2011). The resident has been residing in a nursing home in New York State. The court describes the irreversible nature of the resident's condition and how the progression of the disease increases the risks of developing swallowing difficulties and secondary infections that may lead to death (*Zornow*, 2010). Advanced dementia is generally viewed and accepted as an irreversible and incurable illness, among the leading causes of death in the US (Palacek et al., 2010). Mitchell and colleagues (2009) describe patients with advanced dementia as being at "end-stage" while not always appropriately recognized as such. Consequently, these patients are also at risk for receiving less than optimal palliative care. Therefore, based upon this evidence, we may comfortably conclude that Mrs. Zornow is likely approaching the end of her life, although she may not meet the definition of terminally ill for the purposes of the MHB or other statutory criteria.

In her early illness and prior to being admitted to the nursing home, we learn from the court record that Mrs. Zornow was taken care of by her daughter, Carole Zornow, who has petitioned the court to be her guardian (Makofsky, 2011; *Zornow*, 2010). There are six other siblings who are involved in their mother's care issues. The court appointed Carole Zornow and her brother, Douglas, as temporary co-guardians in July, 2010. The final order of the court appoints Carole Zornow and a Catholic agency to be co-guardians for Mrs. Zornow.

Capacity, prior directives, and surrogacy We can infer from the court's decision that at the time this matter came before the court in May 2010, Mrs. Zornow probably did not have capacity to make decisions. She had never appointed a health care agent under New York State Law (Makofsky, 2011; *Zornow*, 2010). However, under the Family Health Care Decisions Act that became effective in June, 2010, a guardian is a legally authorized surrogate under the law. Therefore, the guardians appointed by the court for Mrs.

Zornow act as public health law surrogates under the Family Health Care Decisions Act.

With respect to prior directives, Mrs. Zornow had a DNR order and two MOLST orders, executed successively on September 15 and September 18, 2009 (Makofsky, 2011; Zornow, 2010). It is not entirely clear from the court decision who consented to these orders, i.e., whether it was Mrs. Zornow herself while she had capacity or whether "clear and convincing evidence" was used to complete the MOLST forms, which is permissible under New York State law.

The judge in the case, however, appeared unfamiliar with MOLST orders and their legal basis in state law. A MOLST order is a medical order for life-sustaining treatment signed by a physician that has been consented to by the patient (or, if the patient does not have capacity, by the surrogate), and documents the patient's wishes about future care. It is modeled on the national POLST paradigm, or Physician Orders for Life-Sustaining Treatment. The New York Public Health Law was amended in 2008 to permit alternative DNR forms. The MOLST form is an approved New York State Department of Health form that can be used to document DNR, DNI, and Do Not Hospitalize orders, as well as election of certain levels of care (full treatment, limited interventions, comfort care). The MOLST/POLST paradigm is also supported by a strong evidence base that demonstrates its effectiveness in assuring that patient wishes are honored (Hickman et al., 2009; Hickman et al., 2011; Hickman et al., 2010), although a recent research study reported that there is some variation in consistency rates between treatments and POLST orders for feeding tube decisions (63.6%) as compared to other types of decisions (resuscitation, 98%) (Hickman et al., 2011). Charles Sabatino of the American Bar Association and Naomi Karp of AARP (2011) recently collaborated in writing a comprehensive report about POLST that describes its history, how it differs from traditional advance directives, state-by-state developments, and community partnerships that have been instrumental in building support for the paradigm.

The two MOLSTs for Mrs. Zornow contained orders not to initiate the administration of artificial nutrition and hydration, and not to transfer Mrs. Zornow to the hospital unless she had pain or symptoms that could not be controlled in the nursing home (Makofsky, 2011; Zornow, 2010). MOLST orders are appropriate for seriously, chronically ill individuals who may have less than a year to live. Therefore, the MOLST order was an appropriate planning tool for Mrs. Zornow. If Mrs. Zornow were not able to consent to the

MOLST orders herself due to lack of capacity, in the absence of a surrogate, clear and convincing evidence of her wishes could have been used as a basis for completing the MOLST orders. Her son Donald presented evidence at some point that his mother had given verbal instructions to him and his siblings that she did not want life-sustaining artificial nutrition and hydration if she were no longer able to take in food or water orally, although a daughter presented conflicting evidence (Makofsky, 2011; *Zornow*, 2010).

Proposed and alternative treatments The central issue in this case is artificial nutrition and hydration, which is a medical treatment under the applicable statute. The court revoked Mrs. Zornow's prior MOLST orders and limitations on treatment. The surrogate therefore is faced with evaluating two options under the life-sustaining treatment standards of the Family Health Care Decisions Act: consenting to the administration of artificial nutrition and hydration or forgoing life-sustaining artificial nutrition and hydration where the latter would result in Mrs. Zornow's dying a natural death. The second option of forgoing treatment does not mean that Mrs. Zornow would receive no care. The patient still has a right to palliative care.

For a patient who is neither terminally ill nor unconscious and has an irreversible or incurable condition, as is the case for Mrs. Zornow, the standards under which the surrogate must evaluate these two options are the reasonably known wishes of the patient, or if not known, the patient's best interests including the patient's values, and religious and moral beliefs (NY PHL 2994-d[4][a][i]). Additional standards under the Family Health Care Decisions Act that govern life-sustaining treatment decisions are as follows:

> Treatment would involve such pain, suffering or other burden that it would reasonably be deemed inhumane or extraordinarily burdensome under the circumstances **and** patient has an irreversible or incurable condition, as determined by attending physician with concurrence (NY PHL 2994-d.5.)

It should be noted that this standard does not contain any language that explicitly addresses medical futility. In New York, the Family Health Care Decisions Act eliminated the express futility language in the former DNR law (N.Y. PHL Art. 29-B) that provided a separate basis for physiologic evaluation of futility. However, this change does not bar consideration of futility under the standards. The standards are written more broadly to take account of physiologic bases for futility, as well as qualitative assessment of suffering and illness burden (Morrissey, 2011b). Decisions that do not relate to CPR that fall under this standard for residents in a nursing home also have to be reviewed by the institutional ethics review committee (NY PHL Art. 29-CC).

Goals of care, promise for recovery, and evaluation of suffering burden Mrs. Zornow's case calls for evaluation of her suffering and illness burden under the applicable standards. What does that evaluation involve? In order to properly evaluate suffering and illness burden, it is important to know the patient's goals of care. This is a dialogue that continues over time because goals of care change as the patient's clinical course changes. In light of Mrs. Zornow's advanced dementia and irreversible and incurable illness trajectory, the goals of care that would be discussed with the patient's family or surrogate decision maker fall into three possible domains: prolonging life; improving or maintaining quality of life and/or functional status; or potentially modifying or reversing the disease process (Community-wide Clinical Guidelines for Percutaneous Endoscopic Gastrostomy Tube Feeding, 2010).

Values and appropriateness of treatment Decisions about artificial nutrition and hydration, especially tube feeding, tend to create tension and conflict for patients, families, and surrogate decision makers because of the emotional responses involved in making such decisions (Morrissey, 2011a; Sulmasy, 2006). Family members may discern benefits in the use of a feeding tube and rely on such benefits to the extent they would expect that such treatment might allow them to spend more time with their loved ones and help relieve them of feelings of guilt about forgoing treatment options. Discussions about feeding tubes also raise a spectre for the family of choosing between care or no-care options for the family's loved one (Palacek et al., 2010)—a dichotomy that is not well-founded and the source of serious misconceptions about hospice and palliative care.

In Mrs. Zornow's current clinical health status, it is unlikely she would experience benefits in any of the three domains from the proposed treatment. The questions that have to be asked and carefully weighed about the patient's care are:

- *Will treatment make a difference?*
- *Do burdens of treatment outweigh benefits?*
- *Is there hope of recovery?*
- *What does the patient value?* (Bomba, Morrissey, and Leven, 2011).

Mrs. Zornow's clinical, psychosocial, and emotional health status have to be assessed when considering these questions with respect to the proposed medical treatment in light of her suffering and illness burden. Evaluation of pain and suffering requires a multidimensional assessment (Altilio, 2004; Morrissey, 2011a). In conducting such a comprehensive assessment, it is necessary to determine if the burdens that artificial nutrition and hydration would impose on Mrs. Zornow's already compromised systems, compounded by her already existing illness burden, would be outweighed by the benefits.

There is strong evidence that frail elderly residents in nursing homes are at high risk for feeding tubes, and that feeding tube interventions are a medical treatment that is associated with poor outcomes for such persons (Finucane, Christmas and Travis, 1999; Mitchell et al., 2007, 2009; Palacek et al., 2010). Finucane and colleagues (1999) provide clinical evidence that feeding tubes in patients with dementia do not improve survival and can increase risk of aspiration pneumonia, infections, and pressure sores, while providing no clear benefits in terms of improving function or providing comfort. These complications can heighten the patient's pain and suffering. Based upon the clinical evidence, feeding tubes would likely not make a difference in Mrs. Zornow's illness course in terms of recovery, and might actually shorten her survival time.

The alternative for Mrs. Zornow is oral, or careful hand feeding (Palacek et al., 2010). The benefits of oral feeding are enjoyment of the taste and texture of the food, even if what is offered is altered in texture or consistency, and the additional benefits of social interaction that oral feeding brings. There is evidence that everyday acts of feeding and being fed unassisted by technology draw upon maternal dimensions of existence involving maternal holding and relational intimacy (Morrissey, 2011c), essential constituents of good hospice and palliative care. In a study of pain and suffering among frail elderly women, Morrissey (2011c) reported that feeding is a multidimensional lived experience connected to life course maternal foundations and enacted empathic care sought by seriously ill persons at the end of life. Research has also demonstrated that family members find relief in participating in "comfort feeding" (Palacek et al., 2010).

The goals of care discussion for Mrs. Zornow should focus on, among other things, what Mrs. Zornow would value (NY PHL Art. 29-CC). Prior directives, even if not legally valid as stand-alone documents, may be used by the surrogate decision maker as evidence of patient wishes and values. In light of Mrs. Zornow's clinical course as an advanced dementia patient with no promise of recovery, as well as the values her prior directives would appear to reflect not to be subjected to prolonged suffering, discussion about goals of care should focus largely on palliation and comfort care—maintaining the patient's quality of life to the extent possible, reducing pain levels, and preventing and relieving suffering. Aggressive treatments such as surgery, dialysis, chemotherapy, or feeding tubes would, in most cases, be medically inappropriate for an advanced dementia patient. Mrs. Zornow is an appropriate candidate for assessment for hospice care.

New CMS guidance on feeding tubes The U.S. Department of Health and Human Services, Centers for Medicare & Medicaid Services (CMS), has recently made changes to survey guidance for feeding tubes that delineates the following potential benefits or adverse effects of feeding tubes:

> The use of a feeding tube may potentially benefit or may adversely affect a resident's clinical condition and/or psychosocial well-being. Examples of some possible benefits of using a feeding tube may include:
>
> • Addressing malnutrition and dehydration;
>
> • Promoting wound healing;
>
> • Allowing the resident to gain strength, receive appropriate interventions that may help restore the residents' ability to eat and perhaps return to oral feedings.
>
> Examples of some possible adverse effects of using a feeding tube may include:
>
> • Diminishing socialization, including, but not limited to, the close human contact associated with being assisted to eat or being with others at mealtimes;
>
> • Not having the opportunity to experience the taste, texture, and chewing of foods;
>
> • Causing tube-associated complications; and
>
> • Reducing the freedom of movement related to efforts to prevent the resident from pulling on the tube or other requirements related to the tube or the tube feeding.

(CMS, State Operations Manual [SOM], F tag 322, Survey & Certification [S&C]: 11-37-NH).

Further, under this CMS guidance, "avoidable" and "unavoidable" use of feeding tubes is defined as follows:

- "Avoidable" means there is not a clear indication for using a feeding tube or there is insufficient evidence that it provides a benefit that outweighs associated risks.

- "Unavoidable" means there is a clear indication for using a feeding tube or there is sufficient evidence that it provides a benefit that outweighs associated risks. (CMS, SOM, F tag 322, S&C: 11-37-NH).

This guidance may be helpful to nursing home staff in communicating to families the benefits and risks of feeding tubes for their loved ones as illustrated in *Matter of Zornow*.

Unjust demand for medically and ethically inappropriate care Mrs. Zornow's case represents a common scenario. Nevertheless, conflicts such as the ones that arose in this case usually are resolved informally or at the ethics committee level before they reach the courts. We should continue to see the courts as arbiters of last resort.

Similar to the facts of the *Zornow* case, below are the facts of a case provided from a nursing home in Western New York that presents an example of very aggressive medical interventions at the end of life:

> The patient was an 82-year-old male previously incarcerated for murder but paroled years ago. He suffered a debilitating stroke four years ago and subsequently was institutionalized for long term care. During his four years in a skilled nursing facility, the patient became deeply religious and simultaneously convinced that he was going to hell for the murders (he admitted to staff that he'd only been convicted in one of several) he'd committed as a younger man. No amount of pastoral care involvement or discussion of redemption could sway his beliefs, which ultimately became an obsession of sorts. He eventually articulated that he wanted "everything done" in order to delay his trip to Hell. When he lost capacity from a series of small strokes in the SNF, a public Guardian of Person was appointed to his case, about a year ago.

> About six months ago, the patient, who had a long history of COPD, developed pneumonia and then respiratory failure, requiring intubation and mechanical ventilation. The Guardian of Person, knowing of the patient's request that all available treatments be done, requested that the hospital care team follow the patient's previously-stated wishes, so the patient received, in addition to his mechanical ventilation, artificial feeding/hydration and then suffered through several pneumothoraces requiring surgical intervention before dying about three months ago. The patient received very aggressive treatment at the end of life without any likely benefit beyond living "longer" (and, in his belief, avoiding the Devil for a little longer). The hospital care team bridled repeatedly at the aggressiveness of care for the patient's underlying frailty, as they believed that the care was "a waste" of time and money, especially as caregivers came to understand why the patient had requested such aggressive care.

This case demonstrates, as did Mrs. Zornow's, how important social history and social and cultural contexts are to end-of-life decision making. This elderly man's life course experience in the criminal justice system emerged as a critical part of his decision-making process at the end of life. Appropriate social, emotional, and spiritual supports in dealing with the struggles this individual faced are core constituents of good end-of-life care.

Health care justice What steps should be taken when health professionals are faced with requests for treatment interventions that clearly exceed reasonableness in terms of what is medically and ethically appropriate care? Benefits-burdens analysis and evaluation of the patient's suffering are essential tools in clinical ethics. What is also essential is a discussion of health care justice and equitable allocation of scarce resources. The costs of providing medically inappropriate and oftentimes harmful interventions to patients at the end of life cannot be justified on ethical grounds when there are many members of the society who have unmet needs for adequate health care (Jennings and Morrissey, 2011).

In light of these ethical concerns, I endorse the recommendations of the New York State Bar Association Health Law Section Summary Report on Health Care Costs (2009) to: (a) promote clinical practice guidelines in end-of-life care to help reduce use of costly modalities of questionable benefit to the patient; (b) fund comparative effectiveness research to evaluate drugs and treatments used at the end-of-life and their relative costs; (c) formalize in law and policy a definition of treatment that provides no medical benefit other than prolonging death or suffering as "nonbeneficial treatment"; and (d) ensure immunity for decisions to cease nonbeneficial treatment as approved by an ethics committee, or in the alternate, if found consistent with nationally recognized clinical practice guidelines (Davino et al., 2009). Building upon these recommendations, I call for a four-pronged approach to deal with the problem of unreasonable and unjust demand:

- early education for professionals and the community about advance care planning and palliative and end-of-life options;
- improved care coordination, communication, and interdisciplinary team care planning processes;
- ethics consultation and ethics committee review policies, procedures, and practices; and
- consideration of supply-side policy making at the provider systems level consistent with a growing paradigm shift away from individualistic, rights-based frameworks to more communitarian, social, and relational models of care in end-of-life decision making.

RECOMMENDATIONS FOR A FOUR-PRONGED APPROACH

Education There is a widespread consensus that we need to lay much stronger foundations for our health care professionals and our communities in palliative and end-of-life care education and training, particularly in the area of ethics and ethical dilemmas. Content that focuses only on new laws and regulations is not sufficient. The really important education is translating mandates into implementation of meaningful person-centered care on the ground for patients, families, and their health care professionals situated in different health care settings, especially as patients make care transitions from one setting to another. Funding for education and training is desperately needed and will go a long way to relieve the dissemination of misinformation in both the health and legal systems that may be contributing to bad outcomes for patients and families.

Improved care coordination, communication, and interdisciplinary team care planning processes Consistent with the POLST/MOLST evidence-based paradigm and process for documenting goals of care discussions, the decision process about artificial nutrition and hydration and levels of care, such as those at issue in *Matter of Zornow*, as well as other forms of life-sustaining treatment, should begin with early conversations with social workers and other members of the interdisciplinary team. These professionals can explain care options to families and surrogates, including the option to provide "comfort only" feeding to patients for whom tube feeding is not medically or ethically appropriate (Palacek et al., 2010). Goals of care and preference-sensitive treatment decisions can be translated into medical orders and reviewed periodically by the patient's physician and other health care professionals. One of the strengths of social work involvement in the POLST/MOLST program is the opportunity to improve communication and care coordination among patients, physicians, family members, caregivers, and health care agents or surrogates. Communication has been identified as critically important to patient-centered care, the shared decision-making process, and preference-concordant care. Furthermore, effective communication may help to avoid futility disputes (Bomba, Morrissey, and Leven, 2011; Fins, 2006).

Ethics consultation and ethics committee review In New York State, the Family Health Care Decisions Act now mandates that certain cases be reviewed by institutional ethics review committees. In nursing homes, all life-sustaining treatment decisions that involve patients who are neither terminally ill nor permanently unconscious (except for decisions about CPR) are required to be reviewed by the ethics committee. The decisions of the ethics committee in these cases are binding. Even if reviews are not mandated, or in the event of a conflict between a physician and patient, or between surrogates, anyone connected with a case may refer to the ethics committee for advice. Many facilities that have the necessary trained and qualified staff will make ethics consultations available without convening the full ethics committee. Ethics consultations and ethics committees should be seen as essential resources for patients, families, and health care professionals to help resolve disputes where conflict may seem intractable. Ethics committee members must also receive appropriate training instructing them in the serious responsibilities they assume in serving in this role (Morrissey, 2011b). With regard to the two cases referenced in this chapter—*Matter of Zornow* and the case of the 82-year-old parolee who ended up in the hospital—each would have been reviewed by the respective institutional ethics committee under the mandates of the Family Health Care Decisions Act. Assuring that ethics committee members have immunity from liability for their good faith participation in the ethics committee process is also a *sine qua non* of policy making in this area.

Supply-side systems level change Hospice care is a model of care that effectuates change at the system level. Hospice is both a philosophy of care and a delivery system. Patients who consent to and transition into hospice care

are informed that they are forgoing primarily curative care. Decisions about care made at the systems level such as in the hospice model relieve crisis and conflict at the bedside. Robert Burt advances three "countervailing schemes" to alter decision-making processes:

- No one should be socially authorized to engage in conduct that directly, purposefully, and unambiguously inflicts death, whether on another person or on oneself.
- Decisions that indirectly lead to death should be acted upon only after a consensus is reached among many people. No single individual should be socially authorized to exercise exclusive control over decisions that might lead to death, whether that individual is the dying person, the attending physician, or a family member acting as health care proxy.
- As much as possible, end-of-life care should not depend on explicit decisions made at the bedside of a specific dying person, but rather should be implicitly dictated by systems-wide decisions about available resources, personnel, and institutional settings—that is, by setting up default pathways that implicitly guide and even control caretaking decisions in individual cases (Burt, 2005, p. S11).

Burt's proposed end-of-life decision-making scheme would support the paradigm shift that is already occurring in palliative and end-of-life care toward more communitarian, social, and relational models of care. Such models recognize autonomy, but in the larger social ecological context of community.

Hospitals and nursing homes can begin to make systems decisions that are modeled on hospice care, such as what level of resources to allocate to ICU units, perhaps limiting access to days spent in the ICU, or integrating palliative care into standards of care, thus making palliative care accessible to all residents. As Burt suggests, changes at the systems level will help to mitigate conflict-laden and emotionally stressful end-of-life choices for families and surrogates at the very time when they need to be investing their emotional resources in relational time and communication with their loved ones.

CONCLUSION

Unjust demands for futile, nonbeneficial or marginally beneficial treatments by family members or surrogates are not uncommon, and usually arise from communication failures about goals of care for the patient. There are a number of approaches for avoiding futility disputes, or resolving them when they arise, including (a) comprehensive ethics training for professionals, ethics committee members, families, and surrogates; (b) strengthening communication, interdisciplinary care planning and care coordination; (c) embedding ethics consultation and ethics review committee practices in health care facilities; and (d) effectuating supply-side policy changes at the systems level about end-of-life decision processes to open up space for patients and families to invest their social, emotional, and spiritual resources in meaningful relationships.

The author gratefully acknowledges Dr. Patricia Bomba for her consultation on the Community-wide Clinical Guidelines for Tube Feeding, and Dr. Stephen Evans for his case contribution from Western New York

Editor's Note: On December 13th, 2011, the New York State Supreme Court, Monroe County, decided that "the guardians were correct in their decision to proceed with medically assisted nutrition." (Transcript, p. 25, Matter of Zornow, *2011, NY Slip Op 52455(U)).*

Mary Beth Morrissey, *PhD, MPH, JD, is a postdoctoral researcher for the Hartford Risk and Resilience Project of the Fordham University Graduate School of Social Service. Dr. Morrissey's research interests are devoted to health and mental health policy, public health and community health education, health care decision making, pain and suffering, hospice, palliative and end-of-life care, and vulnerable subgroups of older adults including frail elderly nursing home residents and older adults in prison. Dr. Morrissey has over 20 years of experience as a practicing health care attorney, and concentrates her practice to the intersectionality of health law and policy, public health, gerontological social work research, and ethics. Dr. Morrissey is chair of the Policy Committee of the Aging and Public Health Section of the American Public Health Association, Aging Issues Chair of the Policy Committee of the Public Health Association of New York City, and a member of the National POLST Paradigm Research Committee. In addition, she is active in legislative advocacy and coalition-building at the state and grassroots levels, currently serving as President of the Westchester End-of-Life Coalition and founder and Chair of the Collaborative for Palliative Care.*

REFERENCES

Affordable Care Act (Patient Protection and Affordable Care Act). (2010). Pub. L. No. 111–148, 124 Stat. 119; Pub L. No. 111–152, 124 Stat. 1029.

Altilio, T. (2004). Pain and symptom management: An essential role for social work. In J. Berzoff and P. R. Silverman (Eds.), *Living with dying: Handbook for end-of-life health care practitioners* (pp. 380–408). New York: Columbia University Press.

Bern-Klug, M. (2010). Trends in the characteristics of nursing homes and residents. In M. Bern-Klug (Ed.), *Transforming palliative care in nursing homes* (pp. 84–106). New York: Columbia University Press.

Bomba, P., Morrissey, M. B., & Leven, D. C. (2011). Key role of social work in effective communication and conflict resolution process: Medical orders for life-sustaining treatment (MOLST) program in New York and shared medical decision making at the end of life. *Journal of Social Work in End-of-Life and Palliative Care, 7*(1), 56–82.

Bossuyt, N., Van den Block, L., Cohen, J., Meeussen, K., Bilsen, J., Echteld, M., Deliens, L., & Van Casteren, V. (2011). Is individual educational level related to end-of-life care use? Results from a nationwide retrospective cohort study in Belgium. *Journal of Palliative Medicine, 14* (10), 1135–1141.

Burt, R. (2005). The end of autonomy. In B. Jennings, G. Kaebnick, & T. H. Murray (Eds.), Improving end of life care: Why has it been so difficult? *Hastings Center Report Special Supplement, 35*(6), S9–S13.

Byock, I. (2002). Meaning and value of death. *Journal of Palliative Medicine, 5*(2), 279–288.

Callahan, D. (2011). Rationing: Theory, politics, and passions. *Hastings Center Report, 41*(2), 23–27.

Centers for Medicare & Medicaid Services, Survey and Certification Letter 11–37- NH: Issuance of Revisions to Interpretive Guidance at F tag 322, as Part of Appendix PP, State Operations Manual.

Community-wide Clinical Guidelines for Percutaneous Endoscopic Gastrostomy (PEGs)/ Tube Feeding (2010). Retrieved from http:// www.compassionandsupport.org/pdfs/patients/advanced/PEGs_Final_ Guidelines_12.14.07.pdf

Davino, M., Kornreich, E., Tichy, J., Goings-Perrot, J., Brocks, J., Gebbie, … Lavigne, P. (Fall 2009). Health law section summary report on healthcare costs: Legal issues, barriers and solutions. *New York State Bar Association Health Law Journal, 14*(2), 126–138.

Fins, J. J. (2006). *A palliative ethic of care: Clinical wisdom at life's end.* Sudbury, MA: Jones and Bartlett.

Finucane, T. E., Christmas, C., & Travis, K. (1999). Tube feeding in patients with advanced dementia: A review of the evidence. *JAMA, 282,*1365–1370.

Hickman, S. E., Nelson, C. A., Moss, A. E., Hammes, B. J., Terwilliger, A., Jackson, A., & Tolle, S. W. (2009). Use of the physician orders for life-sustaining treatment (POLST) paradigm program in the hospice setting. *Journal of Palliative Medicine,12*(2), 133–141.

Hickman, S. E., Nelson, C. A., Perrin, N. A., Moss, A. H., Hammes, B. J., & Tolle, S. W. (2010). A comparison of methods to communicate treatment preferences in nursing facilities: Traditional practices versus the physician orders for life-sustaining treatment program. *Journal of American Geriatrics Society, 58*(7), 1241–1248.

Hickman, S. E., Nelson, C. A., Moss, A. H., Tolle, S. W., Perrin, N. A., & Hammes, B. J. (2011). The consistency between treatments provided to nursing facility residents and orders on the Physician Orders for Life-Sustaining Treatment form. *Journal of American Geriatrics Society, 59*(11), 2091–2099.

Jennings, B. (2007). Public health and civic republicanism: Toward an alternative framework for public health ethics. In A. Dawson, A., and M. Verwij (Eds.). *Ethics, prevention, and public health.* Oxford: Oxford University Press (pp. 30–58).

Jennings, B. J., & Morrissey, M. B. (2011). Health care costs in end-of-life and palliative care: A quest for ethical reform. *Journal of Social Work in End-of-Life and Palliative Care, 7*(4), 300–317.

Jennings, B., Ryndes, T., D'Onofrio, C., & Baily, M. A. (2003). Access to hospice care: Expanding boundaries, overcoming barriers. *Hasting Center Report Special Supplement,33*(2), S3–S7.

Makofsky, E. (2011). Advance directive news: Topsy-turvy health care decision-making. *New York State Bar Association Elder and Special Needs Law Journal, 21*(4), 43–44.

Matter of Zornow, 31 Misc. 3d 450, 919 N.Y.S.2d 273 (Monroe Co. 2010); 2010 N.Y. Slip Op. 20549.

Medicare Payment Advisory Commission (March 2011). *Report to Congress: Medicare payment policy*. Washington, DC: Author.

Mental Hygiene Legal Service, Second Judicial Department (2011). MHL Article 81 and related matters: Collected cases (current through August 2011), New York.

Mitchell, S. L., Teno, J. M., Kiely, D. K., Shaffer, M. L., Jones, R. N., Prigerson, H. G., ... Hamel, M. B. (2009). The clinical course of advanced dementia. *New England Journal of Medicine, 361*(16), 1529–1538.

Morrissey, M. B. (2011a). Phenomenology of pain and suffering at the end of life: A humanistic perspective in gerontological health and social work. *Journal of Social Work in End-of-Life and Palliative Care, 7*(1), 14–38.

Morrissey, M. B. (2011b). Educating ethics review committees in a more humanistic approach to relational decision making. *New York State Bar Association Health Law Journal Special Edition: Implementing the Family Health Care Decisions Act, 16*(1), 65–67.

Morrissey, M. B. (2011c). Suffering and decision making among seriously ill elderly women (Doctoral dissertation, Fordham University). Retrieved from http://fordham.bepress.com/dissertations/AAI3458134/

Morrison, R. S., & Meier, D. E. (2011). *America's care of serious illness: A state-by-state report care on access to palliative care in our nation's hospitals.* New York: Center to Advance Palliative Care.

Morrison, R. S., Dietrich, J., Ladwig, S., Quill, T., Sacco, J., Tangeman, J., & Meier, D. E. (2011). Palliative care consultation teams cut hospital costs for Medicaid beneficiaries. *Health Affairs, 30* (3), 454–463.

N.Y. Pub. Health Law, Ch. 45, Art. 29-CC (McKinney, 2011).

Office of Inspector General, Department of Health and Human Services. (July 2011). Medicare hospices that focus on nursing facility residents. Washington, DC.

Palecek, E. J., Teno, J. M., Casarett, D. J., Hanson, L. C., Rhodes, R. L., & Mitchell, S. L. (2010). *Journal of American Geriatrics Society, 58*(3), 580–584.

Prainsack, B., & Buyx, A. (2011). *Solidarity: Reflection on an emerging concept in bioethics.* UK: Nuffield Council on Bioethics.

Sabatino, C., & Karp, N. (2011). *Improving advanced illness care: The evolution of state POLST programs.* Washington, DC: AARP Public Policy Institute.

Sen, A. (2008). Why and how is health a human right? *Lancet, 372,* 2010.

Sulmasy, D. P. (2003). Health care justice and hospice care [Special supplement]. *Hastings Center Report, 33*(2), S14–S17.

Sulmasy, D. P. (2006). End-of-life care revisited. *Health Progress,* 50–56.

Temel, J. S., Greer, J. A., Muzikansky, A., Gallagher, E. R., Admane, S., Jackson, V., ... Lynch, T. J. (2010). Early palliative care for patients with metastatic non-small-cell lung cancer. *New England Journal of Medicine, 363,* 733–742.

Teno, J. M., Mitchell, S., Gozalo, P., Dosa, D., Hsa, A., Intrator, O., & Mor, V. (2010). Hospital characteristics associated with feeding tube placement in nursing home residents with advanced cognitive impairment. *JAMA, 303*(6): 544–550.

Tuohey, J. G. (2010). POLST orders are not dangerous. *Ethics and Medics, 35* (10), 3–4.

United Nations. (1948). *The Universal Declaration of Human Rights.* Retrieved from http://www.un.org/en/documents/udhr/

US Conference of Catholic Bishops (2009). *Ethical and religious directives for Catholic health care services,* 5th ed. Washington, DC: USCCB.

Wronka, J. (2008). *Human rights and social justice: Social action and service for the helping and health professions.* Thousand Oaks, CA: Sage.

Zoloth-Dorfman, L. (1993). First, make meaning: An ethics of encounter of health care reform. *Tikkun, 8*(4), 23–26.

CHAPTER 13

When Family Is the Issue

Kelly Komatz and Alissa Hurwitz Swota

When making health care decisions for a child, the standard by which such decisions are directed is the best interest standard. That is, one should make the decision that is in the best interest of the child. Determining what is in a child's best interest, weighing the various interests and values at stake, and making sure to allow all stakeholders to have a voice in the decision-making process, is an unbelievably difficult task. This degree of difficulty increases exponentially when the interests and values of the stakeholders do not align with one another. In general, all children have an interest in maintaining stable family relationships, early bonding, and avoiding pain and suffering. However, that is but one component of a child's best interest. In addition to these general interests, there are also the specific interests of *this particular child* who is embedded in *this particular family*. While health care providers are able to add valuable insight into how to fill out the general interests of children, the child and the child's family are the only ones able to provide insight into the child's specific fears, values, and beliefs. The "heavy lifting" in the decision-making process lies in figuring out how to marry the general interests of a child with the specific interests of this child, and emerge with a coherent conception of a medical treatment plan that will be in this child's best interest. In Debbie's case, not only was there discord concerning what was in fact in her best interest, the goals of care that the family espoused shifted substantially as Debbie's disease progressed.

CASE STUDY

Debbie is a 12-year-old female who was previously healthy with a negative past medical history for any significant illnesses or surgery. When Debbie started junior high school, she became aware that she was unable to keep up with her classmates during school while changing classes; her legs just seemed weak and tired. When Debbie tried out for the volleyball team she noted that she had difficulty with the drills and grew tired before the end of practice. This condition prompted an evaluation by the pediatrician and multiple specialists. Eventually Debbie was diagnosed with mitochondrial disease. Mitochondrial disease is a progressive condition that causes early death due to mitochondria's failure to produce sufficient energy for cells to function properly, leading to organ system failure. At this time there is no known cure for mitochondrial disease. Debbie, her parents, and her sibling understood the diagnosis and the physical changes that would eventually occur during the course of the disease process, but they were not prepared for the difficult choices they would face along the journey of living with a progressive, fatal condition.

At first, the medical decisions related to the progression of Debbie's condition seemed relatively straightforward and Debbie's parents agreed to several non-invasive medical interventions without hesitation. The goal of such interventions was to help Debbie to continue to enjoy her life despite loss of functions. When Debbie had increasing difficulty swallowing liquids, an evaluation was done to assess Debbie's anatomy in order to have a gastrostomy tube placed through her abdominal wall directly into her stomach. This allowed Debbie to continue to receive nutrition in a liquid form, especially during periods of illness or days when swallowing was more difficult. Over a period of a year, Debbie experienced further physical decline due to the medical complications related to the progression of her disease. She was no longer able to ambulate on her own and needed to be in a wheelchair. No longer able to eat or drink anything by mouth, Debbie became totally dependent on her gastrostomy tube feedings for her nutrition and fluids. In addition, Debbie had very limited use of her upper extremities and at times would go for days without being able to move her arms or hands or to even hold her head up. During a hospitalization for pneumonia requiring intubation, it became difficult to extubate Debbie; the decision was made to place a tracheotomy to assist with maintaining Debbie's airway. Debbie initially was able to breathe on her own through the tracheotomy. However, over the course of several months, Debbie experienced further decline. With increasing muscle weakness and unable to breathe on her own, Debbie became dependent on the ventilator 24 hours a day.

Debbie's family had consistently made medical decisions throughout the course of Debbie's disease with the goal of ensuring that Debbie maintained a high quality of life. However, the focus changed as Debbie experienced further decline and began to enter into a phase of her disease that would result in her death. At this time, Debbie's family began to make decisions with the primary goal of keeping

Debbie alive for as long as possible. In short, the goals of care appeared to change from a focus on the quality of life to a focus on the quantity of life.

As Debbie's mitochondrial disease progressed it robbed her of the ability to communicate; Debbie was no longer able to even mouth any words. Interaction with others consisted of an occasional small change in her facial expressions to indicate comfort or discomfort. Anti-anxiety medications were initiated in light of Debbie's past responses to interventions such as bathing, suctioning secretions, medications, and chest physiotherapy to keep her lungs clear. Debbie's father consistently complained of the sedative effects of the pain medications; he noted that he was often unable to discern whether his daughter was awake or asleep. In general, he often disagreed with the recommended medication regimen. Debbie's medical condition did not allow her to open her eyes at all. Even before she had declined to this state, her parents would tape her eyes open during her normal awake times in order for her to see the television, watch movies, or be able to see a person reading a book to her. The ventilator did all of Debbie's breathing for her and so where the ventilator would make certain "sounds" when she was awake and attempting to breathe on her own, her muscle weakness was such that this was no longer a sign of Debbie being awake. While Debbie's mother was with her 24 hours a day, 7 days a week, and was intuitive to Debbie's cycles, at this stage even her mother had great difficulty knowing when she was awake or asleep or in any distress.

The medical team caring for Debbie began to experience more difficulties in working with Debbie's family, particularly her father. The team spent a great deal of time with her father, educating him and answering questions related to his daughter's care. The issue of ensuring Debbie's comfort, especially given her inability to communicate, was consistently highlighted by the health care team. Debbie's father believed that she had some awareness of her surroundings as evidenced by her brain activity. He felt that by using the medications to keep Debbie comfortable, both from pain due to her condition as well as anxiety, the physicians were interfering with the one sign that assured him that his daughter was still alive. Several meetings were held, both among members of the health care team and between medical staff and family. These meetings centered on pursuing a treatment plan that would emphasize being awake as much as possible (which meant very low doses of pain medications) versus ensuring Debbie was comfortable (with the understanding that one of the side effects of the pain medications was sedation). The health care team championed the latter plan of care, while Debbie's family pushed for the former. Needless to say, the meetings in which these divergent goals of care were discussed often ended with all parties frustrated and further entrenched in their respective positions.

The situation in caring for Debbie escalated when her father insisted that Debbie start receiving total parenteral nutrition (TPN) in order to extend her life. This required the placement of a percutaneous intravenous catheter that requires special care and opens a patient up to risks, including infection and blood clots. The intravenous nutrition requires weekly laboratory studies to ensure that the appropriate balance of electrolytes is given. This request, coupled with the conflict surrounding the level of pain medication, increased the divide between the health care providers and Debbie's father.

FACTORS TO CONSIDER IN THE DECISION-MAKING PROCESS

If the concept of family-centered care is to be taken seriously, then the patient must be considered as but one part of a larger whole. That is, the patient, here the child, is a part of a family. In determining what is in a child's best interest, one cannot divorce the child from her context. To do so is to make nonsense of a robust understanding of the best interest principle. Specifically, discerning what is of harm or of benefit to the child entails recognizing that the interests of the child are inextricably tied to members of her family. For example, starting a child on a treatment plan that requires hospital stays and clinic visits several times a month will have a profound impact on her parents and siblings. Will her parents have to take off of work to get her to her appointments and stay with her in the hospital? Do her parents have jobs where they can even take off such extensive periods of time? If her parents begin to miss work and lose their jobs, will they also lose their medical insurance and the means with which to pay their bills? In cases where the child is battling a terminal condition, familial interests are even weightier, since family members will have to live with their decisions after the child dies. Failure to recognize the interconnectedness of families is not only unrealistic, it is irresponsible. Thus, when espousing the idea of family-centered care, one needs to recognize that accurate considerations of harms and benefits to the child entail consideration of the interests of her family.

It is important to review the family dynamics as they relate to Debbie's care. Debbie was the eldest child with one younger sibling. Debbie's father was the main breadwinner and the person through whom the medical insurance was possible. Debbie's mother remained at home, caring for Debbie 24 hours a day, 7 days a week. Even as Debbie's condition worsened, she was not eligible for in-home shift nursing, placing more responsibilities on the mother. As Debbie's disease progressed, the medical intensity of her care increased. This high level of care made it so that Debbie's sibling was unable to participate in extracurricular activities. In short, Debbie's disease ravaged not just Debbie, but her whole family. Yet while all of these factors are important and need to be considered in the decision-making process, the patient must take center stage. Debbie's case presses family-centered care to the limits. While the health care team realized that Debbie's family will live with their decisions after Debbie has died, this does not give them license to make any and every decision they would like. Here especially, Debbie's basic interest in avoiding pain and suffering seemed to be neglected, according to members of the health care team. Even more, it was the members of the health care team who had to partner in caring for Debbie, even though they did not agree with many of the care decisions. On the other hand, Debbie's family understood decisions that aimed at extending Debbie's life as the right decisions, and any actions that would risk abbreviating Debbie's life as morally unacceptable.

Professional Standards and Autonomy

Health care providers must strike a fine balance between respecting the wishes of the family and maintaining their own personal and professional values. This case pushed this balance to the limit. Debbie was being cared for by providers trained in pediatric palliative medicine, providers intimately aware of the vexing issues that arise in caring for patients with life-limiting conditions. From the beginning, Debbie's providers went out of their way to engage the family and involve them in the process of developing a treatment plan. While the relationship between providers and Debbie's parents was very good for a long time, toward the end of Debbie's disease course the relationship began to sour. This turn mirrored the shift in the goals of care expressed by Debbie's parents. When the primary concern switched from quality to quantity of life, and Debbie's father made consistent, persistent requests to decrease her pain medications, health care providers began to grapple with conflicts between their fundamental values, professional standards, and respecting the preferences of the family. Providers were forced to struggle with their respective professional standards which promoted the idea of keeping a patient out of pain. Here especially, health care providers were experts in managing a patient's pain and took that to be their primary goal in caring for a patient; to allow their patient, a child no less, to suffer when palliation was available seemed beyond the pale. Further when Debbie's father asked for additional invasive treatments including placing his daughter on TPN, requiring placement of a percutaneous intravascular catheter and weekly blood chemistries, health care team members started to voice concerns about providing "futile" care that served only to subject Debbie to further "torture." It became progressively more difficult for them to continue caring for Debbie day after day while she was experiencing pain that could have easily been allayed and initiating additional treatment regimens that they believed to be "futile." What drove health care team members to continue their involvement in Debbie's care was the fact that they had grown close to her over the years and believed that leaving her now, during the last chapter of her life, would be tantamount to abandoning her in a time of need. However, continuing to care for Debbie in light of the constraints set forth by her family caused tremendous moral distress for health care team members. Health care providers are not void of any values of their own; we cannot and should not ask providers to check their values at the door. What we can do is ask that the values that influence a provider's ability to care for a patient be made transparent and try to ensure that such values not overwhelm the decision-making process.

Not too long after TPN was started and negotiations aimed at increasing the level of pain medications Debbie was receiving were completed, Debbie died. Was Debbie a victim in her family's zealous pursuit of a futile goal? Should the courts have gotten involved? Were health care providers driven to administer care that flew in the face of their personal values? These are all questions that those involved in caring for Debbie continue to grapple with. To be sure, some of those same questions have probably pained Debbie's family. The true test to how one responds to such questions comes when faced with a patient similar to Debbie.

CLINICAL ADVICE

Often, conflicts arise in the clinical setting because of poor communication. To be sure, this miscommunication can occur between the health care team and the family, and also among members of the health care team. Interestingly, in Debbie's case, health care team members excelled in communicating with each other and with the family. In analyzing Debbie's case, it is useful to point out not only what went wrong, but also, what went right— communication fell in the latter category. What follows is some advice to help foster a good relationship and clear communication between health care providers, patients, and families.

At the outset of the relationship, health care providers must work to clarify the goals of care. During this process, and it will be a process, providers must discern what patients (where applicable) and families hope to achieve through a particular treatment plan. In addition, providers can help guide patients and families through complex medical information and guide them toward options that are obtainable, rather than have families set unachievable goals. Throughout the relationship, providers should revisit these goals. New test results and changes in condition are some of the points at which revisiting the goals of care make sense. At the outset of the relationship, health care providers must recognize that they too have biases regarding treatment plans and such biases should be transparent during the decision-making process. That is, instead of allowing these biases to operate subterraneously during the process of developing a treatment plan and clarification of the goals of care, providers need to be up front about such biases (as it is only natural to have them) not only with patients and families, but also with themselves. Overall, by focusing on engaging the family at the outset of developing a treatment plan and partnering with them every step of the way, a solid foundation on which to build a trusting relationship is built.

Author's Note: This understanding of a child's best interest and the components thereof come from Christine Harrison (Presentation on Pediatric Bioethics, Jacksonville, Florida, November, 2008).

Kelly Grace Cronin Komatz, *MD, MPH, FAAP, FAAHPM, is board certified in pediatrics and in hospice and palliative medicine. She is assistant clinical professor of pediatrics at the University of Florida College of Medicine in Jacksonville, FL. Dr. Komatz is the medical director of Community PedsCare of Community Hospice NE Florida and of the Pain and Palliative Care Consult Service at Wolfson Children's Hospital. Dr. Komatz is involved in numerous national organizations, including serving on the section on bioethics of the American Academy of Pediatrics and the special interest groups on both pediatrics and ethics of the American Academy of Hospice and Palliative Medicine.*

Alissa Hurwitz Swota received her PhD in philosophy from the University at Albany, SUNY, and completed her post-doctoral fellowship in clinical ethics at the Joint Centre for Bioethics, University of Toronto. She is currently the bioethicist at Wolfson Children's Hospital in Jacksonville, Florida. She is also an associate professor of philosophy at the University of North Florida where she codirects the Center for Ethics. She has published several articles and chapters on ethical issues in medicine. Her research focuses on ethical and cultural issues at the end of life, advance care planning, and pediatric bioethics.

CHAPTER 14

Ethical Dilemmas When the Patient Is an Infant: Uncertainty and Futility

Brian S. Carter

Tell all the Truth but tell it slant—
Success in Circuit lies
Too bright for our infirm Delight
The Truth's superb surprise

As Lightning to the Children eased
With explanation kind
The Truth must dazzle gradually
Or every man be blind—

— Emily Dickinson

Care for newborns and young infants is often colored and complicated by prognostic uncertainty. At times such care may first be questioned in fetal life, with the diagnosis of a grave or concerning lesion. Pinter (2008) suggests that categories of malformation severity may be helpful in determining which fetuses might be carried to term, and which might be considered for termination. These categories would be based upon the likelihood of cure, with or without associated physical, cognitive or social and behavioral disabilities and impairments—in essence providing for an exercise in determining an acceptable quality of life. Among conditions most likely to lead to pregnancy termination, one recent study from France noted the high prevalence of brain malformations (Rouleau et al., 2011). What is the caregiver's responsibility to convey the "truth" about what is known, while balancing the reality of not having absolute certainty about outcomes before or after birth? How can truth and hope be held in tension by patients, families, and caregivers?

Is the use of futility language a help or hindrance in this place? And how do all parties react and respond to changing, or emerging, truths in time?

CASE STUDY

Annabella Grace was born at term to parents who already cared for a healthy 3-year-old and a 16-month-old with the sequelae of shaken baby syndrome (child abuse with resultant brain injury, caused by her biological father who was now in jail). While Annabella's mother, Miranda, was young, she certainly was not inexperienced. Early in her pregnancy, Miranda had a normal obstetric ultrasound. Her pregnancy progressed largely uncomplicated, but on the day of her delivery she was found to have a uterine fundal height and size greater than her known gestational dates and a repeat ultrasound was performed. It revealed polyhydramnios (too much amniotic fluid) and Annabella was noted to have a number of porencephalic cysts present throughout her brain—indicative of severe brain injury—and some enlarged ventricles (naturally occurring fluid-filled spaces in the brain). Annabella's parents were informed of these findings and counseled by her obstetrician to see a maternal-fetal medicine (MFM) specialist, because her polyhydramnios posed a threat for her uterus given a past history of cesarean delivery. While at the MFM's office in a large tertiary academic medical center, Miranda received further counseling from a neurosurgeon and a neonatologist; neurological problems were expected after birth, and Annabella's survival was questioned. Her parents "heard" that she had a fatal condition—one from which she was either not expected to survive, or to have devastating neurological injury and impairment. As a result, they prepared for the worst.

Annabella was born pink and active, and was beautiful in the eyes of her entire family. She was microcephalic and had irritability, perhaps even seizures, but she breathed and received initial intravenous fluids and then nasogastric tube feedings. An extensive diagnostic laboratory and imaging evaluation of Annabella occurred in the neonatal intensive care unit (NICU). Her cranial MRI confirmed likely intrauterine multifocal hemorrhagic strokes with destruction of much of her gray and white matter. An EEG was obtained to determine if she was having seizures and, indeed, this was the case. She was treated with anti-epileptic drugs, but repeated EEGs remained abnormal, demonstrating persistent seizure activity. While her initial head and body growth were normal for her gestational age, she was thought to possibly have suffered from an intrauterine infection, though this was never proven. Her neurological examination was abnormal, especially as it related to increased muscle tone, occasional stiffness of her arms and legs, jerky and jittery movements from time to time, and the absence of some key "primitive" neurological reflexes.

Annabella's prognosis for long-term survival and neurologic stability were believed by all of her clinicians to be poor. Her neurologist predicted that if her seizures did not stop, she would surely die. The eventual condition of refractory seizures and severe brain damage, clinically known as infantile spasms, was predicted by her neurologist. With this grave prognosis, her managing team in the NICU, in conjunction with her neurologist, agreed that a palliative care referral and hospice care were best for Annabella and her family. At the end of her first postnatal week of life, Annabella and her family were seen by the pediatric palliative care team. Transfer to an inpatient hospice was arranged and Annabella left the NICU.

After she was transferred to an inpatient hospice facility with a pediatric team, four days passed and Annabella's parents asked to take her home with a hospice nurse to follow-up daily. Comfort measures were ensured, anti-epileptic medications, sedatives, and morphine were also prescribed, and she went home tolerant of some oral feeding as well as naso-gastric tube feeding. She had a decidedly good couple of weeks at home, but at age four weeks she had a serious apnea event at home and her parents, described by one clinician to have "panicked," called 911 for emergency services. They asked the paramedics to give her oxygen and transport her to the children's hospital, later stating that they "couldn't just not do anything." Both the emergency medical personnel and the hospice nurse were initially confused, given her home hospice care regimen, her accepted "do not intubate/do not resuscitate" status, and the fact that Annabella had already recovered from her apnea and did not actually require emergent airway or cardiovascular support. However, she was transferred by air-ambulance to the local children's hospital emergency department. There she was evaluated, monitored, and a care conference was held to revisit treatment goals and her home hospice care. She was discharged within hours and seen by her pediatrician for followup the next day.

ANALYSIS

While a number of pieces of this case may be considered ethically problematic, the problem of uncertainty, and how different ethical values held by independent caregivers might result in conflicting courses of action for Annabella, bears some attention. Is it a matter of determining which values, or principles, should be given priority? Should this determination be based primarily on tensions between competing goods, such as nonmaleficence—avoiding harm and respect for life—regardless of any predictive quality of life ascertainment, or is it something deeper?

From one perspective, Annabella's case may represent a failure of communication and shared decision making. Included in this perspective is the admitted limits of prognostication in many pediatric conditions, especially when the child is so very young. When an outcome is uncertain, but includes the possibility of death, how this is framed in early conversations with parents may have a significant effect on how the information is received, and what decisions ultimately follow (Haward, Murphy, and Lorenz, 2008). While it may have seemed that Annabella's parents and health care team began their journey together (even prenatally) by agreeing on goals of care focused on giving her a chance at life, in time it appeared that her parents and health care team eventually came to see "giving her a chance at life" differently—and likely ascribed different meaning to what this meant, what was important, and what actions should follow.

The fact that health care professionals deal with uncertainty in prognosis on a daily basis certainly must color their approach to patients such as Annabella. They may consider that certain interventions ought to be avoided, as their therapeutic value is limited. But such an interpretation requires that all interventions be viewed in terms of the goals of care. What is it that we want to accomplish for this patient, with this condition, today and in the near future? Alternatively, parents who bear the responsibility of ongoing care at home after their infant is discharged from the hospital or hospice—following treatment decisions—continue to see their child through daily life events, with myriad complexities and even crises. They are quite likely to view their responsibilities as parents to include protecting their child from harm, sustaining and nurturing her, and ensuring she gets everything she needs for as long as she lives. It may not be, as is often thought by clinicians who are trying to understand why a parent may seem to insist on "doing everything," that parents see such crises as an opportunity to beat the odds. Rather, they may acknowledge limits, but nonetheless want to live out their parental roles and responsibilities in what is most certainly a different sense of "normal" but one that, nonetheless, allows them to fulfill their role as "bearers of hope" (Reder and Serwint, 2009).

In Annabella's case, the importance of both a social and family history, as well as taking time to ascertain and clarify certain values in the beginning, was most important. Here, the palliative care team would learn that Miranda has a brother who suffered paraplegia after an automobile accident—and Miranda grew up caring for a disabled sibling. Her 16-month-old child, the victim of nonaccidental trauma (child abuse) with severe neurological sequelae had already, in her mind, beaten the odds that were initially voiced by the health care team attending to her, having lived without the severity of neurodevelopmental problems predicted and bringing value to her family.

Annabella can quite possibly live for an extended period of time—but will likely die prematurely. Her family knows this but chooses to focus on goals of making her life as normal as possible while she is with them. Surely the goals for her care may need to be revised over the years; her parents have already made some modifications, as she engages now in rehabilitative services. It might be said that her family was more inclined to adapt her goals to her changing circumstance—her *not dying*—ahead of the hospice, palliative care, and other health care team members. In this manner, they were able to feel they advocated well for her. It is even possible that they may have perceived that her health care team was no longer committed to her in the same manner, and that they constantly focused on limiting treatment—yielding what they stated was a prevailing negative tone when speaking about Annabella's condition. While some health care professionals may resort to this approach when they believe that parents "are in denial" and do not understand the severity of their child's condition, palliative care professionals must balance, or hold in tension, what seem to be dual duties of truth telling and not abandoning hope. Benzein, Norberg, and Saveman (2001) noted a particular value of the lived experience of hope for adult cancer patients in palliative home care that involved not only "hoping for" something, but also "living in hope." Living in hope meant having confirmative relationships with loved ones in their families and sharing in the experiences of being at home, with these family members, caregivers, familiar things, and pets. If for these patients their home provided a source of "feeling at home," it is reasonable to posit that similar hopefulness might be experienced by parents eager to have their fragile child at home. In their work, these investigators revealed a tension that was held by patients between hoping for something (e.g., a hope of getting cured), and living in hope (accomplished as they reconciled their individual comfort with life and death).

The challenge for caregivers is to give an honest assessment of the situation (upholding the rule of telling the truth) and at the same time respect the parent's own choices and their commitment to advocacy. In most instances outside of the ICU environment, health care professionals can express their concerns that a child like Annabella might die without presuming, or declaring, that they know when, in fact, a life will end. Caregivers need to be cautious about their own need for closure driving them to expect that decisions be made immediately, or in the near term. Except in cases where there is a clear consensus on what is in the child's medical and social best interest, professional caregivers have a duty based upon the principle of autonomy to respect the parents' values. Shared goals can still be pursued, even when such differences exist, if parents are assisted in understanding how a current situation, while presenting new challenges, remains consistent with the overall diagnosis and prognosis. In this case, Annabella's continued survival and new need for seizure control differs from past experiences. Parents need to have their previous experiences, decisions, and values respected and validated, but they also require clinicians and others to honor their own process that allows them to live through and with the decisions they make for their child. In addition to autonomy-based respect for the parents, this approach is also based on beneficence in caregivers honoring their duty to support the well-being of the family.

If clinicians are not sensitive to how blunt their commitment to truth-telling can be, their own use of language that includes phrases such as "this is futile," or even "we should all just give up since there is no chance of curing her," might send mixed messages. Futility must be evaluated in terms of a stated goal. "Giving up" might suggest that other options truly exist and the child is being kept from them. Caregivers need to be able to present options for treatment that include a palliative focus and make it clear that they are not giving up. They must be mindful of the unequal power that exists between parents and professionals and use transparency in their working with parents to validate their feelings and support their concerns while continuing to address an appropriate balance of advocacy and interest on behalf of the child. An avoidance of adversarial postures, such as in the pursuit of legal action, should minimize a tragic polarizing of postures between parents and caregivers, in which the child's best interests are only rarely ensured. Rather, health care professionals should ask themselves what is necessary to facilitate the support of the child and family during their difficult times and determine what actions—truly measures of generosity and compassion—will allow parents and professionals to preserve their integrity.

The language of futility, or what in other instances is referred to as "unwarranted care," raises many issues that are thorny for clinicians and families alike. In the context of a young infant or child, who socially and culturally is not supposed to die before her parents, and for whom absolute certainty in prognosis is not the norm, it may be best to avoid the term. Instead, attention should be focused on the clarification of goals and discerning right action in a culturally sensitive, patient and family-centered manner that honors stated or elaborated values. Why is this best?

- Not all patients agree that futility negates advance life support, such as mechanical ventilation or dialysis.
- Clinicians (of all disciplines) don't identify futility reliably or consistently.
- With medical advances, survival estimates for most conditions may become obsolete quickly.
- Rigid notions of futility lead to self-fulfilling prophecies.

Additionally, caregivers need to realize that there are consequences for patients and families when clinicians use the concept of futility without careful consideration. The patient and family may be marginalized and no longer considered or allowed to feel that they have a place as significant participants in future decision making. It can worsen communication among all concerned, and raises questions such as, "Futile for whom?" or "Futile in relation to what?" Futility language can introduce suspicion and distrust, resulting in a questioning of clinicians' diagnostic and prognostic accuracy, and even whether they have some other agenda. To some, futility language may sound like concern for the costs of care more than patient-centered care. This language may sound like giving up, dashing hope, not caring, or frankly, abandonment. Futility language can stand in the way of important family-centered end-of-life care and procedures. If a clinician uses futility to cease further deliberation, it communicates a lack of any respect for the moral, social, or ritualistic value of certain practices at the end of life, even cardiopulmonary resuscitation (Zier et al., 2009).

There are also consequences for health care professionals when futility is used without caution. Clinicians may question their purpose and value. When futility means different things to different people, it fractures communication within the health care team, and between the care team and families. Seeds of suspicion may be planted, and distrust of certain clinicians, families, and clinical scenarios follow. It may even contribute to staff turnover. Finally, it takes away from what caring professionals bring to their next clinical encounter, contributes to the stress-burnout-depression continuum, and brings about moral angst, which is one of many manifestations of caregiver suffering.

DECISION

Annabella's parents actively participated in decisions to support her life and make it as rich as possible. Through clear communication and shared decision making, they let clinicians know that they wanted Annabella to have the best quality of life possible for as long as she lived. This meant decisions to place a feeding gastrostomy tube, seek rehabilitative care with physical and occupational therapy, and continue to take medication for control of her seizures. To date, she is thriving. Though affected by spasticity and evolving cerebral palsy with infantile spasms (her seizure disorder), she is gaining weight and increasingly interactive with her family. Her parents are encouraged by her developing response to human interaction. And while they understand that her longevity of life may be limited, her quality of life has already been improved.

AFTERWORD

Annabella's pediatrician was admittedly a little baffled and initially didn't know what to think about her trip to the emergency department or her new direction of care. Her parents wanted ongoing attention to her needs and care and clearly understood her likely lethal condition, but also reminded everyone involved of the uncertain timespan until her passing. The family's initial goals for Annabella had focused on supporting her until she died, but those goals were evolving to find ways to extend her life as long as possible. At that point, the family felt that hospice care did not provide them with the opportunity to focus on this life-extending treatment, so they chose to disenroll Annabella from hospice care. Since that time, she has continued to receive regular neurology care and treatment for seizures, had a laparoscopic feeding gastrostomy tube placed, and has been evaluated in the spasticity clinic, where she was started on an anti-spasticity medication and physical therapy. She is also being evaluated for her evolving cerebral palsy by a pediatric orthopedist.

Conclusion

Annabella's case is instructive in many ways. Lessons learned by caregivers include a recognition of the need for parents to hear the full spectrum of possibilities when addressing likely outcomes—not simply an expected early death. Health care providers need to have a plan for what to do next when early predictions are inaccurate and the infant's life and illness course changes. When caregivers fail to consider and address all reasonable possibilities with parents, frustration, confusion, anger, and guilt may follow. These reactions may be shared by parents and caregivers. What palliative care clinicians can focus on is both learning and then modeling how to "expect the unexpected" and adapt to "a new normal." In many ways this is akin to advance care planning as seen in adult palliative care.

Brian S. Carter, MD, is a professor of pediatrics in the Division of Neonatology at the Monroe Carell, Jr. Children's Hospital at Vanderbilt University Medical Center in Nashville, TN. He received residency and fellowship training in pediatrics and neonatal-perinatal medicine in Denver, CO, and has been trained in clinical ethics and in palliative care. His honors include membership in the Alpha Omega Alpha Honor Medical Society, receipt of the 2003 National Hospice and Palliative Care Organization (NHPCO) Research Award, and presenting the William A. Silverman Lecture in Ethics at the 2008 Pediatric Academic Societies meeting. He serves on the Vanderbilt University Medical Center Ethics Committee, has done ethics consultation, and has been active in both professional curriculum development and broad community educational activities in both clinical ethics and pediatric palliative care.

References

Benzein, E., Norberg, A., & Saveman, B. I. (2001). The meaning of the lived experience of hope in patients with cancer in palliative home care. *Palliative Medicine,15*, 117–126.

Dickinson, E. (1961). Tell all the Truth but tell it slant. In T. Johnson (Ed.), *Complete poems of Emily Dickinson* (pp. 506–507). New York: Little, Brown and Company.

Haward, M. F., Murphy, R. O., & Lorenz, J. M. (2008). Message framing and perinatal decisions. *Pediatrics, 122,* 109–118.

Hoffmann, P. B., & Schneiderman, L. J. (2007). Physicians should not always pursue a good "clinical" outcome. *Hastings Center Report, 37*(3), 3.

Pinter, A. B. (2008). End-of-life decision before and after birth: Changing ethical considerations. *Journal of Pediatric Surgery, 43,* 430–436.

Reder, E. A. K., & Serwint, J. R. (2009). Exploring the concept of hope for parents and health care professionals during a child's serious illness. *Archives of Pediatric and Adolescent Medicine, 163,* 653–657.

Rouleau, C., Gasner, A. , Bigi, N., Couture, A., Perez, M. J., Blanchet, P., ..., Encha-Razaui, F. (2011). Prevalence and timing of pregnancy termination for brain malformations. *Archives of Disease in Childhood, Fetal and Neonatal Edition, 96:F,* 360–364.

Zier, L. S., Burack, J. H, Micco, G., Chipman, A. K., Frank, J. A., & White, D. B. (2009). Surrogate decision makers' responses to physicians' predictions of medical futility. *Chest, 136*(1), 110–117.

Additional Resource
Strong, C., Feudtner, C., Ballard, M. K., Carter B. S., & Dokken, D. L. (2000). *Goals, values, and conflict resolution.* In B. S. Carter, M. Levetown, and S. E. Friebert, (Eds.). *Palliative care for infants, children, and adolescents: A practical handbook,* (2nd Ed., pp. 26–55). Baltimore, MD: Johns Hopkins University Press.

CHAPTER 15

Whose Suffering Is It?
An Ethical Reflection on the
Decline and Death of a Child

Timothy R. Arsenault

My parents tried to make things normal, but that's a relative term. The truth is, I was never really a kid. To be honest, neither were Kate and Jesse. I guess maybe my brother had his moment in the sun for the three years he was alive before Kate got diagnosed, but ever since then, we've been too busy looking over our shoulders to run headlong into growing up. You know how most little kids think they're like cartoon characters—if an anvil drops on their heads they can peel themselves off the sidewalk and keep going? Well, I never once believed that. How could I, when we practically set a place for Death at the dinner table? (excerpted from Jodi Picoult's novel, *My Sister's Keeper*, 2004, p. 9)

The life-limiting illness and death of an infant, child, or adolescent can leave a long shadow over the lives of their surviving loved ones. Hospice and palliative care has an enormous opportunity to serve dying children and their families, yet negative assumptions, misinformation, intensified emotions, and financial anxieties can present strong barriers to timely referral, effective interventions, and bereavement support. The care of infants, children, and adolescents with life-limiting illness and that of their families is problematic medically, emotionally, spiritually, and ethically. The challenges to support autonomy, to speak the truth, to relieve suffering, to do no harm, and ensure that limited resources are distributed justly, often create dilemmas of conscience. The lingering memories of struggling to do the right thing can have a lasting impact on the lives of those who have been at decisional crossroads along the journey from diagnosis to death, and even into bereavement. This reality is equally true for family members as well as professional care teams.

It is estimated that over 440,000 infants, children, and adolescents are living with life-threatening conditions in the United States (Levetown and Orloff, 2010). While much is understood about the decline and death of adults, the decline and death of children can be from a variety of clinically complex sources. These sources may include metabolic deficiencies, genetic anomalies, developmental defects, brain injury, perinatal infections, childhood on-set illness, rare cancers, or neurological conditions. Care is often expensive, in settings separated from family, pets, peers, and familiar surroundings. Often through the progress of the illness the goal and hope to cure persists even as death approaches.

While hospice and palliative care provide best interdisciplinary practices addressing the multiple layers of childhood terminality, children and their parents often face the choice between curative treatment and the cessation of all cure-directed care to allow admission into hospice with comfort measures only. Most current payer sources do not support concurrent curative measures and palliative end-of-life care. Some state programs have grasped the concept that children with advanced illness or disability may be best served by a hybrid model of care that supports both palliative care and curative measures. Section 2302 of The Patient Protection and Affordable Care Act of 2010 notes that "Concurrent Care for Children does allow states to offer concurrent palliative care alongside curative care for children who medically qualify for hospice care." Many states have implemented this care provision, others are in the process of implementing, and a few have not due to litigation. Also, children and adolescents with rare diseases and anomalies are desirable candidates for clinical trials and experimental treatments. Desperate parents and caregivers cling to every hope for a remission. Given these barriers and disincentives, less than 1% of dying children in the US are ever served by hospice care (Levetown and Orloff, 2010).

Ethical challenges are compounded when dying children or adolescents seek to understand their disease process and participate in setting direction for their care plan. The novel *My Sister's Keeper* by Jodi Picoult (2004) is the compelling story of two sisters. One sister, Anna, was conceived for the express purpose of providing bone marrow for her older sister, Kate, also a minor, who is battling a rare form of leukemia. Anna, now 13, has spent a lifetime of invasive medical procedures to provide life-extending tissue for Kate. Anna is now expected to donate a kidney to save her sister. As the story unfolds, Anna is seeking medical emancipation from her parents, particularly her mother, who has been a fierce advocate for Kate. For a while, the reader assumes that the emancipation is being sought because of the long history of painful procedures. Eventually, the writer reveals that the sisters have developed a pact to end all procedures because Kate is exhausted and wants to die. This truth could not be heard by their mother who continues to fight the emancipation in fear of losing Kate. The compelling plot takes many twists and turns, exposing the dynamics of a hurting family. While a work of fiction, the story invites the reader into the all-too-real world of a dying adolescent and the complex layering of relationships, decisions, medicine, and in some cases, court action.

In 2009, the case of Daniel Hauser captured national attention. The then 13-year-old had fled Minnesota with his mother, Colleen Hauser, to avoid court-ordered chemotherapy for Daniel's Hodgkin's lymphoma. Doctors had testified that Daniel had a 90% chance of being cured through chemotherapy and radiation and a 95% chance of dying without it. The boy and his parents resisted chemotherapy and radiation for religious reasons. Daniel claimed to be a medicine man in his faith and insisted that only natural healing methods should be employed.

Daniel's parents were accused of medical neglect and Daniel ended up in the custody of County Family Services. Court testimony revealed the convergence of several ethical issues: religious freedom, the validity of alternative therapies as medical treatment, the voice of a minor child in directing his medical care, parental rights involved in the medical treatment of their child, and the right to refuse unwanted treatment that the family perceived as toxic.

The case resolved when the family consulted with an elder in Nemenhah, a Native American spiritual organization. Without elaborating on the details of their consultation, the Hausers agreed to at least five rounds of chemotherapy and radiation, while receiving acknowledgment that alternative medicine would be included when possible. With the application of traditional and alternative therapies along with psychological and spiritual counseling, Daniel experienced remission of his lymphoma.

CASE STUDY

Alex was just 11 when diagnosed with Ewing's sarcoma, a rare form of bone cancer. When Alex was eight, his father had committed suicide under a cloud of family secrets. With his father's death, Alex became the "man of the house." Alex had no siblings and lived alone with his mother, June, on the edge of poverty. There was a deep love between mother and son; Alex was both son and spousal surrogate to his mother. June would not allow any discussion of prognosis as she could not bear the thought of losing the remaining love of her life. Alex, not wishing to cause additional stress to his mother, agreed to experimental treatments and drug trials resulting in extreme side effects and repeated hospitalizations.

The moral distress of staff rose with each trip to the hospital; after some time, the hospital palliative care team was consulted by the attending hospitalist. The team social worker gently approached Alex with the question of what his wishes would be should he experience cardiac arrest. He said he was not prepared to answer and the social worker left the "Five Wishes" Advance Directive document with him as a tool for him to use for reflection and consideration. This was a rare moment when June was away from Alex's bedside and out of the hospital.

Alex called his mother, and June, in turn, called the hospital administrator, insisting that there be "no negative talk or visitors in Alex's room." The palliative care social worker was disciplined for bypassing June and never got to see Alex again. A few weeks later Alex died in the hospital due to his advanced disease and complications related to the toxic effects of the aggressive treatments he was receiving. June had to be hospitalized, overcome with grief and anger.

ANALYSIS

At the age of eleven, Alex was old enough to understand the nature of his illness and his prognosis. Even though June, as Alex's parent, was his health care decision maker, Alex was not consulted about his treatment plan and was shielded from meaningful dialogue about his condition. June stood watch over Alex and monitored nearly every conversation with him.

The hospital staff was caught in the dilemma of honoring June's parental rights and the desire to share the terminality of his condition with Alex. Staff watched as Alex's suffering was magnified not only by the disease process but also by the side effects of the treatment he was enduring.

The case was further complicated by the suicide of Alex's father, Michael. It was later discovered that Michael had watched his own father suffer and die from bone cancer with his pain poorly managed. Michael's worst fear was that something would happen to his only son. A suspicious slow-healing break in Alex's arm led the family to speculate that it could have been caused by cancer. Michael could not bear the thought of watching Alex endure the same suffering as his grandfather, and believed that perhaps there was a genetic connection that Michael transmitted to Alex. Michael took his life before there was a definitive cancer diagnosis for Alex. The prospect of another cancer death in the family was just too much for Michael to bear.

The moral distress of the hospital staff and the palliative care team was intense. This response was not due to fatigue or burnout; these competent, engaged clinicians felt that they had tools at the ready to serve Alex and his mother. Yet they felt powerless to intervene on Alex's behalf and felt stonewalled by June's edict to protect Alex (and herself) from all perceived negativity. The palliative care team social worker, who felt she acted in Alex's best interest, was disciplined for bypassing June. This decision was a clear administrative signal to the rest of the staff and only served to drive their moral distress underground.

Alex, so bonded with his mother, could not bring himself to oppose his mother's desperate hope for a cure. He willingly subjected himself to experimental treatments and endured life-threatening side effects with a team of research clinicians encouraging the continuation of treatment in the hope that a remission would be triggered.

In one sense, June and Alex received what they wanted: an aggressive, curative care plan. However, the outcome was a difficult death for Alex, with no plan to support life closure or bereavement. In the end, Alex died as a result of toxic side effects of treatment with his symptoms poorly managed. The palliative care team was kept at arm's length. June's grief was overwhelming. She ended up in the hospital's behavioral unit under heavy sedation.

The only place where staff was able to process their moral distress and grief was the staff break room and in hushed hallway conversations. Many of the staff were outraged at the disciplinary action imposed on the social worker and yet others respected the need to support patient and parent autonomy, even when it did seem to cause more suffering. Some felt the disciplinary action was heavy-handed, while others felt the social worker, even with good intent, stepped over her boundaries. The controversy remained behind the scenes but became a wedge between those with opposing viewpoints. Departmental leadership sensed unrest, but did not have the tools or time to help staff unpack their distress. A pall of grief descended over the floor where Alex and June had spent so many days. The hands-on care staff was heartbroken at the death of this little boy who bravely endured so much and tried so hard to live so as not to add to his mother's suffering.

Another issue raised by this case is the distribution of resources. The total costs related to hospitalizations were absorbed through Medicaid and the hospital's not-for-profit charitable commitment to treat regardless of the ability to pay. The cost of experimental treatment was underwritten by the drug company providing it. This raises the question of distribution of resources. In the view of a desperate mother and cure-seeking researchers, it was a wise investment. In the view of others, all these funds could have been better utilized elsewhere. It also raises the question: was Alex's consent to receive experimental treatments truly informed and free?

AFTERWORD

While June was undergoing intense therapy soon after Alex died, a hospice volunteer who also had had a young son die began to visit her. At first, June refused visitors, but softened in time. A healing bond began to form between these two women who exchanged stories about the loves of their life.

One of the staff involved in Alex's care approached the hospital chaplain, who also served on the hospital ethics committee. The chaplain offered to facilitate a debriefing for those closely involved in Alex's death. This process prompted the hospital administration to open dialogue with the ethics committee and the human resources department about how they might collaborate to address the issue of staff moral distress and grief. While the case had been unusual for this growing hospital, administrators knew it would not be the last. Internal support mechanisms were needed to address grief and unrest before they became destructive diversions of energy.

Because of a recent merger, the hospital ethics committee was undergoing a reorganization and had missed opportunities to become involved in this case. At the time of the case, it was not widely known how to access the ethics committee and how to seek a consultation. Alex's death sparked renewed interest in the staff to receive ethics education and revive the committee. Because of the case, a stronger ethics committee was developed comprising a cross section of staff representative of the merged facilities. An internal marketing campaign helped to raise staff awareness and provided clear instructions on how to access the committee and how to prepare for a consultation.

LESSONS LEARNED AND LARGER IMPLICATIONS FOR END-OF-LIFE CARE

Hospice and community clinicians working with children need to have a special understanding of and respect for the developmental stages of children and their unique life circumstances when providing treatment and support. Assessing competence, providing "kid-friendly" information, and seeking age-appropriate assent should be a standard of care. However, age level is no guarantee of the presence or absence of emotional or spiritual maturity. Some children young in age can be "old souls" capable of great wisdom beyond their years. Other children, in mid to late adolescence, when greater maturity would be assumed, can display great immaturity and complete deference when it comes to decision making. Fear, undue pressure, broken parental bonding, confusion about medical terms, and the lack of understanding of consequences of choices, may all have a role to play in the landscape of children assenting to care.

Unresolved grief and family secrets are often part of the landscape surrounding parents and caregivers struggling to cope with the fact that their child is dying. Effective support operates at "the speed of trust." Fostering skills in clinicians and volunteers that quickly promote trust building helps to create the atmosphere of safety and openness that leads to sharing the back stories that have led up to the current crossroads. Painful truths can only be told and heard in an atmosphere of trust.

Part of the genius of the hospice movement is the integration of volunteers into the fabric of providing care. Volunteers with life experiences help to create a safe, credible, and compassionate community of care, especially those who have survived suicide and child loss.

Social networking is opening a whole new arena for seriously ill children and adolescents. Most teens easily navigate the Internet and can find like-minded teens with similar experiences. With guidance and direction from a hospice or palliative care team, cyber communities of support are springing up online. Naturally, support can be found for hurting parents as well.

The hospice and palliative care community needs safe venues for staff and volunteers to process moral distress when it happens. Ethics committees, besides providing case consultation, can also be helpful in providing "round table" opportunities for open discussion when necessary. Some hospitals have adopted a process model called "Schwartz Rounds®," which offers step-by-step guidance in helping staff and volunteers reflect on events that raise challenges of conscience.

Internal grief support for staff and volunteers needs to be one of the key benefits available to anyone working in health care. The rapid turnover of patients and families, the high-tech environment of care, and the intense emotions of stressed families can wear on professional and volunteer caregivers. Bedsores, which come about as a result of constant physical pressure and compromised nutrition, can serve as a rich metaphor. "Bedsores" can form on the caregiver's spirit if ways to relieve pressure and nourish the inner life are not found.

Advocacy with government and third-party payers on behalf of seriously-ill children and their families is crucial. Sick children do not move through curative, palliative, and end-of-life care as if it were a clear, sequential continuum. The illness of a child can leave a family emotionally and financially devastated. Payment structures ought to support true interdisciplinary care that fosters hope and comfort.

Strategic partnerships across a community's care continuum are critical in the movement of children and adolescents from curative treatment to palliative and end-of-life care and then into bereavement support for survivors. Of course, bereavement does not begin only after a death. Bereavement begins with a life-threatening diagnosis. Agencies operating in silos and competitive enclaves are of little help when histories have to be shared over and over and vital information is at risk of being lost in the handoff. Hospice partnerships with schools, children's hospitals, and the mental health community will serve to strengthen the wellness of a community. Hospice may not be perceived as a wellness initiative; but it is well known that the stress of caring for ill children, struggles of conscience, and unresolved grief can lead to poor physical and mental health outcomes. A hospice and palliative care organization deeply engaged with its community, helping to educate on choices, and relieving grief, can have an enormous impact on wellness. Hospice cannot underestimate the power of community education and gatherings that help to demythologize hospice care and diminish fear. A robust teen volunteer program can do wonders to reinforce the view that hospice "is about living." Creative ideas such as displaying children's art in hospice facilities, opening meeting rooms to schools and nonprofits, running a camp for bereaved kids, offering meaningful internships, and the like, can all work to penetrate hospice awareness into a community. These activities counteract the perception that hospice is a negative, bleak, last stop on life's journey.

CONCLUSION

In an ideal world, steps might have been taken even before Alex's diagnosis that could have led to better outcomes for everyone involved. Michael's father would have been served by an interdisciplinary hospice team that would have managed the pain and symptoms of his cancer, with Michael's dad driving the plan of care. The hospice team would have begun bereavement counseling with Michael's family upon admission. Trusting relationships with the local hospice would have begun there, and perhaps Michael's anxiety and guilt could have been addressed and a suicide avoided. Perhaps Alex could have attended a school group or bereavement camp to help him adjust to the loss of his granddad. Even if hospice did not come on the scene until after Michael's suicide, perhaps June and Alex could have received support through a widows' or suicide survivors' group sponsored by the hospice.

When the news of Alex's diagnosis came, hospice and palliative care counselors could have been referred in and allowed to visit based on the history of trust already established. June and Alex could have processed the significance of their relationship and could have thoughtfully evaluated the benefits and burdens of experimental treatment.

As Alex declined, perhaps he could have been connected to a community of cyberfriends to companion him. June could have been introduced to other parents who experienced similar challenges, and trusted volunteers could have helped with the details of managing life outside the hospital.

Again, with trust as the solid foundation, the truth of Alex's terminality could have been shared and experimental treatment discontinued. Alex's final weeks could have been lived out in comfort, accomplishing his wishes and goals and receiving the support of uniquely trained and experienced counselors.

June's grief over Alex's death could have been eased by the strength of other parents who have been down this same road. Counselors and volunteers could have helped with the preparation of a celebration of Alex's life. June's first year without Alex would be supported by regular visits and invitations from her circle of fellow parents, and June could find the courage to live on and to not have been troubled by her decisions about Alex during her own dying.

Timothy R. Arsenault, MA, is the director of spiritual care for Suncoast Hospice and cochairs the hospice's Bioethics Committee. In 2007, Arsenault helped establish a partnership with a local hospital system for Clinical Pastoral Education. Prior to joining Suncoast in 1994, he spent 23 years in pastoral ministry in a variety of settings. He has been a secondary school instructor, college lecturer, pastor, ministry supervisor, director of a retreat and conference center, and spiritual director. He cofounded the Audire Program, a three-year training institute for spiritual direction ministry. Arsenault is a member of Spiritual Directors International, the Council of Hospice Professionals, and the Florida Bioethics Network.

REFERENCES

American Academy of Pediatrics Committee on Bioethics. (1995). Informed consent, parental permission, and assent in pediatric practice. *Pediatrics, 95*(2), 314–7.

Brockman, L., & Moreno, M. (2008). Withholding information from an adolescent. Retrieved from http://virtualmentor.ama-assn.org/2008/08/ccas3-0808.html

Devettere, R. J. (2000). *Practical decision making in health care ethics: Cases and concepts.* (2nd Ed.) Washington, DC: Georgetown University Press.

Doka, K. J., Jennings, B. , & Corr, C. A. (2005). *Living with grief: Ethical dilemmas at the end of life.* Washington, DC: Hospice Foundation of America.

Fernandez, C., Fraser, G., Freeman, C., Grunfeld, E., Gupta, A., Stephen, L., ...Schacter, B. (2011). Principles and recommendations for the provision of healthcare in Canada to adolescent and young adult-aged cancer patients and survivors *Journal of Adolescent and Young Adult Oncology, 1*,(1), 53–59.

Freyer, D. R. (2004). Care of the dying adolescent: Special considerations. *Pediatrics, 113*, 381–388.

Gross, T. (June 2010). Challenges and practicalities of obtaining parental consent and child assent in pediatric trials. *Regulatory Rapporteur, 7*, 6.

Larcher, V. (2005). ABC of adolescent consent, competence, and confidentiality. *BMJ, 330*, 353–356.

Levetown, M., and Orloff, S. (2010). *Ethical Issues in the Care of Infants, Children and Adolescents.* Unpublished manuscript.

Nelson, R., & Fost, N. (2011). Ethics in pediatric care. Retrieved from http://drugswell.com/wowo/blog1.php/2011/04/27 /

Picoult, Jodi. (2004). *My Sister's Keeper.* New York: Atria Books.

Shaw, M.. (2001). Competence and consent to treatment in children and adolescents. *Advances in Psychiatric Treatment, 7*, 150–159.

President's Council on Bioethics. (2005). *Taking care: Ethical caregiving in our aging society.,* Washington, DC: Author.

Tait, A. R., Voepel-Lewis, T., & Malviya, S. (2006). Do they understand? (Part II): Assent of children participating in clinical anesthesia and surgery research. *The Journal of Pediatrics, 149*, 1, Supplement, S25–S30.

Waz, W. (December 2010). The need to know: Disclosure of information to pediatric patients. Retrieved from The Center for Bioethics and Human Dignity, http://cbhd.org/content/need-know-disclosure-information-pediatric-patients

Additional Resources:
For more information on "Schwartz Rounds®" go to
http://www.theschwartzcenter.org/

For more information on the Five Wishes document, go to
http://www.agingwithdignity.org/five-wishes.php or call 1-888-5-WISHES.

CHAPTER 16

Informed Decision Making and the Adolescent Patient

Kristin Meade and Sarah Friebert

CASE STUDY

Megan is a 16-year-old girl with cystic fibrosis (CF) whose recent disease trajectory has been worsening significantly. She has been admitted to the hospital for pulmonary infections and "tune-ups" with increasing frequency over the past 18 months, and her baseline pulmonary function has declined steadily after each episode. Megan and her family have been meeting with the pulmonary team to discuss the possibility of lung transplant and to outline her goals of care. During one of these meetings, Megan expresses that she has no interest in lung transplant or in being kept alive "on machines" should her respiratory status deteriorate to the point where intubation and mechanical ventilation are necessary.

Megan had an older brother with CF who died at age 22 while awaiting a lung transplant. She and her family were present as he died in the ICU on a ventilator. She also has a sister who is healthy.

Megan's parents are unwilling to "lose another child to this horrible disease." They want to do whatever they can to optimize Megan's chances to receive healthy lungs and to stay alive as long as possible. The palliative care team is consulted to help the pulmonary team and the family work through a mutually agreeable plan of care.

As these discussions are progressing, Megan develops overwhelming sepsis and is admitted to the pediatric intensive care unit (PICU) for stabilization and treatment.

Cases such as these pose unique challenges to the team of providers caring for adolescent patients, as these patients are often caught in the difficult place of having the capacity to make their own health decisions, but lacking the legal power to do so.

Adolescence is, by definition, a period of profound transition from the near complete dependence of childhood to the self-determination of adulthood. As such, it is a period defined by emerging cognitive and problem-solving abilities, evolving emotional maturity, and growing psychosocial skills. It is a time when children begin to cement their own moral and personal values. All of these skills are necessary to face the unpredictable and complex challenges of adulthood, but none of these skills is magically mastered at the age of 18. Instead, mastery is a gradual and step-wise process that begins long before the age of 18, and continues well into the third decade of life, or beyond.

Making serious and complex medical decisions requires the use of all of these evolving faculties. Unfortunately, however, not all serious and complex decisions wait until adulthood. For adolescents like Megan, facing serious medical illnesses, important decisions need to be made during this crucial period of development. Navigating these situations requires a complex balancing act—acknowledging the amazing expertise adolescents possess about their own health, while also recognizing their limitations. In this chapter, we will explore how medical decisions are made for this unique population, including situations when there may be disagreements between adult caregivers and adolescent patients.

Despite medical progress, many adolescents will face serious medical challenges; an estimated 3,000 will die annually as the result of chronic illnesses, including cancer, cardiovascular diseases (e.g., congenital heart disease), pulmonary diseases (e.g., cystic fibrosis), AIDS, renal disease, metabolic disorders, neurologic diseases (e.g., muscular dystrophy or spinal muscular atrophy), and congenital anomalies (Xu, Kochanek, Murphy, and Tejada-Vera, 2010). While some of these children have associated cognitive limitations, many of them have the ability to participate in their own health care decisions.

Adolescence is defined as the period of life from the beginning of development of secondary sexual characteristics to the termination of growth. Dramatic physical changes are accompanied by equally dramatic cognitive changes, including the enhanced development of logical and abstract reasoning, the refinement of new social skills needed for the creation of meaningful long-term relationships outside of the family, and the emergence of self-image and identity. While living with a serious, chronic illness can impart great, albeit untimely, wisdom, it is also important to acknowledge that illness itself can impede normal development. With the demands of intensive medical treatments and doctor's visits, the associated physical changes or limitations, and the constant emotional burdens, serious illness can interfere with the typical peer interactions necessary for normal development. This in no way implies that adolescents with chronic illness are poorly adjusted, but merely emphasizes the far-reaching effects of the diagnosis of a serious or chronic illness.

To understand decision making for the adolescent, it is first important to understand the principles that apply to decision making for adults. The long-established principle of *autonomy* dictates that a competent adult patient over the legal age of 18 has the right to make his or her own medical decisions. In the United States, autonomy is such a highly valued principle that overruling it, even if a choice may cause significant harm or death, is tantamount to battery and must only occur in an extremely limited set of circumstances. For adults, competency—a legal term—is presumed. In practice, providers determine whether a patient is able to make his or her own decisions by assessing capacity—a medical term.

Decisional capacity requires four things—that a patient (a) be able to understand the medical information provided to him; (b) be able to appreciate the consequences of his decision; (c) be able to demonstrate reasoning when reaching a decision; and (d) be able to express a decision that is consistent with his priorities and beliefs (Schlam and Wood, 2000). If a patient can demonstrate these skills, respect for the principle of autonomy necessitates that his or her own wishes are followed. However, in situations where a previously competent adult has been deemed to lack decisional capacity, medical decisions must then be made by a surrogate using the principle of *substituted judgment*; that is, the surrogate attempts to reach a decision that most closely reflects the best understanding of a patient's previously stated wishes and values.

As children and adolescents have not met the legal age of competency, they do not possess the legal right to make their own decisions or consent to treatment (except in cases of emancipation, which will not be discussed here). Therefore, surrogates—usually parents or primary caregivers—must legally make all medical decisions on behalf of a child. Because true informed consent can only be given for oneself, these surrogates for children provide informed *permission*. The presumption, unless proven otherwise, is that the surrogate is making decisions based on the best interest of the child. The best interest standard stems from a beneficent ethical goal: to protect a vulnerable population (children) from harm—ostensibly from the harm of their own poor or immature decisions. However, this legal precedent ignores the general consensus that most adolescents, as well as some older children, have decisional capacity long before the age of legal competency. As such, an ethical approach dictates that they should be given input in decisions about their own health. Even in cases when a child does not possess decisional capacity, the goal is to have the child participate in her own health care decision making to whatever degree she is able and interested, and to *assent* to treatment whenever appropriate.

In practice, the goal of including children in their own health care decision making does not come without challenges. There are no checklists to determine competency and capacity in children and adolescents. So how does one determine the best way to involve a child or adolescent in decision making at a developmentally appropriate level? Even more challenging, how does one respond if a child does not agree with parent or health care provider decisions (i.e., expresses dissent)? This chapter looks at how to honor the ethical principles of autonomy and self-determination in the adolescent patient within the legal constraints of society.

Most of the data (American Academy of Pediatrics Committee on Bioethics, 1994, 1995; Freyer, 1992; Ross, 1997; Weir and Peters, 1997) suggest that adolescents over the age of 14 have the skills necessary for decision-making capacity. These skills—understanding medical information, appreciating the consequences of decisions, and reasoning—are those for determining capacity in adult patients. One additional factor to highlight in this age group is that of voluntary choice. Adolescents must be able to show that they are making their choice independent of (not because of or in spite of) the authority figures in their life—particularly parents and physicians. The general consensus among pediatric health care providers, psychologists, ethicists, and lawyers is that adolescents, age 14 and older, should be presumed to have decision-making capacity, unless proven otherwise (Freyer, 2004). Children younger than 14, on the other hand, should be presumed to *lack* decisional capacity, *unless proven otherwise;* this implies, therefore, that providers should seek to determine whether these children have the ability to make their own decisions. A subset of older children, and potentially a large subset, will meet these criteria, particularly as the medical illness itself will impart an invaluable perspective and knowledge that healthy peers would lack.

In 2004 David Freyer published a sentinel article in the journal of *Pediatrics* focusing on end-of-life decisions for the adolescent patient. In this article, he argues that adolescents who have shown decisional capacity "have the functional competence to make *binding* medical decisions for themselves, including decisions relating to the discontinuance of life-sustaining therapy and other end-of-life issues." If all parties agree, this is the ideal situation, as the child will feel empowered to make a decision in consensus with, and with full support from, his or her family and medical team. This position also argues for the term "modified substituted judgment," in which an adolescent who meets criteria for decisional capacity is given full and binding authority to make decisions, and the parent, following the wishes of the child, is able to provide the legal authority to execute that wish. Conflict arises, clearly, in cases where a parent, who has legal authority, and a child, who may have ethical or moral standing, disagree about the proper decision. If these decisions are ethically but not necessarily legally binding, how do we resolve disagreements? While this all-or-nothing approach may have some advantages, another way to approach these situations is using the principle of shared decision making, where all sides—the child, the caregiver, as well as the physician—have a valid say in all decisions. The American Academy of Pediatrics' (AAP) 1995 Policy Statement on "Informed Consent, Parental Permission and Assent in Pediatric Practice" stresses the importance of shared decision making:

> Decision-making involving the health care of older children and adolescents should include, to the greatest extent feasible, the assent of the patient as well as the participation of the parent and the physician. Pediatricians should not necessarily treat children as rational, autonomous decision makers, but they should give serious consideration to each patient's developing capacities for participating in decision-making, including rationality and autonomy. If physicians recognize the importance of assent, they empower children to the extent of their capacity. (p. 315)

The key to shared decision making is the use of a graduated level of input, where the weight of the child or adolescent's view is dependent on the individual's abilities and experiences. Over time, as a child or adolescent becomes more sophisticated, he should be given an increasingly larger say in the decisions about his health. Age, while important, is not the sole factor, as multiple other equally important factors evolve in a similar, but independent, manner. The first of these factors is intellectual ability. Though intellectual abilities generally increase with time, there is high variability across a population. Complex decision making, by definition, requires that an individual have the intellectual capacity to comprehend difficult medical information and use it to weigh risks and benefits, burdens, and long-term implications. As children can demonstrate their growing ability to reason and understand, they should be given greater input into their medical decisions.

The second factor is that of emotional maturity. Children vary widely in their ability to appreciate how their fears and insecurities shape their decisions, how their decisions impact others in their families and community, and how to balance short-term comfort with long-term benefits. This category would also include spiritual maturity, as children and adolescents establish their own values and priorities based on their evolving beliefs about the purpose of life and the meaning of suffering.

Third, an individual's personal experience with an illness should have a profound impact on his or her ability to participate in medical decision making. The wishes of adolescents who have lived with the cruelties of a chronic illness for the bulk of their lives should certainly be given greater standing than those of adolescents newly diagnosed with an illness, with little understanding of the future reality.

Finally, the proximity to end of life also influences the degree to which patients without the legal ability to consent should have their health care decisions honored. Protection of the vulnerable from their own poor decision making takes on a different significance when the child is not going to survive; most experts agree in these circumstances that the adolescent's wishes and decisions should be given more weight than in situations where cure is still a reasonable expectation. Taken together, these factors will determine the degree to which an individual patient can participate in his or her own medical decisions, appropriate for his or her ability level.

One additional point to highlight is that shared decision making requires that an older child or adolescent's opinion, if elicited or expressed, must be treated as valid. As stated in the 1995 AAP Policy, "we note that no one should solicit a patient's views without intending to weigh them seriously." Asking for the child's opinion, but then subsequently disregarding his thoughts, will only serve to devalue the child's growing autonomy and undermine trust.

As mentioned above and in Megan's case, medical decision making in this population has the potential for significant conflicts, particularly when the wishes of a child or adolescent differ from that of an adult caregiver. Ideally, most of these conflicts can be solved without resorting to legal action by using an interdisciplinary team and employing a family-centered approach. With rare exceptions, legal intervention should be the last resort.

When trying to resolve disagreements, teams should be very deliberate in requiring that both parties genuinely listen to and acknowledge the views of the other. For Megan, the first step involves facilitating a conversation between Megan and her parents, allowing each to express their hopes and goals, as well as their reasons for choosing their respective positions. Ideally, these conversations occur in advance of significant changes in health status or times of crisis. In reality, however, it is often an acute event (such as a PICU admission) that precipitates discussion and the ensuing conflict. Legally, of course, the parents' wishes would prevail; however, pediatric health care providers have a fiduciary duty toward their child patients to advocate for their voices to be respected. One effective strategy in situations like this is to encourage the parents to enable their daughter to exert control over her own body and her own disease—control that has likely been lacking throughout most of her life. While the family may ultimately not be able to save their daughter, they can honor her autonomy and personal integrity by allowing her to make her own health care decisions and choose her end-of-life path.

Following this approach allows the team to genuinely honor the strengths that each side brings. For caregivers, it is important to appreciate the long-standing devotion they have shown to the child, to recognize the intensity with which they will fight for their child's life, and to acknowledge that these caregivers will have to live with any decision for the remainder of their lives. For the adolescent, it is key to acknowledge the individual's suffering and unique perspective of his or her experience with illness. In addition, it is important to educate families about the ethical principles underlying decision making in a nonjudgmental way that emphasizes the emerging autonomy of their child. By creating mutual understanding through effective communication, the team can usually allow the adolescent patient and his or her family to come to a mutually acceptable consensus.

Another more common, but fortunately less emotionally charged, challenge is trying to determine the best way to share serious medical information with children and adolescents of all developmental levels: effective, empathic, bidirectional communication. Full exploration of this topic is out of the scope of this chapter. However, it is imperative that children and adolescents receive sufficient developmentally appropriate and culturally-sensitive information about their conditions in order to participate actively in their treatment. In particular, adolescents like Megan cannot make informed decisions for themselves unless they understand:

1. The name of their condition, how and why it occurs, and whether and how it is treatable.
2. The range of usual life expectancy.
3. The anticipated illness trajectory, likely symptomatology, impacts on quality of life, and likely causes and mechanisms of death.
4. Types of disease-modifying treatments available, along with their short- and long-term benefits, and known and potential burdens.
5. Expected complications of illness and treatment, and their outcomes.
6. Possible treatments to prevent and relieve suffering.
7. The supports available for them and their families, friends, and community (Graham, Levetown, and Comeau, 2011, p. 140).

In addition to outlining the minimum requirements for informed health care decision making, this focus on communication allows us to highlight the importance of an interdisciplinary team. By utilizing the team psychologist, child life specialist, or other provider who has formed a strong bond with the child, the team should be able to share medical information in a way that is developmentally appropriate, while also providing the patient with the sense that his or her views are valid and important.

An additional challenge is that of nondisclosure requests. In these situations, families request that health information, typically bad news, not be shared with their children, for fear that the news would be too upsetting or would cause them to lose hope and "give up." Through a step-wise approach that generally begins with prevention, most such requests can be effectively handled without eroding trust. Except in certain cultural and religious traditions, it is unusual for families to be as adamant about keeping information from adolescents as occurs with younger children. Nevertheless, exploring what the family is afraid will happen, and what the adolescent already knows, is an effective starting place when this dynamic occurs. Further discussion of this complex issue can be found in the Reference section below; see in particular the work of Zieber and Friebert (2008).

Working through serious medical decision making in the adolescent population certainly comes with many challenges; most significant among them is the difficulty of balancing the ethical and moral principles of autonomy with the legal constraints of adolescence, all within a developmentally diverse set of patients. However, when it is done effectively, it can be an intensely rewarding experience. Shared decision making not only empowers the patient to take control of his or her own health, but honors the invaluable role of the parent or other caregiver. For patients like Megan, the opportunity to actualize control over their own bodies and conditions through autonomous health care decision making is a right and a gift that represents the least we can offer them in their suffering. Regardless of age, adolescents with chronic or complex conditions deserve no less.

Kristin Meade, MD, is currently working at Duke Hospital as an assistant professor of medicine in palliative medicine. She completed her medical training at Stanford University School of Medicine, followed by residency in the combined program of internal medicine and pediatrics at Duke University and a fellowship in pediatric palliative care at Akron Children's Hospital. She has a strong interest in medical ethics and is an acting member of the Duke Hospital Ethics Committee and the Clinical Ethics Consult Subcommittee. Her research focus is on the ethical principles guiding the use of intensive care for children and young adults with complex, chronic medical conditions.

Sarah Friebert, MD, is the founder and director of the Haslinger Family Pediatric Palliative Care Center at Akron Children's Hospital in Akron, Ohio, where she holds an endowed leadership chair in pediatric palliative care and directs the ACGME-accredited palliative medicine fellowship training program. In 2008, the Center was selected as a pediatric Palliative Care Leadership Center by the Center to Advance Palliative Care. Dr. Friebert is chair of the Section of Hospice and Palliative Medicine of the American Academy of Pediatrics, a member of the board of directors of the American Academy of Hospice and Palliative Medicine, and serves as consulting pediatric medical director for the National Hospice and Palliative Care Organization. Dr. Friebert is associate professor of pediatrics at Northeast Ohio Medical University. Her research interests include:

ethical decision making, spirituality in children, models of effective care delivery, and interventions to reduce symptom distress in children and families facing life-threatening conditions.

REFERENCES

American Academy of Pediatrics Committee on Bioethics. (1995). Informed consent, parental permission, and assent in pediatric practice. *Pediatrics, 95,* 314–317.

American Academy of Pediatrics Committee on Bioethics. (1994). Guidelines on forgoing life-sustaining medical treatment. *Pediatrics, 93,* 532–536.

Freyer, D. R. (1992). Children with cancer: Special considerations in the discontinuation of life-sustaining treatment. *Medical and Pediatric Oncology, 20,* 136–142.

Freyer, D. R. (2004). Care of the dying adolescent: Special considerations. *Pediatrics, 113,* 381–388.

Graham, R. J., Levetown, M., & Comeau, M. (2011). Decision making. In B. S. Carter, M. Levetown, & S.E. Friebert (Eds.). *Palliative care for infants, children, and adolescents,* (2nd ed.) (p. 139-168). Baltimore, MD: Johns Hopkins University Press.

Ross, L. F. (1997). Health care decision making by children: Is it in their best interest? *Hastings Center Report, 27,* 41–45.

Schlam, L., & Wood, J. P. (2000). Informed consent to the medical treatment of minors. *Health Matrix: Journal of Law-Medicine, 10,* 141–174.

Weir, R. F., & Peters, C. (1997). Affirming the decision adolescents make about life and death. *Hastings Center Report, 27,* 29–40.

Xu, J., Kochanek, K. D., Murphy, S. L., & Tejada-Vera, B. (2010). *National Vital Statistics Report, 58,* 1–134. Retrieved from: http://www.cdc.gov/nchs/data/nvsr/nvsr58/nvsr58_19.pdf

Zieber, S., & Friebert, S. E. (2008). Pediatric cancer care: Special issues in ethical decision making. In P. Angelos (Ed.). *Ethical issues in cancer patient care,* (2nd ed.) (p. 93–116). New York: Springer.

FURTHER READING

American Academy of Pediatrics Committee on Bioethics and Committee on Hospital Care. (2000). Palliative care for children. *Pediatrics, 106,* (Pt 1):351–357.

Friebert, S. (2008). Palliative care. In W. L. Carroll, J.L. Finlay, (Eds.). *Cancer in children and adolescents* (p. 513–522). Sudbury, MA: Jones and Bartlett Publishers.

Virtual Mentor. (2010). Pediatric palliative care. American Medical Association Journal of Ethics; 12,7: 517–602; www.virtualmentor.ama-assn. org/2010/07/pdf/vm-1004.pdf

CHAPTER 17

Does Dementia Change the Equation? Advance Directives and Dementia

Charles A. Corr, Karen M. Corr, and Susan M. Ramsey

The phrase *advance directives* applies to a wide range of instructions that one might make orally or in writing about actions one would or would not want to be taken if one were somehow incapacitated and unable to take part in making decisions concerning issues involving health care at the end of life (Doukas and Reichel, 2007). Since 1991, the Patient Self-Determination Act has required that individuals being admitted to a health care facility that receives federal Medicare or Medicaid funds be informed of their right to accept or refuse treatment and to execute a written advance directive (Zucker, 2007). Such individuals must also be told about the options available to them to implement those rights (Urich, 2001). Even so, many do not exercise their right to complete an advance directive—but that, too, is within their rights. One reason may be that any advance directive depends on an individual's cognitive capacity and willingness to address ahead of time the implications of his or her possible incapacitation and death, as well as what that might mean for the lives of family members and close friends.

LIVING WILLS

Although they lacked legal standing when they first appeared in the 1970s, early living wills were intended as a means whereby persons who were competent decision makers could convey their wishes to professional care providers, family members, and friends about interventions they might or might not wish to permit in the event of a terminal illness. Typically, living wills express concerns about two areas. One is the possibility of finding oneself in a situation in which one would be unable to take part in making important decisions. The other addresses the context of dying in which one might be in an unfamiliar or alien environment, among strangers who might have their own individual or professional views of what should or should not be done, and who might not understand, appreciate, or agree with the wishes of the person who wrote the living will.

In general, living wills focus on a request to withhold or withdraw interventions that merely prolong dying when one is in an incurable or irreversible condition with no reasonable prospect of recovery; they characteristically do not call for direct killing or active euthanasia. Living wills usually contain language such as: "I am not asking that my life be directly taken, but that my dying not be unreasonably prolonged." The primary goals are to refuse certain kinds of cure-oriented interventions ("artificial means" and "heroic measures") when they are no longer relevant ("futile care" that can no longer be expected to produce a cure); to request that dying be permitted to take its natural course; and to ask that suffering associated with life-threatening illness be mitigated with effective palliative care, even if such palliative care should have a collateral or side effect of hastening the actual moment of death.

The broad legal context for living wills is the well-established right to privacy and the right of competent decision makers to give or withhold informed consent and to accept or refuse interventions even when that might affect the timing of the individual's death (Alderman and Kennedy, 1997; Annas, 2004; Rozovsky, 1990). So-called "natural death" legislation now endorses the legal status of living wills in all 50 states and the District of Columbia. Typically, such legislation

- specifies the conditions under which a competent adult is authorized to sign a document of this type;
- stipulates the form such a document must take to have legal force;
- defines what sorts of interventions can or cannot be refused—for example, interventions undertaken with a view toward cure, which may or may not include hydration or nutrition;
- authorizes oral or written repudiation of the document by the signer at any time;
- requires that professional care providers either cooperate with the document's directives or withdraw from the case and arrange for alternative care (consenting to do so is thus legally protected, whereas failure to do so is theoretically subject not merely to potential malpractice liability but also to penalties that could extend in principle to loss of professional licensure); and

- stipulates that death resulting from actions authorized by the legislation is not to be construed as suicide for insurance purposes.

Legislative models have been proposed (e.g., President's Commission, 1982) that typically

- relate to all competent adults and mature minors—not only those who are dying;
- apply to all medical interventions without limiting the types that may be refused;
- permit the designation of a substitute or surrogate decision maker in a manner similar to that described in the following section;
- require health care providers to follow the directives of the individual and incorporate sanctions for those who fail to do so; and
- stipulate that palliative care be continued for those who refuse other interventions.

This model exceeds the scope of early living wills and includes features now more typical of durable powers of attorney.

Potential difficulties have led to criticisms of living wills (see Fagerlin and Schneider, 2004). For example, like any document written down in advance, living wills may not anticipate every relevant feature that might arise in a complex, life-threatening situation. Partly for this reason, their significance and force may be subject to interpretation or dispute among the family members and professional care providers they seek to guide. Nevertheless, individuals are usually advised to make out a living will according to the laws of the jurisdiction in which they reside and to couple it with a durable power of attorney in health care matters.

DURABLE POWERS OF ATTORNEY IN HEALTH CARE MATTERS

State legislation authorizing "durable powers of attorney for the making of decisions in health care matters" (sometimes called a "health care proxy") is grounded in the well-established legal doctrine of "power of attorney" whereby one individual authorizes another individual (or group of individuals) to make decisions and take actions on behalf of the first individual in specific circumstances or for a specified period of time. Historically, a power of attorney continued in force only while its author remained competent. A "durable" power of attorney is one that endures until it is revoked; that is, it continues in force even (or especially) when the individual who authorized the designation is no longer able to act as a competent decision maker.

Reputed advantages of durable powers of attorney are that they empower an agent (a surrogate or substitute decision maker) to make decisions on behalf of an individual in any and all circumstances the document covers, and the agent can be instructed to refuse all interventions, to insist on all interventions, or to approve some interventions and reject others. The first advantage attempts to minimize problems arising from changing circumstances and competing interpretations of written documents; the second allows the person authorizing the agent—and the agent—some degree of freedom in choosing which interventions to accept and which to refuse. Legislation authorizing durable powers of attorney in health care matters has been approved in most jurisdictions in the United States.

Five Wishes

An organization called Aging with Dignity developed a document that combines many of the best elements of living wills and durable powers of attorney in health care matters. The "Five Wishes" document is specially designed to be easy to understand, simple to use, personal in character, and thorough. This document asks the person filling it out to express desires about these issues and provides guidance on each of them: (a) the person I want to make health care decisions for me when I can't make them for myself; (b) the kind of medical treatment I want or don't want if I am close to death, in a coma, or have permanent and severe brain damage and am not expected to recover from that situation, or I am in another condition under which I do not wish to be kept alive; (c) how comfortable I want to be; (d) how I want people to treat me; and (e) what I want my loved ones to know.

The "Five Wishes" document currently meets the legal requirements of a majority of states under their living will and durable power of attorney in health care matters regulations; in other states and countries it can be used to help individuals offer guidance to their care providers. The document is available in English or Spanish, and there are bilingual versions in two dozen languages.

Dementia

According to the Alzheimer's Association (2011, p. 5),

Dementia is caused by various diseases and conditions that result in damaged brain cells or connections between brain cells. . . . To meet *DSM-IV (Diagnostic and Statistical Manual of Mental Disorders, Fourth Edition)*, the following are required:

- Symptoms must include decline in memory *and* in at least one of the following cognitive abilities:

1. Ability to generate coherent speech or understand spoken or written language;

2. Ability to recognize or identify objects, assuming intact sensory function;

3. Ability to execute motor activities, assuming intact motor abilities, sensory function and comprehension of the required task; and

4. Ability to think abstractly, make sound judgments and plan and carry out complex tasks.

- The decline in cognitive abilities must be severe enough to interfere with daily life.

Dementia refers to a broad category of neurodegenerative diseases for which there is no known cure, that lead to irreversible cognitive impairment and are fatal. Dementia contrasts with *delirium*, which is characterized by sudden onset and significant fluctuations in mood that can be induced by certain medications, medication interactions, vitamin deficiencies, or other conditions such as urinary tract infections or pneumonia. Many persons with delirium may regain lost functions when treated properly. Some other chronic disorders, like Parkinson's disease or amyotrophic lateral sclerosis (Lou Gehrig's disease) involve progressive loss of control over bodily functioning not usually accompanied by cognitive impairment, although dementia can develop in the late stages of these diseases.

Alzheimer's disease (AD), perhaps the best-known type of dementia, is a chronic and progressive brain disorder primarily affecting memory, thinking, behavior, and the ability to perform everyday activities. Typically beginning with mild cognitive impairment (MCI), AD advances more or less gradually and inexorably until affected individuals can no longer function or care for themselves and inevitably die.

The Alzheimer's Association (2011) has estimated that there were 5.4 million persons living with AD in North America in 2010, of which some 5.2 million were age 65 or older (roughly 1 in 8 in this age group). In 2007, AD was identified as the sixth leading cause of all deaths in the United States, leading to 74,632 deaths and a death rate of 23.7 per 100,000 (Xu, Kochanek, Murphy, and Tejada-Vera, 2010). AD is the fifth leading cause of death for individuals age 65 or older. Nevertheless, AD deaths may be underreported when the immediate cause of death is ascribed to complications arising from dementia, such as aspiration pneumonia from being bed-bound at the end of life or falls associated with wandering. Also, many persons with AD have unrelated health problems that can lead to debilitation and death. Thus, the distinction between dying *from* AD and dying *with* AD may not be very clear (Ganguli and Rodriguez, 1999).

It is important to note that AD and dementias of all types are not a part of normal aging, and only about 15% of individuals with MCI go on to develop AD. Still, AD and other forms of dementia are primarily found among older adults; after age 65, the likelihood of developing AD or other dementias doubles every five years. Whereas most other leading disease-related causes of death have shown a gradual decrease in numbers in recent years, deaths from AD have increased by nearly 66 % since 1980. AD is a particularly challenging cause of death because at present it cannot be prevented, cured, or slowed in any appreciable degree.

Numbers of deaths from AD have risen rapidly in recent years, partly as a result of improved identification and awareness of this condition, partly because of changes in the way diseases are classified in the international coding system, and partly because of increases in the population of older adults (and especially older females) who are most likely to experience AD.

CASE STUDY
Early Dementia with Intermittent Periods of Lucidity
George and Sylvia Stock were in their early 60s when George began to display memory problems and symptoms of confusion. This alarmed Sylvia because she was in frail health; George had always been the strong member of the pair and took care of most practical problems they faced. Earlier the Stocks had been urged to complete advance directives and to establish revocable living trusts so that either could act for the other if one became unable to participate in

decision making. They had not acted on this advice despite the encouragement they received from their daughter, Linda, a nurse who lived in town. Both George and Sylvia were initially puzzled and sometimes frustrated or annoyed by his memory lapses and what appeared to be problems with uncertainty, misunderstandings, and bewilderment. They did not think these were of much consequence, although it was hard to maintain that view as George's sporadic forgetfulness became more persistent. In one of George's several brief periods of lucidity, Linda shared with them the Alzheimer's Association's ten warning signs of AD. Sylvia told George she worried that things seemed to be changing more rapidly, and George agreed. They sought a consultation with a geriatrician who confirmed what they had only suspected. Linda obtained more literature about dementia to share with her parents and her brother, Joe, who lived in another city with his wife and children (e.g., Kuhn, 2003).

Advanced Dementia

As George's dementia progressed, he developed problems in driving, got lost one day while out walking, and left some food cooking on a stove. At this point, George's behaviors seemed to change from day to day or even moment to moment. Sylvia had to prod George to take the medications he needed and she kept watch over him so he would not wander off at night or when he wasn't properly dressed for inclement weather. That was a burden to her, but it became much worse when he began to display outbursts of irritation and rapid mood swings. His personality now seemed so different from the kind, gentle man to whom she had been married for so many years. Foul language and aggression toward others drove many of their former friends away. It was especially hurtful when George could no longer recognize family members or sometimes mistook them for long-dead relatives.

Finally, when George could no longer take care of his daily needs and both Sylvia and Linda had become worn out, they had to consider placing him in a health care facility. Linda's brother Joe thought this wasn't really needed, but Linda told him he didn't know what it was like trying to care for their father on a day-to-day basis. In fact, the long-term care facility they chose provided a pleasant and secure environment for George. His needs were met and he adjusted well to his new surroundings. Eventually, he even made friends with a female resident and they spent lots of time together watching television, walking around, or just holding hands. Gradually, however, his decline continued, he lost weight, his health worsened, and his needs increased greatly.

ANALYSIS

The primary ethical dilemma that arises in dementia is which health care decisions should be made and who should make them. When George finally agreed to complete an advance directive, he discussed his wishes concerning care with his wife and daughter, and he and Sylvia each completed individual advance directives naming Linda as their agent. All this was to the good.

As his dementia progressed, however, George gradually lost the ability to care for himself and to perform activities of daily living. In principle, Sylvia and Linda then jointly faced a series of difficult decisions; in practice, however, because Sylvia was growing increasingly frail and had always been a rather anxious person, she turned more and more to Linda for guidance and became increasingly reliant on her daughter's decisions. Linda sought to involve her brother in all important decisions, but she did not find him to be of much help. Among the important decisions they faced were: the need to place George in a suitable institution; how to respond when he developed an acute infection; what to do when he failed a swallowing evaluation and placement of a feeding tube was recommended; and how to deal with other aspects of his treatment and issues of resuscitation should they arise.

From time to time, Joe would fly into town to visit his parents and, as he said, to "help out" with some of these decisions. In the early stages of George's dementia, these brief visits tended to invigorate both George and Sylvia for short periods of time. That led Joe to believe that things were not all that bad and that Linda was perhaps overstating the challenges she and her parents faced. For Linda, these visits by her brother made it more difficult to know what was best to do. Disagreements with Joe and his efforts to persuade Sylvia to agree with him undermined Linda's confidence that her convictions about how to care for her father (and mother) were well founded. She gained some reassurance, however, by talking to her father's geriatrician and a good friend who was a nurse practitioner. Both of these professionals had extensive experience with dementia patients and both offered practical guidance at each step of a long journey.

DECISIONS AND CONSEQUENCES

Linda and Sylvia made some principal decisions concerning treatment for George, some of which evoked increasing objections from Joe.

From the outset, Linda and Sylvia decided to do all they could to keep George in the familiar environment of the family home. In this, they responded to guidance that themes of loneliness, isolation, and fear are often found in persons in the early stages of dementia. As a result, Linda and Sylvia reassured George that he would not be abandoned and that they continued to love and value him as a cherished member of their family. Reading from Kuhn's book, (2003, p. 86), that "awareness of decline in mental abilities is often coupled with appreciation of the remaining gifts in one's life," Linda and Sylvia worked diligently to share valued activities with George and to give him the gift of their presence.

As George's dementia progressed, Linda and Sylvia eventually found themselves unable to continue to provide the care he needed at home. They decided to place George in a health care facility that specialized in caring for residents with dementia. This was not a decision they found easy to make as it represented a major change in the lives of all three of them. They felt guilty about not being able to fulfill wishes expressed by George earlier that he die at home and not be put in a nursing home. In fact, guilt was and continued to be a major theme in their lives from this time forward, especially for Linda, who was basically responsible for most of the decisions that had to be made concerning George's care. Even though she knew she was speaking for her father when he could no longer do so, she had to constantly remind herself she was upholding values they had always shared. Recalling comments George himself had made in the past approving similar decisions involving other family members and friends confirmed Linda's conviction as she faced each new challenge, but she could never shake off some lingering sense of guilt and grief as she made choices on behalf of her father.

When George was lucid and appeared to be able to continue to function with their assistance and with help from friends, neighbors, their church group, a community day care program, and an in-home service, Linda and Sylvia were able to concentrate on the present. They came to believe they could continue on in this way for some time even as they tried not to think too far into the future. In the end, however, the care that George needed, his increasingly erratic and difficult behavior, and the burdens placed on all of them were too much for Linda and Sylvia. Joe seemed to believe it wasn't really necessary to institutionalize George and he expressed some concern about the costs of long-term care, but he went along with this plan.

As they planned for George's care when he was placed in the nursing home, Sylvia and Linda had consulted with their geriatrician who would follow him in long-term care. In so doing, they learned that their state was one of about a dozen in which they could develop with the geriatrician what she called Physician Orders for Life-Sustaining Treatment (POLST) (Nisco, Mittelberger, and Citko, 2011; Sabatino and Karp, 2011). As she explained, the POLST model is specifically designed for individuals with a chronic, progressive illness and would help clarify treatment options and preferences for George throughout each stage of his disease. A POLST would document those decisions on a standardized medical order form that would be inserted in George's medical records. The geriatrician made clear that an order like this is readily recognized by health care professionals, such as those who provide various types of care to individuals in the community. In George's case, the POLST would officially guide all aspects of his treatment and complement his advance directives, even accompanying him to hospital or medical appointments, should these occur. The POLST would be reviewed on a regular basis and adjusted if necessary.

Somewhat later, as his dementia continued to progress, George became incontinent and developed a urinary tract infection. At that point, George was no longer able to participate in decisions about his care, but his family unanimously agreed with the staff recommendation to treat this acute outburst. This was a relatively easy decision for the family to make.

Much later, staff at the long-term care facility recommended that George be given a swallowing evaluation. The reason for this was that, even though he continued to be able to feed himself somewhat, George had begun to display escalating episodes of coughing, congestion, and choking. Efforts had been made to modify George's diet to soft foods and altered liquids, as well as to offer assistance to him in eating, but these did not seem to improve the situation. As a result, some staff became concerned that George might experience incidents of aspiration pneumonia. Without fully understanding what was involved in this recommendation, Sylvia and Linda agreed to having this evaluation performed by a qualified speech-language pathologist.

When George failed the swallowing evaluation, the family faced a decision as to whether or not to authorize the placement of a feeding tube. They were told that tube feeding might help to minimize some of the difficulties George was currently facing, thereby improving to some degree the quality of his life and perhaps also how long he would live. They were also told, however, that it would not have any effect on his underlying and progressive dementia, it would restrict his mobility even further, and it would probably mean that he would no longer be allowed to take anything by mouth. Also, placement of a feeding tube would provide nutrition and hydration, but it would not rule out the possibility of aspiration of tube feedings.

Sylvia and Linda were unsure how to proceed. They had put off making a decision on that point when they drew up the POLST order, but now they sought advice from the professionals who had helped them earlier in the course of George's disease and from a trusted clergyperson. From these sources, they learned that other families had responded to challenges like this in different ways. Some families felt that prolonging life under almost any circumstances was their primary duty. For those families, it was almost as easy to agree to feeding tube placement as it had been for Sylvia, Linda, and Joe to agree to interventions to treat George's urinary tract infection. At the same time, Sylvia and Linda were told that other families viewed tube feeding in these circumstances to be an extraordinary intervention, one that did not address George's underlying dementia, might have unexpected outcomes, and was not absolutely required of them. One family member who had faced a similar situation with her mother told Sylvia and Linda that when this issue had been presented to her and her relatives, they were exhausted by their long journey and the many burdens they had faced. As a result, she had viewed this moment as a difficult but critical opportunity to "just let her mother drift off," as she said. So she had refused the placement of the feeding tube for her mother.

Sylvia and Linda shared all of this with Joe and urged him to help with the dilemma they faced. He immediately said he could not face the idea of "letting his father starve to death," as he put it. For Joe, deciding to authorize the placement of a feeding tube was almost an automatic decision. He found stories on the Internet that reported cases in which placement of a feeding tube led to a kind of recovery for some individuals who had later been able to remove the tube and once again swallow their food. For these reasons, Joe pleaded with Sylvia and Linda—especially with his mother—to permit the feeding tube to be placed. When Sylvia chose to withdraw from this difficult decision and "leave things to her children," as she said, Joe even argued that Linda had no right to reject the feeding tube and go against his wishes.

In fact, according to George's durable power of attorney in health care matters, Linda was the legitimate decision maker in these circumstances. Acting as George's agent, Linda made three critical decisions:

1. She brought on board a hospice program that had previously worked in

a cooperative way with the staff in George's long-term care facility and she sought the advice of the hospice interdisciplinary team on a plan of care that would provide her father with the best quality of life possible.

2. She arranged to review the POLST document with their geriatrician and subsequently determined with the staff of the facility that interventions under the POLST document would be restricted to those focused on quality of life.

3. She decided not to permit placement of the feeding tube, saying "I love my father, but I can't see that there is anything to offer here that provides a real, enduring gain for him or for any of the rest of the family."

As a result of these decisions, George did live for some time without the feeding tube and ultimately he died quite peacefully. Sylvia and Linda took comfort that George was receiving the best care available in his situation and was not burdened by interventions that were unnecessary or no longer relevant to his needs.

Sometime later, when Joe and his wife came to town for George's funeral, Joe confessed to Linda and Sylvia that, at his wife's urging and before his father's death, he had spoken by telephone with the geriatrician who had guided George's care. Joe said she had explained to him more fully the role of the POLST document, as well as the potential advantages and burdens if a feeding tube had been put into place for George. In addition, contacts with members of the hospice interdisciplinary team had helped Joe to come to a better appreciation of the challenges and burdens that his mother and sister had faced as George approached the end of his life. Joe said that all of these conversations had helped him to soften his disagreements with the decisions Linda and Sylvia had made. In the end, Joe was pleased that his father had, in fact, died a peaceful death.

CONCLUSION

Many lessons follow from the convergence of advance directives and dementia that is set out in this case study. It is important to note that this chapter only describes *some* of the difficult challenges associated with caring for a person with dementia. No single case can illustrate all possible challenges. No single family represents all the decisions that might be made by other families. Each journey with dementia is an individual pathway through a disease trajectory that is always complex and becoming increasingly prominent in contemporary societies. Nevertheless, there still are some useful lessons to learn from the experiences of this particular family and the decisions they faced.

- Putting in place an advance directive well before problems arise such as those described here can be invaluable. The advance directive should represent the thoughtful wishes of the individual who fills it out as clearly and in as much detail as possible.
- The person chosen to serve as the agent should be a person who understands as fully as possible the wishes of the individual on whose behalf he or she can eventually be expected to act, and the agent should be someone who can be trusted to execute those wishes.
- Copies of the advance directive and the identity of the person chosen to serve as the agent should be shared with the individual's family members, physician, and any individuals who provide care.
- It would be desirable to have a full and frank conversation about the diagnosis and prognosis of dementia as early as possible after that diagnosis has been established. Such a conversation should communicate: the need for advance directives if they are not already in place; the facts about dementia as a progressive, incurable disease that will eventually lead to death; as much of the likely problems and burdens to be encountered that the individual and his or her family members can absorb; and the reality that opportunities may continue to exist for quality in living and meaningful human interactions for some time to come before the disease reaches its final stages. At this point, individuals and their family members should be provided with literature about dementia and about effective coping strategies, as well as resources they can call upon as needed.
- Even when a person with AD remains at home, but especially when it becomes time to consider institutional placement, it is desirable to consider developing and inserting in the medical record a POLST order whenever that option is locally available. Knowledgeable, experienced, and appropriate professionals can be helpful in both the timing and the content of this and related discussions, but in the end the decisions to be made are properly the responsibility of the individual with dementia as long as he or she is competent to make or to participate in making such decisions, or of his or her designated agent when he or she is no longer competent to be involved in such decision making.
- As the disease progresses, additional conversations will be necessary to discuss changes in the individual with dementia, adjustments to POLST orders as necessary, and specific coping strategies for family members

to help both themselves and the individual with dementia; additional literature and resources may be needed to help clarify the issues at hand.

- Whenever possible, individuals with dementia and family members should be helped to anticipate particular developments and important decisions they are likely to face in the near future. One key point in time is when it may soon be necessary to consider relocating the individual with dementia from a home setting to a health care facility; another might be when it is expected that decisions may need to be made concerning interventions to address acute or chronic challenges; a third key point might be when it is desirable to consider reviewing POLST orders or other care plans.

- Individuals, and especially their family members, are likely to need targeted guidance and support when they almost inevitably face the most difficult decisions about quality in living and prolonging the life of the individual with dementia. Those decisions are likely to develop most easily when they have been the subject of prior discussions such as those reflected in advance directives.

- In view of the very long trajectories experienced by most individuals with dementia, it is likely that different professionals, organizations, and institutions of different types may become involved in helping individuals and family members or in directly delivering care themselves. In addition to multiple individuals, these organizations and institutions might include home care and/or day care programs, medical providers, respite programs, nurse practitioners, hospitals, long-term care facilities, and hospice programs. For that reason, it is desirable that they share common and consistent care philosophies so that individuals and their family members are not faced with a cacophony of voices, awkward handoffs, and difficult transitions from one system of providing care to another. All of these care providers need to be aware of the individual's wishes and supportive of them.

- There is an important role here for hospice care in advocating for advance directives in relationship to dementia. Hospice programs can serve as a model of what can be achieved in the care of individuals with dementia, as well as in caring for the family members of such individuals both before and after their deaths (Corr, Corr, and Ramsey, 2004). The principal reason for this is that dementia, particularly in its advanced forms, exhibits a strong fit with the hospice philosophy and its emphases on holistic care and interdisciplinary teamwork. Dementia affects both persons who have the disease themselves and other individuals who are affected because someone they know, love, or provide care for has the disease; it affects each of these people as unique individuals with their own personalities, backgrounds, and lifestyles; it can change their lives physically, cognitively, emotionally, socially, economically, behaviorally, and spiritually; it expresses itself in a very wide range of manifestations, while progressing irregularly and most often over an extended period of time; and it has a strong component of loss and grief, both during the progression of the disease and after the death of a person with dementia.

- While there are limitations in terms of admission requirements for dementia patients to hospice programs, in 2009 it was already the case that diagnoses of dementia including Alzheimer's disease exceeded 11 percent of all admissions to hospice programs (National Hospice and Palliative Care Organization [NHPCO], 2010, p. 7). This is partly because and partly in spite of the fact that hospice use has been "found to be higher for diseases that impose a high burden on caregivers, or diseases for which prognostic accuracy is easier to achieve" (NHPCO, 2010, p. 7). In fact, a recent study found that, "Bereaved family members of people with dementia who received hospice reported higher perceptions of the quality of care and quality of dying" (Teno et al., 2011, p. 1531).

Hospice programs will not be able to care for all dementia patients and should not be expected to do so. Other caregiving systems can and will continue to provide excellent, high-quality care for dementia patients. But hospice programs can play an important role in caring for a significant portion of such patients and their families, as well as in setting standards for such care.

Charles A. Corr, PhD, is vice-chair of the Board of Directors for the Suncoast Hospice Institute, an affiliate of Suncoast Hospice. Dr. Corr is also a member of the International Work Group on Death, Dying, and Bereavement (Chairperson, 1989-1993); the Association for Death Education and Counseling; the ChiPPS (Children's Project on Palliative/Hospice Services) Communications Work Group of the National Hospice and Palliative Care Association; and the Executive Committee of the National Donor Family Council. Dr. Corr's publications include more than three dozen books and articles, along with well over 100 chapters and articles in professional journals in the field of death, dying, and bereavement.

His most recent publications include two chapters in Beyond Kübler-Ross: New Perspectives on Death, Dying and Grief *(Hospice Foundation of America, 2011) and the seventh edition of* Death & Dying, Life & Living *(Wadsworth, 2013), co-authored with Donna M. Corr.*

Karen M. Corr, *RN, MSN, ARNP, is a gerontological nurse practitioner and clinical advisor for Evercare, providing primary care in local skilled nursing facilities in Washington state. Her article, "Taking the Gloves Off: Caring for Confused Patients without Using Restraints" (co-authored with Donna M. Corr, RN, MS), was published in* Nursing94.

Susan M. Ramsey, *MS, CCC-SLP, is a speech-language pathologist and senior rehab director for Premier Therapy Services in Tacoma, Washington. She has practiced as a manager and speech language pathologist in a geriatric setting since 1991 and has presented at local and state levels on the topics of swallowing, its disorders, and management strategies.*

References

Alderman, E., & Kennedy, C. (1997). *The right to privacy.* New York: Vintage.

Alzheimer's Association. (2011). *2011 Alzheimer's disease facts and figures.* Chicago: Author.

Annas, G. J. (2004). *The rights of patients* (3rd ed.). Carbondale, IL: Southern Illinois University Press.

Corr, C. A., Corr, K. M., & Ramsey, S. M. (2004). Alzheimer's disease and the challenge for hospice. In K. J. Doka (Ed.), *Living with grief: Alzheimer's disease* (pp. 227–243). Washington, DC: Hospice Foundation of America.

Doukas, D. J., & Reichel, W. (2007). *Planning for uncertainty: Living wills and other advance directives for you and your family* (2nd ed.). Baltimore, MD: Johns Hopkins University Press.

Fagerlin, A., & Schneider, C. E. (2004). Enough: The failure of the living will. *Hastings Center Report, 34*(2), 30–42.

Ganguli, M., & Rodriguez, E. G. (1999). Reporting of dementia on death certificates: A community study. *Journal of the American Geriatrics Society, 47*, 842–849.

Kuhn, D. (2003). *Alzheimer's early stages: First steps for family, friends, and caregivers* (2nd ed.). Alameda, CA: Hunter House Publishers.

National Hospice and Palliative Care Organization (NHPCO). (2010). NHPCO facts and figures: Hospice care in America. Alexandria, VA: Author. Retrieved from http://www.nhpco.org/research

Nisco, M., Mittelberger, J., & Citko, J. (2011, May). POLST: An evidence-based tool for advance care planning. *Newsline: The monthly membership publication of the National Hospice and Palliative Care Organization*, pp. 1–2.

President's Commission for the Study of Ethical Problems in Medicine and Biomedical and Behavioral Research. (1982). *Making health care decisions: A report on the ethical and legal implications of informed consent in the patient-practitioner relationship. Vol. 1, Report; Vol. 3, Studies on the foundation of informed consent.* Washington, DC: U.S. Government Printing Office.

Rozovsky, F. A. (1990). *Consent to treatment: A practical guide* (2nd ed.). Boston: Little, Brown. (Also see 1994 Supplement.)

Sabatino, C. P., & Karp, N. (2011). Improving advanced illness care: The evolution of state POLST Programs. Washington, DC: AARP Public Policy Institute. Retrieved from http://www.aarp.org/health/doctors-hospitals/info-04-2011/polst-04-11.html

Teno, J. M., Gozalo, P. L., Lee, I. C., Kuo, S., Spence, C., Connor, S. R., & Casarett, D. J. (2011). Does hospice improve quality of care for persons dying from dementia? *Journal of the American Geriatrics Society, 59*, 1531–1536.

Urich, L. P. (2001). *The Patient Self-Determination Act: Meeting the challenges in patient care.* Washington, DC: Georgetown University Press.

Xu, J. Q., Kochanek, K. D., Murphy, S. L., & Tejada-Vera, B. (2010). Deaths: Final data for 2007. *National Vital Statistics Reports, 58*(19). Hyattsville, MD: National Center for Health Statistics.

Zucker, A. (2007). Ethical and legal issues and end-of-life decision making. In D. E. Balk, C. Wogrin, G. Thornton, & D. Meagher (Eds.), *ADEC handbook of thanatology* (pp. 103–112). Northbrook, IL: Association for Death Education and Counseling.

For more information on the Five Wishes document, go to http://www.agingwithdignity.org/five-wishes.php or call 1-888-5-WISHES.

CHAPTER 18

Ethics, End-of-Life Decisions, and Grief

Kenneth J. Doka

E nd-of-life ethical decisions do more than prolong or terminate a life. Decisions made may facilitate the grief process, allowing survivors a meaningful end to the story of a loved one. Conversely, these decisions may haunt survivors long after the death occurs, complicating grief, creating family dissension, inhibiting support, and increasing ambivalence over the nature or circumstances of the death.

The following letter, sent to me anonymously by "John", the son of a woman with terminal breast cancer, illustrates how ethical decisions can complicate the grief of survivors.

Dear Dr. Doka,

I attended the workshop on grief that you presented in Minneapolis and was particularly interested, and moved, by the concept of disenfranchised grief. [The concept of *disenfranchised grief* is discussed later in this chapter.] Two years ago, my mother passed away. Over the days and weeks that followed, there was the usual grief and sadness to work through, but what my sibs and I couldn't tell anyone was that mom ended her own life—and that we helped.

I was next to Mom when she took her last breath, along with my sibs and three of her grandchildren. Suicide wasn't the cause of her death. It would be an inaccurate and unfair description. She didn't want to die; she had to die. She died on her own terms—at home, surrounded by her loved ones.

Our extended family came to know and affirm how Mom died. We had to let most everyone else believe that it was just an extraordinary coincidence that her entire family was at her side. There's enormous dissonance when you feel that you have to mislead friends about the truth—when you don't think you did anything wrong—when there is no shame or guilt.

The "normal grief" of losing a parent was further aggravated by a sense that there are some in society that would disapprove of her decision or feel it was improper or even criminal for us to assist. I don't know that what we did fits a legal definition of "assist," but we supported her in the decision. And I have come to understand that the resulting grief is disenfranchised.

In this case, John faced an ethical dilemma. On one hand his mother was in pain, clearly terminal, and wished to end her suffering. On the other hand, John realized that assisting his mother's wish placed him in legal jeopardy. While he understood the act to be merciful and had the support of his siblings and extended family, his decision still generated an ambivalence that now complicates his subsequent grief. In addition, he still has concerns that the action might arouse investigation and legal prosecution.

The letter indicates a need to process his grief and, in doing so, to explore his role in his mother's decision to terminate her life. Yet, well aware of the potential limits to confidentiality, he has to do it anonymously in a letter—unable to even seek a reply.

Professional help from a counselor at the time of his mother's decision or even after her death seems precluded by the legal ambiguity of Minnesota's laws. John faced a moral dilemma, but any counselor assisting the family at this time would face an ethical quandary. Would a counselor in this situation be mandated to take appropriate actions to forestall such an act? In such a situation, ethical codes suggest a number of actions. First, the patient should be assessed to assure that he or she has the capacity to make such a decision. This entails ensuring that the patient's cognitive abilities are neither impaired by the disease processes nor by the medication regimen, and also that there are no underlying psychological issues including hopelessness, isolation, or depression. Depression is common in life-threatening illness and often untreated (Fins, 2006). Second, these ethical codes affirm that patients have a right to the highest degree of self-determination to consider all alternatives in terminal care (that is when there is no realistic medical option to cure or significantly prolong life) including aggressive treatment, life-sustaining treatment, and palliative treatment, as well as options to withdraw medical care or hasten death. In making such decisions, the responsibility of the counselor is to ensure that the patient exercises informed consent. This not only means that the patient has the capacity to make such a decision but also that the patient is informed of all options that might assist in alleviating pain and suffering. Studies from Oregon, assessing the effects for six years of the Death with Dignity Act that allowed physician-assisted suicide, indicated that hospice referrals increased when patients requesting the option of physician-assisted suicide were presented with viable alternatives (Oregon Department of Human Services, 2004).

These ethical codes also allow counselors to refer patients who wish to consider options to hasten death if such options conflict with the counselor's values. Moreover, many state laws and all ethical codes allow but do not mandate breaking confidentiality to intervene in a patient's efforts to hasten death (Corey, Corey, and Callahan, 2011). In assessing a counselor's responsibility in such situations, counselors may wish to review their organization's policies, seek ethical consultation from their professional associations, and confer with an attorney. Counselors may also seek the patient's written consent to discuss the patient's condition with the treating physician. Naturally, organizations dealing with clients/patients at the end of life will want to develop policies about such situations that are congruent with state laws and professional ethical codes. Moreover, in such situations, organizations also should make efforts to provide emotional support for counselors who may be experiencing grief when a patient dies—particularly when that grief is exacerbated by ethical dilemmas that arise at the end of life.

Positively or negatively, as stated earlier, the end-of-life decisions that survivors make influence grief. This chapter explores that role. It begins with four central assumptions. The first is that the end-of-life decisions, like so many of the factors that influence grief responses, can be facilitating or complicating, perhaps even at the same time. This chapter explores both aspects of end-of-life decisions.

A second assumption is that professional caregivers, as well as families, have a stake in these ethical decisions, and may have opinions as to the best course of action. Staff, especially in long-term care institutions, may develop attachments to the patient. In addition, family and staff may influence the others' decisions. For both family and staff, the aftermath of these actions or subsequent behaviors may generate doubt on the efficacy of these decisions, and may then influence the course of bereavement

A third assumption is that these decisions cannot be understood apart from their context. Prolonged illnesses or sudden deaths each create complications to grief in and of themselves. Moreover, these contexts are not mutually exclusive. As Rando (1993) reminds, persons even within the context of a lengthy illness can die "suddenly"—that is at an unexpected time and manner. The person slowly dying of cancer is not immune from a sudden deterioration or even a heart attack or stroke. This context of the death and end-of-life decisions around that death will eventually influence the experience of grief.

The final assumption is that strategies do exist, both during and after the decision making, that can be helpful to families and staff. These strategies can enhance the possibility that the decision-making process can be facilitative of grief while mitigating complicating features.

COMPLICATING FACTORS

End-of-life decisions can both facilitate and complicate grief—sometimes simultaneously. As noted above, end-of-life decisions cannot be separated from the context in which they occur. Research has indicated that both sudden death, as well as deaths that follow long-term illness, create complications (see Rando, 1993).

Sudden deaths often occur from circumstances such as an accident, suicide, or homicide. While each circumstance creates unique issues for bereavement, all share complicating factors, such as a sense that the death was preventable, as well as a lack of forewarning. These factors also can complicate a sudden death from natural causes such as a heart attack, aneurysm, or stroke. Here, too, there is preventability and lack of forewarning. Ethical decisions, such as terminating treatment or stopping heroic measures, are often undertaken in both shock and grief with little forewarning or forethought.

Other factors may exist when the illness is prolonged. Family caregivers may be highly stressed as they cope with incessant physical, financial, social, and psychological demands of life-threatening illness. Witnessing the slow deterioration and pain of the dying patient may be difficult for the loved ones. Additional ambivalence can result from the stressful and incessant demands of caregiving. The illness experience may generate considerable ambivalence as family members simultaneously wish for death and an end of the suffering while concurrently wishing that the person would remain alive. The person's deteriorating physical appearance itself may cause ambivalence, to the point where family members are repulsed even as they seek to care and to comfort. Ambivalence has long been identified as a factor that complicates grief (Rando, 1993; Worden, 2008).

End-of-life dilemmas themselves can reflect and even generate considerable ambivalence. The individual or family making the decision can be torn between a desire to end suffering and a continued quest to retain hope even in the face of impending death. Individuals or family members may experience conflict between following their own beliefs and choices and honoring the expressed wishes or beliefs of the deceased. The following example, drawn from clinical experience, illustrates this:

> My husband had made it clear that he did not want continued treatment when we knew it to be futile. However, it was hard to accept that. I believed that when there is life, there is always hope. He would not want anything more. Yet, I felt I should continue. I followed his wishes and he died shortly afterward. I still wonder if I should have kept on going.

This suggests another potential factor in end-of-life decisions. Normally, one person within the family system may hold the health proxy. Such a proxy in the United States authorizes a given person to make medical decisions for an individual incapable of making such decisions, generally because the ill individual is unconscious or has diminished capacity. Families may differ in their abilities to communicate with one another and in their opinions about what should be done. The end-of-life decisions can create family conflicts or revive family disputes, making the process of decision making even more complex. These conflicts may actually limit support that family members receive, while generating concurrent crises such as fights that complicate the grief process. In some cases family disagreements and consequent legal actions can generate considerable publicity and debate and even polarize communities, further limiting support and generating increased ambivalence about the decision process. These factors, too, complicate grief (Rando, 1993; Worden, 2008). One woman's comments, drawn from clinical experience, illustrate the impact that these conflicts can have.

> I held his (her father's) health proxy. My sister came in from California. She had wanted (artificial) feeding to continue, so I had kept it so she could be there when he died. Now I knew it was time to stop; but she did not agree. I told her this was Dad's wish. She knew that but still could not let go. Finally after four

265

days, I said 'stop.' Because there was family disagreement, the ethics committee became involved. Dad died a day later— one more painful day, in my opinion. My sister felt she was right since he died naturally—whatever that means—the day before the committee would decide. She left right after the funeral; we have not spoken since.

Some of the decisions that may be made, such as assisting a suicide, can create additional issues for survivors. It may create legal investigations that add to the stress of the loss. The decision may isolate the decision maker from other family members. It may, as the opening letter indicated, disenfranchise grief.

Disenfranchised grief refers to a loss that cannot be openly acknowledged, socially sanctioned, or publicly mourned (Doka, 2002). The individual experiences a loss but can neither share the full circumstances of the death nor receive subsequent support. Thus the end-of-life decisions that individuals render may alienate others within the family system or even risk public censure—disenfranchising their grief.

The manner of death, too, may complicate subsequent grief. Even the decision to terminate life support may not ensure an easy death. Family members may interpret or misinterpret the final actions of the dying person as evidence of pain. Even when the death does not occur with signs of evident distress, families and especially decision makers may still worry about the way the person died. For example, professionals in end-of-life care understand that neither artificial feeding nor hydration is necessarily palliative, and may in fact be more burdensome for the dying person. Yet, decision makers or other family members may still perceive the patient suffering with thirst or experiencing starvation; these images can haunt subsequent bereavement.

Even decisions to continue treatment may generate issues. Families may feel, in retrospect, that they let the person needlessly suffer. They may sense the active disapproval and even isolation of medical personnel. In other cases, the pain and suffering experienced by the dying individual may create a situation where family decision makers wish that they had taken a more proactive role to end suffering.

FACILITATING FACTORS

End-of-life decisions may not only compound bereavement. In some cases, active decision making at the end of life can be a facilitating factor, easing the strains of grief. Parsons and Lidz (1967) have challenged the notion that contemporary Western societies deny death. Instead the authors suggest that Western societies take an activist orientation toward death—accepting its inevitability but trying to control the timing and nature of death.

The hospice and palliative care movement, as well as more open discussions about physician-assisted suicide, can be seen as extensions of this orientation. While all of these movements accept that death occurs, all attempt to assert some control over the way that the person dies, trying to make that death less painful, and in physician-assisted suicide, timed to the patients' choice.

Individual end-of-life decisions also can allow a semblance of control at an otherwise uncontrollable time. This notion of choice may mitigate the sense of powerlessness that one often feels in the face of death. Moreover, these decisions may be the end result of a process that in and of itself is therapeutic. The best end-of-life decisions are made in a reflective process where the individual has to consult with medical personnel as well as other family members. The process can do much to ease subsequent grief. It can allow a process of consensus building that can generate support and ease isolation. It can offer increased information and discussion that acknowledges the inevitability of death and the futility of further medical interventions; this recognition can assist survivors in accepting the reality of death. The decision-making process can provide opportunities to confront painful emotions and finish unfinished business. In some cases, the reflective process provokes strong spiritual reflection as one assesses not only how one's philosophy or theology address the ethical issues involved but also how one's spirituality more directly speaks to the very loss. All of these factors may ease the tasks that one struggles with in grief (Worden, 2008).

Product as well as process may have a role in facilitating grief. Neimeyer (2001) reminds us that the reconstruction of meaning is a major factor in coping with grief. An individual may define the decision-making process as one that enabled a loved one to die a "good" death, perhaps by easing pain or fulfilling that person's wishes and reaffirming one's own responsibility. In such a case, these inferred meanings might offer subsequent comfort. Decisions to allow an autopsy or donate tissue or organs may also confer subsequent benefits, even if meaning cannot be found in the death itself. A person may see that these decisions benefited other persons or allowed medical science to find or confirm new information. Finding benefits also facilitates the grief process (Frantz, Farrell, and Trolley, 2001).

PROFESSIONAL CAREGIVERS: BEYOND ETHICAL ROUNDS
Family members are not the only persons with a stake in decision making. Professional caregivers also may be in deep distress over ethical decisions that are made.

> A woman in the advanced stages of Alzheimer's disease was now dying of cancer. One manifestation of the woman's dementia was that she thought everyone who worked around her was a son, daughter, or parent. She treated them as such, and endeared herself to the staff. The woman's family was actively involved in care. There came a point when the woman developed pneumonia. Based on her clear advance directives and many conversations that family had with their mother, the family decided not to treat the pneumonia. While the family was at peace with the decision, the staff felt considerable distress at her death. The ethics committee reviewed the decision showing the woman's advanced directives. At the conclusion of the discussion, one of nurses stood up and said, "If it is so damn ethical, why do I feel so bad?" (Doka, 1994).

On one hand, the decision not to treat was clearly ethical. The woman's advanced directives were concise and explicit, families members were in accord, the woman's condition was clearly terminal, and the ethics committee reviewed these decisions in a deliberate manner. Yet, staff feelings were never considered. Staff members had become deeply attached to the woman, and experienced grief at her death. The initial intervention simply served to explain the ethical decision making that led to a decision to terminate all treatment. The staff had not been consulted prior to the decision. A review of the decision and a reaffirmation that the decision had been carefully made in conjunction with an ethics committee did little to mitigate staff grief.

Ethical decisions cannot only be dealt with at a cognitive level nor be seen as only the responsibility of families and ethics committees; professional caregiver grief can often be disenfranchised (Doka, 2002). Caregivers can become highly attached to patients. In fact, Fulton (1987) applied the "Stockholm Syndrome"—the long accepted concept that captive can identify with captors—to the care of the dying. To Fulton, the essence of the Stockholm syndrome is that crisis situations intensify the process of bonding. When patients die, professional caregivers may experience profound grief. This grief may be exacerbated when caregivers feel powerless over the decisions made around a person's death. Both the lack of a formal role in this decision-making process and subsequent inattention to caregiver grief can complicate that bereavement, engendering distress and compassion fatigue (Doka, 1994; Puntillo et al., 2001).

IMPLICATIONS FOR PROFESSIONAL AND FAMILY CAREGIVERS

Though ethical decisions at the end of life can have significant effects on the grief reactions of both family members and professional caregivers (Richmond and Ross, 1994; Swarte and Heintz, 1999; Wallwork and Ellison, 1985), there has not been much discussion of the ways that the process by which end-of-life decisions are made and implemented can be more therapeutic. The grief of family members is facilitated when family members are encouraged to have a deliberative and inclusive process. Decisions to terminate treatment arouse strong feelings of ambivalence (Richmond and Ross, 1994; Wallwork and Ellison, 1985). In addition, Foster and McLellan found that individuals report that they rely on family and friends to help make end-of-life decisions. Such consulting is critical to develop a greater level of consensus and subsequent support. This type of process takes time, allowing the family opportunity to weave their decisions into a consistent narrative of the patient's illness and death (Gilbert, 2002).

This process cannot be rushed. Physicians and others must not attempt to apply pressure to families engaged in decision making. Two comments, drawn from clinical experience, illustrate the role of that deliberative process.

> My father's physician kept pushing for us to make decisions to continue treatments long after it was necessary. We continued to ask, "How is this palliative?" He never could answer. Finally he simply said, "It's what I would do for my father." I said, "Fine, but you give us no compelling reason to do it to mine." Even now I am still troubled by his intrusion. My mother, though, was fearful—feeling we should listen to the doctor.

In this case, the doctor's interference with the decision-making process created a note of distress; in the next case, the physician's respect for the family process was clearly appreciated.

> The doctor was wonderful. She laid out the facts, all the options, patiently answered all our questions. It seemed clear that Mom would not emerge from her vegetative state. Yet, we still decided to wait a few days before disconnecting life support. We decided as a family that we would rather wonder if we waited too long rather than worry we terminated support quickly. This doctor understood. When Mom died, we were ready and at peace with our decision.

Moreover, the process may not end with the patient's death. After the death, family members and other survivors may need to review the decisions that they made in the course of the illness. Physicians need to understand this as a critical aspect of care and one that is both necessary and facilitative of the grief process.

This process, however, should not be restricted to family members; staff members, too, have a stake in ethical decisions. They, too, need to be debriefed when patients die, especially when that death follows end-of-life decisions that may be seen as either prolonging suffering or hastening death. These debriefings not only should concentrate on the ethics of the decision-making process but acknowledge the ways that these decisions may influence caregiver grief (see Doka, 1994; Puntillo et al., 2001).

Ethical decisions never arise in a vacuum. Culture, technology, social and individual values, spiritual and religious traditions, and legal struggles are among the many factors that frame ethics. It is critical, then, to recognize the complement of that—ethical decisions do not proceed in a vacuum, either. The Social Ecology Model (Jennings, 2008) offers a corrective to the intense individualism inherent in contemporary ethics. This model emphasizes that the impact of ethical decisions is influenced by, and affects, not only the patient but also varied groups such as family, friends, and even staff. Decisions that have been made may continue to be reconsidered and reviewed long after the choices and the consequences.

Editor's Note: This chapter deals with material originally published in Doka, K. J. (2005). Ethics, end-of-life decisions and grief. In C. A. Corr, K. J. Doka, and B. Jennings,(Eds.), Ethical dilemmas at the end of life. *Washington, DC: Hospice Foundation of America.*

***Kenneth J. Doka,** PhD, MDiv, is a professor of gerontology at the Graduate School of The College of New Rochelle and senior consultant to the Hospice Foundation of America. A prolific author and editor, Dr. Doka serves as editor of HFA's* Living with Grief® *book series, its* Journeys *newsletter, and numerous other books and publications. He has served as a panelist on HFA's* Living with Grief® *video programs for 18 years. Dr. Doka was elected president of the Association for Death Education and Counseling (ADEC) in 1993. In 1995, he was elected to the Board of Directors of the International Work Group on Death, Dying, and Bereavement and served as its chair from 1997–99. ADEC presented him with an Award for Outstanding Contributions in the Field of Death Education in 1998. In 2006, Dr. Doka was grandfathered in as a mental health counselor under New York's first state licensure of counselors. Dr. Doka is an ordained Lutheran minister.*

REFERENCES

Corey, G., Corey, M. S., & Callahan, P. (2011). *Issues and ethics in the helping professions* (8ᵗʰ Ed.). Belmont, CA: Brooks/Cole.

Doka, K. J. (1994). Caregiver distress: If it's so ethical, why does it feel so bad? *Critical Issues in Clinical Care Nursing, 5,* 346–347.

Doka, K. J. (Ed.). (2002). *Disenfranchised grief: New directions, challenges, and strategies for practice.* Champaign, IL: Research Press.

Fins, J. (2006). *A palliative ethic of care: Clinical wisdom at life's end.* Sudbury, MA: Jones and Bartlett.

Foster, L., & McLellan, L. (2002). Translating psychosocial insight into ethical discussions supportive of families in end-of-life decision-making. *Social Work in Health Care, 35*(3), 37–51.

Frantz, T. T, Farrell, M. M., & Trolley, B. C. (2001). Positive outcomes of losing a loved one. In R. A. Neimeyer (Ed). *Meaning reconstruction of the experience of loss.* Washington, DC: American Psychological Association.

Fulton, R. (1987). Unanticipated grief. In C. Corr & R. Pachalski (Eds.), *Death: Completion and discovery.* Lakewood, OH: Association for Death Education and Counseling.

Gilbert, K. (2002). Taking a narrative approach to grief research: Finding meaning in stories. *Death Studies, 26,* 223–239.

Jennings, B. (2008). Dying at an early age: Ethical issues in palliative pediatric care. In K. J. Doka & A. S. Tucci (Eds.), *Living with grief: Children and adolescents* (pp. 99–119). Washington, DC: The Hospice Foundation of America.

Neimeyer, R. A. (Ed). (2001). *Meaning reconstruction of the experience of loss.* Washington, DC: American Psychological Association.

Oregon Department of Human Services (2004). *Annual statistical reports on Oregon's Death with Dignity Act.* Retrieved from: www.dhs.state.or.us/publichealth/chs/pas/pas.cfm

Parsons, T., & Lidz, V. (1967). Death in American society. In E. Shneidman (Ed.), *Essays in self-destruction.* New York: Aronson.

Puntillo, K., Benner, P., Drought, T., Drew, B., Stotts, N., Stannard, D., ... White, C. (2001). End-of-life issues in intensive care units: A national random survey of nurses' knowledge and beliefs. *American Journal of Clinical Care, 10,* 216–229.

Rando, T. A. (1993). *The treatment of complicated mourning.* Champaign, IL: Research Press.

Richmond, B., & Ross, M. (1994). Responses to AIDS-related bereavement. *Journal of Psychosocial Oncology,* 12, 143–163.

Swarte, N., & Heintz, A. (1999). Euthanasia and physician-assisted suicide. *Annals of Medicine, 31,* 364–371.

Wallwork, E., & Ellison, P. (1985). Follow-up of family of neonates in whom life support was withdrawn. *Clinical Pediatrics, 24*(1), 12–20

Worden, W. (2008). Grief counseling and grief therapy, (4th ed.). New York: Springer.

Index

B

C

D

O

P

T

U

W

Z